EAPH   POLITICAL STUDIES 7

POLITICAL DEVELOPMENT IN RURAL TANZANIA

Political Development in Rural Tanzania

TANU yajenga nchi

GÖRAN HYDÉN

EAST AFRICAN PUBLISHING HOUSE

First published in East Africa 1969
by the East African Publishing House,
P.O. Box 30571, Nairobi, Kenya

This work was made possible through a research grant from the Scandinavian
Institute of African Studies, Uppsala, Sweden, and was originally published as
Lund Political Studies 8 by UNISKOL Bokforlaget Universitet och Skola, Lund

Printed offset litho and bound in Kenya by the English Press Ltd.,
Reata Road, P.O. Box 30127, Nairobi

"*While some nations aim at the moon, we are aiming at the village.*"

JULIUS K. NYERERE, 1961

Contents

Introduction

I

Preface

This is a study of the relationship between rural inhabitants in a selected part of Tanzania—Buhaya—and the centre of the political system in which they are members. It is an investigation of how the system is performing in its attempts to solve the problems emerging in this type of societal environment. As the title of the book *TANU Yajenga Nchi*—TANU builds the country—indicates, it is particularly focused on the role of the Tanganyika African National Union, the only lawful party in Tanzania, in the process of national development. The instrument which has been used to measure the performance of the system is a systematic interview survey.

This study aims at shedding some light on the political culture of a new African nation. It is not, like most other studies on Africa by political scientists, focused on the elite level. The attempt is to introduce the common man, and what he believes, as valuable objects of political science research in Africa. In order to understand his situation after independence, an account of the developments during the pre-colonial and the colonial eras have been included.

This book is the product of work which has extended over a number of years. During my research I have accumulated several debts of gratitude. It is unfortunately impossible here to extend personal thanks to everybody. I can only express the hope that all those who have, in some way or another, been involved in the preparation of this book are aware of my gratitude.

I must, however, express in particular my thanks to the Tanzanian government authorities, who allowed me to pursue this research project in their country, and to all those people in Buhaya, who are the actual objects of this study. It is only due to their cooperation and willingness to take time off their ordinary duties that it has been possible to complete this investigation.

I have gained intellectual inspiration from friends in the Department of Political Science at the University of Lund and at Makerere University College, Kampala, Uganda. My indebtedness is particularly great to Professor Nils Stjernquist and Professor James S. Coleman. Both have shown great interest in my research, offered valuable comments in the course of my work, and their support of my study has always been a source of inspiration.

My thanks are also due to Mr Russell Lansbury, University of Melbourne, Australia, for useful observations on the text, and to Mrs Jane Hartley, Kampala, who was alone responsible for the tedious task of coding the field material. I owe my thanks to Mrs. Ebba Skjöld for the arduous exercise of typing and retyping many drafts. Her efficiency has saved me from several worries.

Last, but not least, I wish to thank my wife, Melania, who together with Mr Justin Maeda and myself has made the Kiswahili translation, and whose considerable patience has been tested by me many times over.

Lund, January, 1968.

Göran Hydén

Figure 1. Geographical map of Tanzania. Bukoba and Karagwe Districts, in the West Lake Region, are specially marked.

Chapter 1.   The theory of political development

One of the most significant and recent changes in the discipline of political science, is the growing awareness among its members of the need for a reconceptualization of the functions and purposes of a political system. A rapidly increasing number of books are being published in which the authors, explicitly or implicitly, regard the political system as a creative, purposeful mechanism, through which societal goals are achieved.[1] They have all moved away from the traditional, more narrow view of the political system, or rather the state, as the legitimate organization for the execution of ultimate physical compulsion.[2] Their primary concern is not with the distribution and execution of power, but rather how the political system can contribute to the general development of society. This new outlook is closely connected with the emergence of a more comprehensive developmental approach to politics.[3]

[1] A summary of these tendencies can be found in Gabriel A. Almond and G. Bingham Powell Jr., *Comparative Politics: A Developmental Approach,* (New York 1966) and Lucian W. Pye, *Aspects of Political Development,* (New York 1966). Cf., also Szymon Chodak, "Societal Functions of Party Systems in Sub-Saharan Africa" in Erik Allardt and Yrjö Littunen, *Cleavages, Ideologies, and Party Systems,* (Helsinki 1964), Glen D. Paige, "The Rediscovery of Politics" in John D. Montgomery and William J. Siffin (eds), *Approaches to Development: Politics, Administration and Change,* (New York 1966), J. Roland Pennock, "Political Development, Political Systems, and Political Goods", *World Politics,* (Vol. XVIII, April 1966), Lars Rudebeck, *Party and People: A Study of Political Change in Tunisia,* (Uppsala 1967), Herbert J. Spiro, *Africa: The Primacy of Politics,* (New York 1966); and Henry Bienen, *Tanzania: Party Transformation and Economic Development,* (Princeton 1967).

[2] This definition was first offered by Max Weber, but is still considered valid by many political scientists. Cf., Max Weber, *The Theory of Social and Economic Organization,* edited by Talcott Parsons, (New York 1964), p. 154.

[3] See the *Studies in Political Development* series (Princeton 1963—66) Vol. I, Lucian W. Pye (ed), *Communications and Political Development;* Vol. II, Joseph LaPalombara (ed), *Bureaucracy and Political Development*; Vol. III, Robert Ward and Dankwart Rustow (eds), *Political Modernization in Japan and Turkey;* Vol. IV, James S. Coleman (ed), *Education and Political Development;* Vol. V, Lucian W. Pye and Sidney Verba (eds), *Political Culture and Political Development;* Vol. VI, Joseph LaPalombara and Myron Weiner (eds), *Political Parties and Political Development.* See also Almond and Powell, *op.cit.,* David Apter, *The Politics of Modernization,* (Chicago 1965), Harold D. Lasswell, "The Policy Sciences of Development" *World Politics,* (Vol. XVII, January 1965), A. F. K. Organski, *Stages of Political Growth,* (New York 1965) and Pye, "Aspects . . ." *op.cit.*

At least, theoretically, this "new school" of political scientists view political development not merely in normative and ethnocentric terms. Development is not the transition from authoritarianism to democracy, in the Western sense; nor is it a unilinear process with a fixed goal. According to this more empirical approach, political development is rather reflected in the attempts by a political system to adapt to or manipulate changes occuring within the system itself or in its environment. The focus is on the functions of the system, and in particular on its capacity to solve problems. A recent definition is offered by Almond and Powell:[4]

Political development...(is)... the increased differentiation and specialization of political structures and increased secularization of political culture. The significance of such development is, in general, to increase the effectiveness and efficiency of the performance of the political system.

One reason for the emergence of an extensive literature on political development is the presently widespread consciousness about the role that political factors play in the development of a society. The ideological justification for modern politics is bound to make it affect every individual citizen and every walk of life. This becomes particularly true in those countries, which only recently have embarked on policies aimed at more extensive social, economic and political changes. Exposure to the representatives of a national political party and their ideology may, in several sub-Saharan African countries, be the first incentive towards modernization for members of an isolated rural community. In Western countries, primarily non-political factors have stimulated change in society; politics have been repressive and retarding change. In non-Western countries, where large-scale modernization[5] of society has begun only recently, politics is viewed as a major tool of change; politics in the minds of those executing it is progressive, not repressive.

The situation being thus, the study of political development becomes particularly relevant. There is, however, an additional reason. Too often, people discussing political development juxtapose the prescriptions of the regime or the aspirations of the political leaders with the actual situation in the counry, without calling in question whether this is empirically true. Students run into difficulties, because the availability of facts illustrating the relation between an ideal and a real situation in a country is limited.[6] Thus, the fac-

[4] Almond and Powell, op.cit., p. 195.
[5] "Modernization" should be viewed as an aspect of the developmental process. Implied in the concept of "modernization" is the ability of a social system to innovate by developing new flexible structures and skills to meet the changes brought about. "Development" in addition to this, implies the proliferation and integration of the new values, roles and structures in a society. Cf., Apter, op.cit., pp. 66—69.
[6] This comes out particularly in books, where attempts to typologize political systems,

tual basis on which many of the generalizations about political development and the typologizing of political systems, particularly in Africa, have been made, is still scanty. The vast majority of the books written by political scientists on Africa have been based on information such as ministerial speeches, government documents and interviews with political leaders. There is, of course, nothing wrong with using these types of sources, but it means that the studies have been rather onesided. The books tell what the leaders have said and what the man in the town believes. This clearly indicates that those books cannot tell "the whole story". There has also emerged a growing awareness of the inadequacy of that type of research.[7]

This study in contrast to these works is an attempt to widen our factual basis for the evaluations of political development by presenting "the other side": the opinions of the rural inhabitants, who, in most African countries, constitute approximately 90 % of the total population. They form the foundation on which the new society has to be built.

A primary objective of the study has been to investigate the centre-periphery relationship and to find out to what extent the prescriptions offered by the political leaders for the solution of various problems are conceived of as appropriate and valid by the common man in the rural areas. Has the latter accepted to be part of a wider national community? How does he react to the new regime? Does he approve of government demands for changes in agricultural methods? How does he view the way government allocates its resources? To what extent is he himself a participant in the political system? These are some of the basic questions, relating to the development of the political system, that this study attempts to answer.

Tanzania in East Africa was chosen because, more than most other countries in Africa its government has paid specific attention to rural development problems. This comes out in Chapter 2, where a more extensive presentation of the Tanzanian political system is given. A second reason is that Tanzania offers an interesting example of a country moving slowly but steadily from a position, where the government rather cautiously attempts to combat the developmental problems to another, where the government optimistically

---

or their various sub-systems, are made. The prescriptions of the regime, or the leaders, therefore, become the basis on which the distinctions are made. Cf., e.g., J. S. Coleman and C. G. Rosberg (eds), *Political Parties and National Integration in Tropical Africa*, (Berkeley 1966), E. Shils, *Political Development in the New States*, (The Hague 1962) and G. A. Almond and J. S. Coleman, *The Politics of the Developing Areas*, (Princeton 1960).

[7] See e.g., Aristide Zolberg, *Creating Political Order—The Party-States of West Africa*, (Chicago 1966), p. 145 and p. 153, Harvey Glickman, "Dialogues on the Theory of African Political Development", *Africa Report*, (Vol. XII, May 1967), and Bienen, *op.cit.*, p. 408. Glickman writes e.g., "Indeed it is now quite clear that the problems of micropolitics are 'where the action is'".

and more deliberately launches attacks on these problems.[8] This investigation is also an attempt to answer the question, whether this change in degree of politicization is related to conditions in the rural environment.

Research was conducted in the northwestern part of Tanzania, in two administrative districts, Bukoba and Karagwe, collectively known as Buhaya.[9] Material for the most important section of the book, a case study dealing with the attitudes of the rural inhabitants towards post-independence developments, was gathered mainly through survey research. The choice of method also confines the study to one culturally homogeneous area, thereby making the conclusions more firmly based.[10] It has limited the possibilities to generalize, but hardly to the extent that another method, for the study of the centre-periphery relationship under present conditions, would have offered much better prospects for comparison with other societies.

In order to facilitate the understanding of change after independence, the book contains a description of the traditional political systems in Buhaya, and an analysis of the most important developments that took place in the colonial period. That part has been made rather extensive, because it consists of information about the growth of local political organizations in Buhaya, which has not been presented at any length in other political science literature.[11] It is aimed at throwing some additional light on the political activities in the rural areas of Tanzania before independence.

The developmental approach

The new, more comprehensive, developmental approach to the study of politics is closely connected with the writings of two men, Gabriel Almond and David Easton.[12] Whilst this is not the place to review their theories at

[8] For an extensive account of political and economic development in Tanzania after independence, see Bienen, *op.cit.*

[9] In accordance with Bantu language grammar, *Ba*-Haya, indicates plural—people; *Mu*-Haya, indicates singular—person; *Bu*-Haya showing location, in this case the country; and *Lu*-Haya, denoting language. In the following pages *Buhaya* will be used to cover both Bukoba and Karagwe Districts, unless specified otherwise.

[10] See Appendix I for an extensive account of how the material was gathered.

[11] Local political development trends before the growth of TANU are mentioned in a few articles and papers. See e.g., R. S. Austen, "Notes on the Pre-History of TANU", *Makerere Journal* (No 9, March 1964), pp. 1—6; Lionel Cliffe, "Nationalism and the Reaction to Enforced Agricultural Change in Tanganyika during the Colonial Period", *East African Institute of Social Research Conference Paper,* (Kampala, December 1964); also T. O. Ranger, "Connections between 'Primary Resistance' Movements and Modern Mass Nationalism in East and Central Africa", *University of East Africa Social Science Conference Paper,* (Nairobi, December 1966).

[12] See Almond and Powell, *op.cit;* Gabriel A. Almond, "A Developmental Approach to Political Systems", *World Politics,* (Vol. XVII, January 1965); David Easton,

great length, a few remarks about their more important contributions will be necessary in order to put this study in its proper perspective.

One of the factors behind this new approach, as indicated above, is the growing concern with the environment of the political system, the interrelationship between the political, economic and social variables.[13] The character of the political system also becomes of vital importance for social and economic development. Politics become a means to solve all types of problems and to satisfy human needs in society.[14]

Implicitly, the advocates of the new developmental approach are evaluating political systems according to their capacity to survive, or to be able to master, the many problems of development.[15] To many observers, this becomes equivalent to the maintenance of a state of equilibrium and the advocacy of only gradual and limited change. This is, however, too narrow an interpretation. The new developmental approach, at least in the opinion of the present author, recognizes that a political system is both innovative and problem-solving. It sets its own goals, thereby often increasing the stress in the system. A higher degree of stress may in certain situations be desirable. For instance, an "ideological escalation"[16] from a rather conservative to a more radical view of politics, may well increase the strength of the system in the long run, even if it brings about political strains and conflicts for some time. It can, however, also go the other way. The stresses become too heavy for the system, and instead of progress one gets regression. As has been noted by Samuel P. Huntington, history is full of cases of the decline of political systems and their break-up into less differentiated and less secularized components.[17]

A Framework for Political Analysis, (New York 1965); and David Easton, *A Systems Analysis of Political Life,* (New York 1965).

[13] The term "political system" has become increasingly common in the study of comparative politics and political development. In older texts "government", "nation" and "state" have been used to describe what is today understood as a political system. These older terms, however, are limited by legal and institutional meanings developed in modern Western societies. The concept of "political system" includes not only governmental institutions such as legislatures, bureaucracy and political parties, but all structures in their political aspects (cf., Almond and Powell, *op.cit.,* p. 18). It is used to enable a more comprehensive analysis of political development.

[14] Cf., Pennock, *op.cit.*

[15] The question of system survival is often related to the persistence of a particular regime. As it is used here, however, a system does not "die" until its various components, community, regime and authorities, are completely fragmented. The decline and fall of the Roman empire is one example; the disintegration of the Nigerian Federation 1967, another.

[16] The concept is borrowed from Albert Hirschman; see his *Journeys Toward Progress,* (New York 1965), p. 316.

[17] Samuel P. Huntington, "Political Development and Political Decay", *World Politics,* (Vol. XVII, April 1965).

Political development, therefore, should be viewed as an open-ended process. Recognizing this, political scientists have shown a growing interest in trying to identify the factors in the political system that determine its changes. Since these attempts are of immediate relevance to this study, a brief review is not out of place.

a) *Structure and culture.* As has already been illustrated, the terms "structure" and "culture" are of key importance to the analysis of political development; *structural* differentiation and *cultural* secularization are principal indicators of political development.[18]

A structure consists of a set of *roles*. An individual secretary of a political party, or an individual member of a council of elders, performs a role. The ensemble of roles in a political party or in a local council constitutes a structure.

"Structural differentiation" refers to the processes, whereby roles and structures change, become more specialized or more autonomous, or whereby new types of roles are established and new structures created.[19] Some examples will illuminate this. When a new post is created in a ministry to deal with a new problem, *role* differentiation is taking place. When a political party decides to introduce new organizational units in order to improve its activities *structural* differentiation occurs. Almond and Powell, in discussing the developmental aspects of role and structure, are, however, not only interested in the emergence of new ones or changes in old ones, but also in the changing patterns of interaction among roles and structures.

Political culture consists of the distinctive values, beliefs and attitudes regarding the political system characteristic of the members of a distinguishable political community. In culturally pluralistic societies, and particularly in multi-tribal states in the process of formation and consolidation, one can also refer to the distinctive political *sub-cultures* of the tribal or ethnic units making up the national mosaic. The process whereby values, beliefs and attitudes are inculcated, when individual citizens are recruited into specific roles in society and in the political system is called *political socialization* and *recruitment*.

The secularization of culture is, according to Almond and Powell, the process whereby men become increasingly rational, analytical and empirical in their political actions; when they feel that they can control their environment; when they can test whether a certain proposed course of action is going to produce the consequences which were intended.

b) *Inputs and Outputs.* The structures and culture of a political system are affected by pressures in the environment or by pressures from within the

---

[18] Almond and Powell, *op.cit.*, p. 105.
[19] *Ibid.*, p. 22. In the following review of principal concepts I am citing the overview made by Almond and Powell on pp. 21—30.

system. For example, if the people inhabiting a particular area desire a new school and request the government to provide the means to build it, that request constitutes an input into the political system. If the government responds to this request, its decision and the means used to implement that decision constitute an output of the political system. Depending on the content of the decision there might be changes in the environment, which again will affect the political system. If, for instance, the government refuses to allocate money for building of the requested school, the citizens who have made the request, may become dissatisfied and withdraw their support for the government. This, then, is the *feedback* effect.

That is, in short, the essence of the input-output theory, as presented by David Easton,[20] one of the first political scientists to study politics in explicit system terms. Inputs into the political system consists of requests, or *demands*. These are, however, not enough to keep the system operating. They are only the raw material out of which the finished products are made. Therefore, the system needs energy which can be used in the process of converting inputs into outputs; it needs *supports*.[21]

Inputs do not necessarily come from the society of which the political system is a part. In many systems the inputs are, to a large extent, generated by the political elite itself. This is particularly true in countries where the government wants to promote rapid modernization. Such spontaneous elite iniatives are referred to as *withinputs*.[22]

The outputs of a political system vary, but tend in many cases to correspond to the type of supports mobilized. To what extent they correspond to demands, and how they do it, however, depends on the character of the political system.[23]

---

[20] For the most extensive account, see his most recent work, "A Systems Analysis . . .", *op.cit.*
[21] Almond and Powell subclassify the demands in the following way:
demands for:
(1) allocation of goods and services;
(2) regulation of behavior;
(3) participation in the system;
(4) communication and information;
Similarly, supports are divided into four different types:
(1) material supports;
(2) obedience to law and regulations;
(3) participatory supports;
(4) attention paid to governmental communications; and, manifestation of deference or respects to public authority, symbols and ceremonials.
[22] Easton, "A Systems Analysis . . .", *op.cit.*, p. 55.
[23] The output types according to Almond and Powell are:
(1) extractions, in the form of taxes and services;
(2) regulations of behavior;
(3) allocations of goods and services, opportunities or statuses;

c) *Functions of political systems.* An essential part of the new theory is *functionalism,* as elaborated most explicitly by Gabriel Almond.[24] According to the functional approach, political systems are analyzed and compared with regard to their performance of certain functions postulated as common —logically if not empirically—to all viable political systems. The number and nomenclature of these functions varies according to the particular analyst.[25] This variability is both to be expected and desired in view of the fact that conceptual schemes are neither right nor wrong, only more or less useful for describing and analyzing a particular phenomenon. The following functional concepts have been employed in the recent literature:[26]

1. interest articulation (demand formulation)
2. interest aggregation (demand coordination)
3. rule-making (decision-making)
4. rule application (implementation of decisions)
5. rule adjudication (judicial interpretation of decisions)
6. communication (spread of information about these activities)
7. political socialization (inculcation of political values)
8. political recruitment (manning of specific roles)

Developmental problems and system capabilities

Effective or adequate performance of the foregoing functions is assumed to be an essential characteristic of all stable, established political systems, or at least the minimal requisite for their continued existence as systems. In addition to these analytical categories centered upon the concept "function", there is another set of categories particularly useful for the analysis of the process of formation of new political systems which are based upon the concept "capability".[27] It is assumed not only that all established political systems have developed the structures and are supported by a poli-

---

(4) symbolic outputs, including affirmation of values, display of symbols, statements of policies, etc.

Cf., Fig. 2, p. 22.

[24] See, e.g., Almond's article (1965), *op.cit,* or Almond and Powell, *op.cit.*

[25] Rudebeck, for instance, in his analysis of political change in Tunisia, *op.cit.,* reduces the number of conversion functions to four: (1) articulation of political interests; (2) aggregation of political interests into compromises on which decisions are based.; (3) application of the decisions based on the compromises produced through the aggregation of articulated interests; (4) political communication. It should be noted that neither Almond in his more recent works, quoted above, nor Rudebeck follow the division into input and output functions, which was part of the original 1960 scheme. Cf., Almond and Coleman, *op.cit.*

[26] These concepts are identical to those presented by Almond and Coleman, *op.cit.*

[27] "Capability" as used in this book should be viewed as a quality of the system and referring to the behavior of the political system as a unit in its relation to the society and the international environment. Cf., also Fig. 2.

tical culture to ensure adequate functional performance, but also, and consequentially, that they have acquired a "capability" to solve certain needs or problems generic to all political systems, namely:[28]

1. the problem of national identity
2. the problem of legitimacy of the regime
3. the problem of organization for the purpose of resource extraction
4. the problem of allocating resources
5. the problem of providing participation in the system

Every well-established political system has in the course of its own development generated capabilities—and the institutionalized means for maintaining these capabilities—to cope with these systemic problems. For new national political systems in the process of formation and consolidation, however, these problems are in the nature of basic crises which must be surmounted. They must *acquire* the capabilities in the first place. For this reason one may refer to these systemic problems, generic to all political systems, as "developmental problems" for which they must develop capabilities. In the subsequent analysis, the concepts set forth in the following corresponding pairs of problems-capabilities will be employed:

Table 1. Problems and capabilities

Problem:	Capability:
Identity	Assimilative
Legitimacy	Regulative
Penetration	Extractive
Allocation	Distributive
Participation	Responsive

These concepts are drawn from Almond,[29] but with some adaptations deemed more useful for the purpose of this study. A summary of our analytical scheme appears in Fig. 2.

---

[28] This should be compared with the list of problem areas identified and presented in a paper by Lucian W. Pye, "Typologies and Political Development" read at the 7th World Congress of the International Political Science Association in Brussels, September 18—23, 1967. He talks about the following problems or crises: *identity* —the psychological and social sense of shared nationhood; *legitimacy*—the problem of authority and of constitutional issues in the organization and division of authorities; *participation*—the change from subject to citizen status; *organization*—the building of political parties, the integration of the interest articulation and interest aggregation functions; *penetration*—the capacity of the government to reach into the society in order to facilitate change and mobilize resources; *distribution*—the capacity of the political system to effect mainly economic development but also to distribute material security and justice.

[29] The main difference between the classification of capabilities used here and that

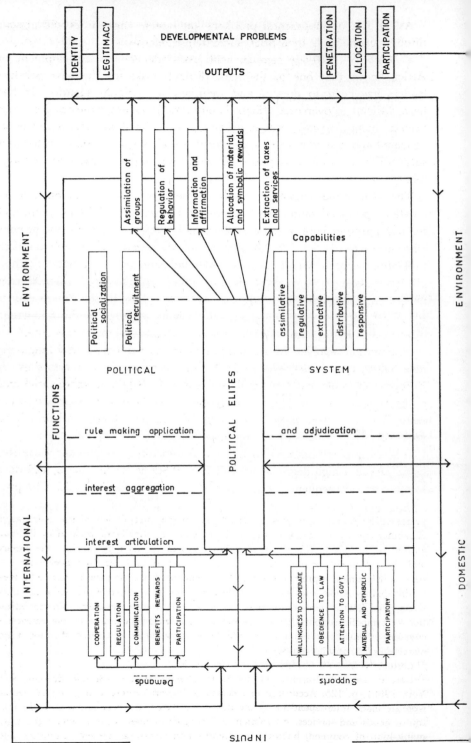

Figure 2. Summary of the analytical scheme used in this study.

As the five developmental problems and system capabilities will appear throughout the book, their brief elucidation is relevant.

a) *Identity.* Anybody familiar with post-independence development in Africa knows that one of the most difficult tasks for the new political leaders has been to create—and maintain—a national identity. It has been difficult to overcome tribalistic outlooks. In many countries there has been an increasing gap between urban and rural inhabitants, rich and poor, educated and non-educated, and so forth. In other words, ethnic, tribal and social differences have continued to constitute major obstacles to development.

The assimilative capability refers to the capacity of a nation-state to create a "political community", to borrow Easton's phrase.[30] For him, and for our purposes here, a political community refers to a group of persons who have agreed to a division of labor for the settlement of their political problems. Deutsch would say that assimilation is gaining ground if, in a given territory, community is growing faster than society.[31] Assimilation progresses if the ability to communicate over wide ranges of subjects is spreading faster among men than is necessitated by their working together directly, and by the limited but direct communication which this entails.

Assimilation involves the learning of many new things; a new language, new habits, new values, and so forth. Such learning is as a rule slow. A European example may serve to illustrate this. In Belgium, where social and economic development has forced people to live and work together, there still exists many differences between the Flemings and the Walloons; both groups have difficulties in accepting each others' customs and values.

It is not implied that national identity is something which, once a country has achieved a high degree of it, will remain stable. It fluctuates, and does so often as a consequence of system performance in another field. The pro-

presented by Almond and Powell, *op.cit.* lies in the introduction of the assimilative capability and the exclusion of the symbolic one, the latter being defined by the two authors as the rate of effective symbol flow from the political system into the society and the international environment. The assimilative capability has been included here as it is almost a prerequisite for the development of a political system. The lack of this quality is likely to lead to the disintegration of the system. The rate of effective symbol flow is here considered part of the distributive capability. The mobilization of symbolic support for the system is regarded as an aspect of the extractive capability. Symbols, in other words, should be regarded as a resource like any other, material goods, services and so forth.

[30] Easton, "A Systems Analysis . . .", *op.cit.*, p. 177.

[31] Karl W. Deutsch, *Nationalism and Social Communication,* (Second Edition, New York 1966), p. 125. According to Deutsch a "society" refers to a group of people who are made interdependent by the division of labor, the production and distribution of goods and services. A "community" consists of men between whom the communication of common, habitual preferences and priorities in men's attention, and behavior, as well as in their thoughts and feelings can take place without difficulty.

blem of national identity can well be intensified as the result of a high rate of mobilization. Ethnic loyalties in the Congo for example, are, to a large extent, the product of modernization.[32]

Most political scientists, however, who have written on political development, believe some sense of national identity to be crucial for the effective functioning of a political system. Ward and Rustow mention "identity" as a major area of crisis in countries undergoing rapid change.[33] Millikan and Backmer specify "national unity" and "political consensus" as the primary prerequisites for new nations.[34]

b) *Legitimacy*. When discussing problems of identity the exclusive concern is with the political community or the problems connected with the *horizontal* dimension of politics; how individual members of the system see themselves in relation to the political community as a whole and its sub-communities, i.e., their feeling towards the nation, the tribe, the religious community, and the clan. The problem of legitimacy[35] refers primarily to the other two major components of the political system in Easton's definition,[36] the regime and the authorities, or the *vertical* dimension of politics; how the members evaluate the values, norms and structures guiding the development of the system, and how they look upon the government authorities who perform the regulatory function in society.

The regulative capability is concerned with overcoming the lack of agreement which exists in many countries about the proper division of authority among various political structures capable of wielding power. But is is also more widely engaged in controling the behavior of individuals in society. The political system has, in Max Weber's own words, the monopoly of "the legitimate use of physical force within a given territory", and as such the responsibility to oppose tendencies to anomie: a phenomenon, particularly serious in countries undergoing quick modernization and social change.

---

[32] A detailed account of this is found in Crawford Young's book, *Politics in the Congo: Decolonization and Independence,* (Princeton 1965), Ch. XI.

[33] Ward and Rustow, *op.cit.,* p. 466.

[34] M. F. Millikan and D. L. M. Backmer, *Emerging Nations,* (Boston 1961), pp. 76—78.

[35] The books in which the problem of legitimacy has been sorted out for special attention are not so many. Among the more recent and important books on the subject are: Leonard Binder; *Iran—Political Development in a Changing Society,* (Los Angeles 1964); and, S. M. Lipset; *America—The First New Nation,* (New York 1963).

[36] Easton's definition of "regime" runs counter to the common conception of a regime. One often talks about "Nyerere's regime" or "de Gaulle's regime" implying their particular governments. Regime in the Eastonian sense, and as used in this study, is referring exclusively to the values, norms and structures of a particular system. "Authorities" is the same as incumbents performing leading political roles in the system.

One might ask why the problem of legitimacy has been singled out for special attention. Almond and Powell, for instance, do not consider it a major developmental problem.[37] One reason for regarding it as a separate problem is the strong tendency particularly in many non-Western cultures to emphasize, that facts must be validated by a legitimate authority before it can be considered credible.[38] Distrust of those who are not in one's own family, tribe or religious group dominates any objective test of truth in traditional societies.[39]

The regulative capability of a political system can be said to be enhanced when there is a widespread belief among its members—as well as among members of other systems—that the existing values, norms and srtuctures are the most appropriate. No system is perfect in the sense that it may engender among all members concerned a sense that everything it does is correct and good. The sense of legitimacy, like that of identity, is constantly in flux. It is quite possible for a system to exist with only a minimum amount of legitimacy; people may simply comply with what is being done out of reasons such as fear of punishment, expediency or indifference. Maintenance of such a system, however, tends to become much more expensive in both a human and a material sense. It is also worth noting that in most new states, government authorities still lack the organizational capacity to ensure effective conformity through fear of punishment.

The roots or sources of the belief in the legitimacy of a regime or its role incumbents are three:[40] ideological beliefs;[41] structural arrangements and performances; and, personal qualities of the role incumbents. Attention should also be drawn to the fact that there exist different constituencies in which a government feels variably keen on establishing its legitimacy; similarly it feels variably anxious to use one or the other source of legitimacy. A government might feel that legitimacy in the eyes of the international community is more important than legitimacy before the masses at home, and concentrates its efforts accordingly. Ghana *under Nkrumah* might be a case in point. Nkrumah's interest rested largely with the pro-

---

[37] Almond and Powell, *op.cit.*, Ch. VIII.

[38] Ithiel de Sola Pool has dealt with this aspect in a chapter "The Mass Media and Politics in the Modernization Process", in Pye's "Communication . . .", *op.cit.*, pp. 234—253.

[39] An article, quoted by de Sola Pool, which gives empirical evidence for this, is Thomas Blair's "Social Structure and Information Exposure in Rural Brazil", *Rural Sociology*, (Vol. XXV, March 1960), pp. 65—75; this paper is, however, by no means the only evidence.

[40] Easton, "A Systems Analysis . . .", *op.cit.*, pp. 289—310.

[41] By "ideology" is here meant any systematic scheme of ideas about human life and nature, regardless of whether it is rational or irrational, based on traditional myth or empirical evidence.

blems of African unity. His actions on the pan-African scene tended to overshadow his interest in the performance in his own country.[42]

Both identity and legitimacy are basic to the development of any political system. If the assimilative and regulative capabilities are poorly maintained, there is always the danger that distribution and participation can lead to the fragmentation of the system. Here, Nigeria and the Congo are cases in point. In these two countries the problems of making the system survive have at certain periods been exclusively prominent, always at the expense of other capabilities. If the sense of identity and legitimacy, on the other hand, is high, a reserve of support for the system, which can be used while performing other activities, is made available.

c) *Penetration.* The problem of penetration is related to the question how a political system can extend its capability to extract energies from the system itself, as well as from its domestic and international environment. A number of definitions of the problem, some of which do not correspond to the one used here,[43] have been given by other political scientists. What is emphasized in this study is the application of politics in promoting changes, which are intended to enlarge the environmental material and human resources available, for the development of the political system.

This developmental problem is particularly serious in the less developed countries, where both material and human resources are scarce. The econo-

---

[42] This comes out in a number of works which within a short time after Nkrumah's fall have been written on the ex-President and his role in politics. See e. g., A. A. Mazrui: "Nkrumah—The Leninist Czar", *Transition,* (No 27, 1966), Henry L. Bretton, *The Rise and Fall of Kwame Nkrumah: A Study of Personal Rule in Africa,* (New York 1966), Bob Fitch and Mary Oppenheimer, *Ghana: End of Illusion,* (New York 1966) and A. A. Afrifa, *The Ghana Coup: 24th February 1966,* (New York 1966).

[43] Lucian Pye defines "penetration" in his book, "Aspects...", *op.cit.,* as involving "the problems of government in reaching down into society and affecting basic policies... The penetration problem is that of building up the effectiveness of the formal institutions by government and of establishing confidence and rapport between ruler and subjects".

Ward and Rustow in their work *op.cit.,* p. 458 also emphasize another aspect. They point to "the motion away" from massive political apathy in traditional and early modernizing societies as a dimension of the process of penetration.

In an unpublished paper for the Political Science Research Programme, Makerere University College in fall 1965, Audrey Wipper suggests that penetration refers to a set of processes of social change through which the central government "brings all areas of the nation under its effective administration and involves the various sectors with its plans, projects, values and aspirations, building up a set of formal institutions to implement its policies and by creating feelings of oneness and confidence between itself and the people".

The difference between these three definitions and the one used here is that the former tend to include under the concept of "penetration" also the problems of regulating the behavior of individuals in society.

mies are primarily based on agricultural production; many of the agricultural products command a low price on the world market. Few people are educated and there are in many countries a lack of motivation for change and a scarcity of technical competence. All these factors tend to restrict the opportunities to draw material and human resources from the domestic society. Many of the less developed countries are therefore also depending on resources obtained from other countries.

It is possible to distinguish between two types of extractions: *balanced* and *unbalanced*. The first type is based on the assumption that penetration downwards in society in order to extract more resources should be done without upsetting a prevailing equilibrium of political goals. The components of the political system are not allowed to be shaken up. The main endeavour is to analyze the possible chain of consequences which might result from certain types of policies and then adapt these policies to the prospective changes. This approach often leads to a more cautious application of political means to achieve change. The extractions which take place are made so as not to offend current political values and structural organization. This approach to the problem of penetration is predominant in Africa among those countries, which Coleman and Rosberg call "pragmatic-pluralistic".[44]

The unbalanced type of extractions put primary emphasis on mobilization of resources rather than upholding an equilibrium between various political goals. One tries to facilitate transformation in society by concentrating the extractive efforts on one part of the system, even if this should mean weakening other parts. Those involved in unbalanced extractions ignore large parts of the total value spectrum of the society for which the change is planned. The "innovators" are not interested in gradually modifying existing policies to bring them in line with expected results. They focus on the immediate and often narrowly defined results of a proposed extractive policy. This approach is most common in those countries which put a high value on rapid social and economic change.[45] In those countries the belief in politics as a creator of profound social and economic changes is particularly strong. Here Lenin's thesis that "political power and inspired willful leadership become the prime movers of history" is an underlying assumption for political action in coping with the problem of penetration. The success of the unbalanced approach, however, is likely to depend very much on whether or not there exists a widespread sense of identity and legitimacy. The dilemma in many countries where the assimilative and regulative capabilities are weak is, as Huntington has pointed out, that "rapid gains in some of the

---

[44] Coleman and Rosberg, *op.cit.*, p. 5.
[45] According to Coleman and Rosberg, these countries are referred to as "revolutionary-centralizing", *ibid.*, p. 5.

most desired areas of modernization ... may have to be purchased at the price of severe loss in political stability".[46]

d) *Allocation.* This problem is related to the capacity of the system to distribute satisfactorily material goods and services as well as symbolic rewards. It is intensified in less developed countries for two main reasons. Generally speaking demands by far exceed what the political and the economic system can produce. Material resources, in particular, are simply not available to meet the constantly rising expectations. Secondly, the prevailing egalitarian values in most societies tend to increase the load of demands on the system. The latter point can be illuminated with a historic comparison. When the European societies a hundred years ago began to undergo extensive social and economic change, the prevailing ideology was still based on the principle of "laissez-faire". The state was not considered to be responsible for promoting the welfare of the people; on the contrary, the road to happiness lay in as little state interference as possible in the affairs of the society. Workers in the industrial cities of Western Europe were left to care for themselves or depend on help from philanthropical societies. Because industrialization preceded demands for an equal distribution of material benefits, the economy of these countries developed a strength of its own. By this means inflationary tendencies could be reduced. In the less developed countries today, however, the economies are still very weak and only slightly developed, while at the same time there are widely spread demands for an equal allocation of material benefits.

It is worth noting, however, that although the demands for equalizing distribution is strong in many African countries the policy of the government might not reflect these demands. Many governments believe that it is necessary to allow some wealth to be concentrated in the hands of people who are able and willing to invest money in order to promote economic growth, if not development.[47] In the countries which are following this kind of policy there is a relative impoverishment of the periphery of political and economic life. This process might well turn out to be a long term threat to constructive social and economic change. The growing difference between well-to-do and less well-to-do members of society may also become a threat to political stability.[48]

In other countries the problem of allocating benefits in a just fashion is getting first priority. Promoting *rapid* economic growth is sacrificed in the

[46] Huntington, *op.cit.*, p. 420.

[47] By "economic growth" is here understood an increase in output (GNP) per capita; by "economic development" the building of institutions, new lines of production, and the dissemination of attitudes essential for a self-sustaining growth.

[48] It is worth remembering that Marx believed that the impoverishment of the social and economic periphery was not a threat to development, but a *precondition* of development as brought about by revolution.

interest of *even* economic development. Steps are taken to avoid making certain areas of the country or certain groups in society impoverished. Generally this type of policy is coupled with a policy of diminishing dependence on foreign aid, or at least certain kinds of foreign aid. This policy also implies large sacrifices for many people. To combat potential dissatisfaction, the system often becomes increasingly preoccupied with the distribution of symbolic rewards and gratifications.

e) *Participation.* The responsive capability relates to the reaction of the system to various kinds of inputs. Participation in the political system varies from country to country. In one system well-organized interest groups and political associations may provide opportunities for extensive participation. In another, such organizations do not exist; a small group of rulers determine exclusively the development of the system. The resultant demands from the domestic environment in the first type of system are likely to be quite high; in the second type, inputs are generated within the political elite.[49]

Again, a historical comparison may illustrate why the problem of participation is particularly serious in the less developed countries today. A hundred years ago in Western Europe the majority of the people had no right to vote or no right to organize themselves for political purposes. The workers and the peasants were kept down by the authorities. Hence the opportunities for inputs from the domestic environment were limited. In many cases, however, this led to illegal participation. When the system itself did not voluntarily respond to the needs of poor people, the latter forced the system to do so by organizing illegitimate means of putting forward their demands, demonstrations, riots and even revolutions.

The implication for the new states, which by and large have been created with wide opportunities for raising demands on the political system,[50] is that sometimes the whole system, but more often the regime and the incumbent authorities, have been put in jeopardy as a result of an "overloading" on the input side.

The responsive capability of the system can, in short, be said to depend on two factors: the number of demands raised in the environment; secondly, the degree to which the system is equipped to meet these demands. In many of the traditional political systems, in which parochial attitudes persisted,[51]

---

[49] Almond and Powell seem to imply that systems without a well organized set of interest groups and political associations necessarily are less responsive to its environment. (Cf., *op.cit.*, pp. 201—03). This seems to me a wrong assumption, since the responsive capability also depends on the attitudes of the political elite. It is quite possible that a system, in which the inputs largely originate within the political elite, can be as responsive to its environment as a system with many interest groups and political associations, provided the elite itself is capable of absorbing the demands.
[50] Almond and Verba in their *Civic Culture,* Princeton, 1963), p. 3, talks about "the participation explosion".
[51] *Ibid.,* p. 16 ff.

expectations and needs—if they existed—were never, or at least hardly ever, politicized. It is still not uncommon to find, that issues which are crucial to certain people do not become politicized, even if a highly developed set of interest groups and political associations does exist. People may have expectations and strong needs, but these do not become inputs until they are transformed into demands for action by the political system.[52]

Development at the grass-root level

The concern with the problems at the grass-root level is new in the study of political development. To political science, rural politics in sub-Saharan African countries is still like an unknown world that needs to be explored. Political scientists have sometimes quoted anthropologists writing on the political organization of a particular tribe, but this type of material has rarely been integrated into a more systematic study of the relation of the centre to the periphery of a national political system.[53] There have been few attempts to bridge the "micro-macro gap" in social science research. We know very little about the place of local political structures and behavior within larger political wholes in Africa. We do not know to what extent the periphery is integrated with the objectives of the political centre.

One purpose of this study, as indicated already, is trying to rectify this situation. It aims at bringing to our attention data obtained at the grass-root level of politics, and putting it into a wider national perspective. Much of the information for this study has been obtained by the present author as a participant observer in these rural communities of northwestern Tanzania, and from written documents. In addition to this, however, survey research has been used in order to obtain some "hard data" on which to base the conclusions.[54]

By using the concept "periphery" to denote the rural areas and its habitants, the impression is easily gained that these are of marginal importance to the development of a society. This is, however, wrong. Several reasons could be stated as to why the rural areas of a less developed country, like

[52] Easton in his "A Systems Analysis", op.cit., p. 40 makes the point that demands can be expressed or implied. In the first case these are most easily detected if they are clearly enunciated orally or in writing. Implied demands are often expressed in actions, such as voting for a particular candidate, etc.

[53] Exceptions are books like David Apter's The Gold Coast in Transition, (Princeton 1955), and his, The Political Kingdom in Uganda, (Princeton 1961), L. A. Fallers, The King's Men, (Oxford 1964), and M. G. Smith, Government in Zazzau, (London 1960). See also Harumi Befu, "The Political Relation of the Village to the State", World Politics, (Vol XIX, July, 1967), pp. 601—20.

[54] For information about how it was gathered, see Appendix I.

Tanzania, and the people inhabiting these areas, are cornerstones in the building of a new society. The economy of the country is almost exclusively depending on agriculture, and, to a large extent, on what is produced in peasant agriculture. Motivations, attitudes and skills of the individual peasant, therefore, become of great significance to the development of the whole society. In a country so heavily dependent on agriculture, the impoverishment of the rural area, by means of migration to the towns, poor communications from the centre, and no incentives to change, constitutes a serious threat, not only to the economy, but also to the functioning of the political system. The results of the lack of political associations in a distant part of southern Italy has already been documented by Edward Banfield.[55] He maintains that only where people can create and maintain corporate political organizations, can they develop a modern economy. Inability to maintain organizations is also a barrier to political progress. As Banfield points out, successful self-government depends upon the possibility of concerting the behavior of large numbers of people in matters of public concern.[56]

Buhaya is situated in the northwestern corner of Tanzania, west of Lake Victoria,[57] and as far as possible away from the national capital, Dar es Salaam. It is inhabited primarily by one tribe, the Haya.

The reasons for choosing Buhaya are many. First of all it is geographically far from the capital, and therefore it provides a particularly ample opportunity to study to what extent government information and policies which originate in the centre of the political system, actually penetrate the periphery.

The Haya people have traditionally had strong links with the kingdoms in Uganda to the north. Their cultural traditions are intimately linked with some of the tribes in Uganda.[58] All this has direct bearing on the problem of identity in Tanzania. To what extent can the Bahaya think of an assimilation with the rest of Tanzania?

The traditional political system was relatively well organized and the traditional authorities, the chiefs, have even in modern times commanded great influence in the area. To what extent have traditional values survived and what are the consequences of this for the problem of legitimizing the new regime?

The old society was highly stratified as a result of the allocation of material rewards by the chiefs. What changes have taken place in the social relations between people?

[55] E. C. Banfield, *The Moral Basis of a Backward Society*, (New York 1958, paperback edition 1967).
[56] *Ibid.*, p. 7.
[57] Cf., map on p. 12.
[58] Cf., Chapter 4.

Due, among other things, to the early settlement of missionaries in the area, Buhaya has become one of the most developed parts of Tanzania. People have engendered new expectations. What are the implications of this for the distributive capability of the political system in a period when sacrifices for the national interest have to be made?

Finally, the Haya people were among the first to organize themselves politically to defend their interest in the colonial period. To the Bahaya the British brought the first popularly elected councils in the local areas. How has this affected the responsive capability and the problem of participation?

The difficulties in establishing any valid grounds for comparison of data based on survey research dissuaded the present writer from field work in any other part of the country. It is hard to account for the differences which might originate in the local traditional cultures, because the anthropological material on most of the tribes in Tanzania do not give full information on aspects relevant for this study,[59] and official statistics at this level do not necessarily make comparisons more firmly based.

It was impossible, for interview purposes, to draw a random sample of the total population in the two districts. Statistics which would render it possible were not available. The main reason for not doing it, however, was because of a desire to make a systematic comparison between different, representative types of parishes in Buhaya. Have not people living near Bukoba, the only town in the region, different attitudes from those living far away in the countryside? What impact has education had on people? In those parts where the educational tradition is long, have people different values from those living in parts where educational facilities more or less are the products of independence? Is there not a clear distinction between people involved in a monetary economy and those who have not yet completely entered into a life based on modern economic exchange?

Instead of a random sample of the total population five village areas or parishes[60] have been selected: Bugombe, Kitendagulo, Bwatangabo, Kabagunda, and Kiruruma, which all differ according to the following basic variables:[61]

---

[59] The anthropological documentation is most extensive on those tribes which all belong to the most advanced in the country: the Chagga, the Haya, the Hehe, the Nyakyusa, the Nyamwezi and the Sukuma peoples. A comparison based on material from these tribes would not have been representative for Tanzania, anyway.

It should be emphasized, of course, that I did not choose Buhaya as an area representative of Tanzania as a whole. As stated above, it was selected on specific grounds to illuminate the problems of political development in the rural areas. See also Appendix I.

[60] A "village" in Luhaya is *kyalo*. Since pre-colonial times villages have for administrative purposes been arranged into parishes; "parish" in Luhaya is *nkungu*. I will alternately use the local and the English words in this study.

[61] Cf., Appendix II.

— distance from Bukoba;
— regular bus connections with Bukoba;
— number of schools in the area;
— age of educational institutions;
— degree and type of commercial activities.

It is also worth noting that of the five parishes, four are in Bukoba District, Bugombe (Kiziba chiefdom), Kitendagulo (Kyamtwara chiefdom), Bwatangabo (Kianja chiefdom), and Kabagunda (Ihangiro chiefdom), and one, Kiruruma (Karagwe chiefdom) in Karagwe District.

A complete account of the characteristics of the parishes is given in Appendix II. A summary of that information is given in the following table:

Table 2. Social, economic and geographical characteristics of the five parishes and their inhabitants, based on local statistics and information gathered through survey research.

	Bugombe	Kitendagulo	Bwatangabo	Kabagunda	Kiruruma
local statistics:					
distance from town	23	2	37	60	103
regular bus connections	two	many	six	one	none
number of schools[62]	9	9	12	7	3
age of schools[63]	38	60	26	30	12
degree of commercial activities	conside-rable	conside-rable	conside-rable	conside-rable	little
average land unit	2	2	3,5	3,5	4
research—generated data:					
age distribution	mainly old	young and old	mainly old	mainly young	mainly young
occupations	mainly farmers	varying	all farmers	varying	mainly farmers
land acquired mainly through	inheri-tance	inheri-tance	inheri-tance	inheri-tance	purchase
size of coffee farm	mainly middle-size	small and middle-size	middle-size and large	mainly small	small and middle-size

[62] In the parish and schools within 7 miles of the parish.
[63] Only the oldest school is recorded here.

	Bugombe	Kitendagulo	Bwatangabo	Kabagunda	Kiruruma
language knowledge[64]	Luhaya+ Kiswahili	Luhaya + Kiswahili	Luhaya + Kiswahili	Luhaya only	Luhaya only
spread of education[65]	60 %	68 %	61 %	54 %	28 %
religious distribution	mainly Catholic	mainly Catholic	mainly Catholic	Catholic + Prot.	mainly Catholic
media exposure[66]	not so often	often	not so often	not so often	not so often
geographical mobility[67]	high	high	high	some	some
membership in TANU	76 %	54 %	75 %	65 %	75 %

Bugombe, Kitendagulo, and Bwatangabo roughly constitute one category. These parishes are quite near Bukoba; bus connections are numerous. The impact of education is reflected in a fairly large number of educated people and persons who speak Kiswahili. Commercial activities are considerable. Land holdings are, however, quite small in Bugombe and Kitendagulo.[68] They are all situated in the most densely populated eastern part of Buhaya, and representative for the various types of communities in this area.

Kabagunda and Kiruruma form a second category, although it is true that Kabagunda in some respects is closer to the other three parishes than to Kiruruma. Both are distant from Bukoba and bus connections are few. Commercial activities are not so extensive, although in Kabagunda, thanks to the existence of a fishing market within its boundaries, the shops are numerous. On the whole, however, the purchasing power of the local population as in Kabagunda is low. Education is more recent in these two parishes and the majority of the population speak only the vernacular. Land is no problem, at least around Kiruruma, where the soil, moreover, is fertile. The population density is low. Kabagunda is representative of a distant parish, where fishing to a large extent has taken the place as the most im-

[64] This reflects the predominant pattern in the village. In Kabagunda, for example, however, almost as many know both Kiswahili and Luhaya as there are people knowing only the vernacular.
[65] Any formal education is here considered.
[66] "Often" means that a majority of the respondents read a newspaper or listen to radio at least once or twice a week; "not so often" that the majority listens or reads less than that.
[67] "High" mobility means that a large percentage of the respondents have travelled outside their home district and outside the country; "some" mobility means that the majority have travelled only outside the district or their home village.
[68] Cf., information given in Chapter 3 and 4.

portant commercial activity. Kiruruma is typical for the economically backward areas of western Buhaya.

Thanks to the good records kept by the parish authorities it was possible to make a random sample from the list of taxpayers in each village area.[69] 15 per cent was regarded as satisfactory to secure a high degree of representativity.[70] In all, 328 people were interviewed in the course of 1965. Their answers constitute the raw material for the analysis made in Part III.

Those who are familiar with systematic interviewing in countries where the population is predominantly illiterate know that survey data must be treated with some caution. Bias often tends to increase in direct proportion to the difficulties of the interview situation. No secrets are made of the difficulties encountered. Sampling bias, translation problems, inexperienced interviewers, reluctant and startled interviewees, ambiguous coding categories and related factors can all introduce error into the data. The present writer has had his share of these problems (and others as well; cf., Appendix I). On the other hand, the data is consistent and uniform. The general direction of the survey data is therefore reliable, although a given response of 25 % might as easily have been 20 % or 30 %.

As a complement to this survey, second interviews were carried out late 1965 with a selected number of the original interviewees to obtain more information on some topics which were only briefly dealt with in the original questionnaire.

In addition to the systematic interviews with the local commoners, interviews were held with local leaders and elders in order to obtain enough background material. Minutes from local VDC meetings and other records were also made available to the present author in the five areas. All these activities were done prior to the systematic interviewing. For full information on how the data was collected, and the problems involved in this process, see Appendix I.

The organization of the book

By way of introduction the next chapter will be devoted to a presentation of the Tanzanian political system; the factors explaining its special qualities, and the steps which have been taken by the system to overcome the developmental problems.

[69] Since principally the men are registered as tax-payers, the respondents in the survey are almost all male. Enough women are included, however, to confirm whether any considerable difference in political outlook exists between members of the two sexes.
[70] Cf., Appendix I.

Part II will deal exclusively with Buhaya. Chapter 3 gives the general background information. The following chapter is a presentation of the traditional systems. In Chapter 5 follows an account of the policies pursued by the colonial powers, Germany and England, in Buhaya. Then comes a description of the early reactions to colonial policies in the area; how a new political consciousness was first created. The last chapter in that part deals with the growth of TANU in Buhaya.

In Part III, the survey data will be presented and analyzed. Five chapters are arranged in order to reflect the attitudes of the local Haya population to various aspects of the five developmental problems identified above.

A summary in Kiswahili follows after the conclusions in Part IV.

Chapter 2. # The Tanzanian political system

As a way of putting the study of political development in Buhaya in its proper context this chapter will be devoted to a presentation of the Tanzanian political system; the environmental factors that explain the general political development in post-colonial Tanzania; the steps that have been taken to overcome various threats to development. When studying political development political scientists have been trying to locate similarities and differences between various national systems. According to the performance of the system or its sub-systems, e.g., the party system, typologies have been created. Distinctions have been made between "revolutionary-centralizing" and "pragmatic-pluralistic" systems,[1] between "mobilization" and "reconciliation" systems,[2] and between "mass" and "elite" systems.[3]

There has been some uncertainty about what type of system Tanzania most resembles. This uncertainty can partly be explained by the fact that there have been significant changes, not in the values of the regime but in the way the leaders of the country have decided to tackle the developmental problems. Another reason is that even superficially Tanzania is no "clear" case. In two recent publications,[4] the American political scientists, Rupert Emerson and Henry Bienen, tend to put Tanzania within the "pluralistic" category. The latter, however, takes issue with the present typologies.[5] He finds them misleading and inadequate. The empirical evidence he presents, mainly from studying intra-party relationships, shows that after independence TANU has become less disciplined and monolithic. The low level of economic development, according to Bienen, simply makes a "revolutionary-centralizing" system impossible. Another observer of East African politics[6] has already earlier expressed a similar view.

[1] Coleman and Rosberg, *op.cit.*, p. 677.

[2] Apter, "The Political Kingdom...", *op.cit.*, pp. 22—24; also his "The Politics...", *op.cit.*, p. 25 ff.

[3] Rudebeck, *op.cit.*, pp. 14—22. Some of the qualities generally attributed to "revolutionary-centralizing", "mobilization" or "mass-oriented" systems are: power resides at the top, generally in the hands of a single leader; the party demands a fundamental commitment on part of the individual; the aim is to create new political structure; combined with this is a strong preoccupation with ideology to give necessary changes perspective.

[4] See R. Emerson, "Parties and National Integration in Africa" in LaPalombara and Weiner, *op.cit.*, pp. 281—287; also Bienen, *op.cit.*, pp. 3—19.

[5] Bienen, *op.cit.*, p. 4.

[6] Albert Meister, *L'Afrique peut-elle partir?*, (Paris 1966), pp. 421—43.

A weakness of the present typologies, already indicated in the first chapter.[7] is that they are based on the prescriptions of the regime, on the intentions and aspirations of the leaders. Ideally, therefore, a structure may be tight, but empirically it turns out to be loose. This is, for instance, Bienen's quarrel with those who unreservedly put Tanzania in the "revolutionary-centralizing" category.

In order to find out to what extent there exists some congruence between the aspirations of the leaders and the prevailing attitudes among rural inhabitants in a distant part of the country, it is necessary to offer a more detailed presentation of the Tanzanian political system as it is reflected in the policies aimed at challenging the developmental problems. As will be seen below, there is no doubt that the political leaders have acted in the spirit of a "revolutionary-centralizing" ideology, at least in some principal respects. They have attempted to achieve a major structural reconstruction and a cultural innovation. New structures have been created to take the place of old ones. Attempts have been made to adjust social and political behavior to a new ideology of socialism. Calls have been made to discard old habits and adopt new motivations more feasible for a country aiming at rapid development. At the same time Tanzanian leaders have closely supervised and controlled the flow of inputs and outputs. Demands on the political system have been regulated by the creation of a commitment to the nation and to the regime. By and large, one may say that the government authorities in Tanzania have intended to achieve a major structural differentiation and a cultural secularization in order to improve the capacity of the political system to combat the many problems with which it is faced.

The following account is not primarily an exhaustive review of events in Tanzania after independence. Certain events, which no doubt are significant in the Tanzanian context, have been selected to illustrate how various aspects of the key developmental problems have entered the political system and which prescriptions the government authorities have proposed for their solution.

The problem of identity

The rate of assimilation into a common nationhood in many new African countries has been rather slow. The Cameroons, Congo-Kinshasa, Nigeria, Sudan, and Uganda have suffered considerably from the persistence of tribalistic or ethnic feelings in politics, often intensified by economic differences

[7] Cf., p. 15.

and a high rate of mobilization in a situation where people have not developed a sufficient ability to communicate with each other.[8]

Conditions for national assimilation in Tanzania have been more favorable than in most other African countries. Particularly two environmental factors are worth noting: (1) the distribution of tribes; and, (2) the existence of a common language, Kiswahili.

Tanzania has no single major tribe, which has tended to dominate others, like the Baganda in Uganda. The largest tribe, the Sukuma, inhabiting a wide area south of Lake Victoria, constitute roughly one twelfth of the total population, according to the national census of 1957.[9] The total number of tribes is around 120, some of which nowadays have less than 10.000 members. Among other large tribes in Tanzania are, the Nyamwezi, the Ha, the Makonde, the Gogo, the Haya, and the Chagga; these constitute *each* between three and five per cent of the grand total.

All the major tribes are inhabiting areas in the geographical periphery of the country. The tribes living in the coastal areas around Dar es Salaam are small and have not been notably affected by the spread of modernization.[10]

The largest proportion of civil servants and politicians in the capital are therefore recruited from the, so-called, up-country tribes. Dar es Salaam has become a genuine melting-pot, where no particular tribe has obtained a prominent position at the cost of others. In this respect, Dar es Salaam differs from the other two East African capitals, Kampala in Uganda, and Nairobi in Kenya. Kampala is located in Ganda territory. A widespread feeling among the Baganda has been that the central government, dominated by members of other tribes, has no right to give directions to them. These feelings were publicly expressed in the Buganda Parliament, the *Lukiiko,* in the fatal months of early 1966, when the Ganda kingship was de facto abolished.[11] A similar situation, although not as critical as in Kampala, exists in Nairobi, where members of the Kikuyu tribe often regard themselves as having priority to new employment opportunities in that town. Nairobi (an old Masai word) is nowadays located almost in the heart of Kikuyuland;

---

[8] See, e.g., Young, *op.cit.,* particularly Ch. XI; and Immanuel Wallerstein, "Ethnicity and National Integration in West Africa", *Cahier d'Etudes Africaines,* (No 3, October 1960), pp. 129—39.

[9] East African Statistical Department, *Tanganyika Population Census 1957,* (Nairobi 1958); also cited in J. Clagett Taylor, *The Political Development of Tanganyika,* (Los Angeles 1963), p. 29.

[10] Cf., e.g., N. Miller, "Village Leadership in Tanzania", *EAISR Conference Paper* (December 1964).

[11] *Uganda Argus,* (Kampala), May 21, 1966. This preceded a major intervention by the central government-controlled army, which aimed at abolishing the symbol of resistance of the Baganda to national integration—the traditional kingship and its incumbent, Kabaka Mutesa II. He is now living in exile in England.

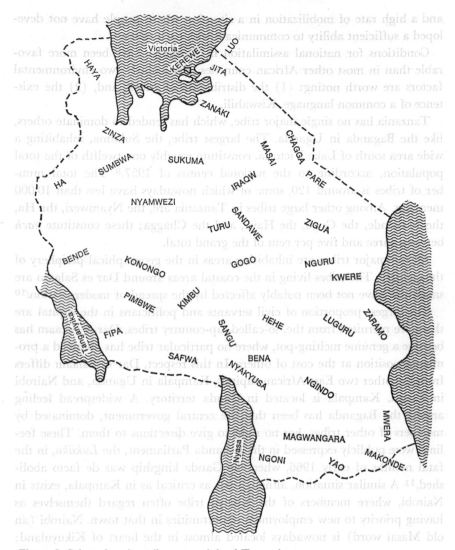

Figure 3. Selected major tribes on mainland Tanzania.

consequently, the members of this tribe constitute the largest group of Africans in the city.

Another reason, why Dar es Salaam is different from Kampala and Nairobi is the prevalence of a common language, Kiswahili; this language is spoken also in other countries, including Kenya and Uganda, but has no official recognition there similar to that in Tanzania. Tribal languages, therefore, dominate much more in these two countries. The problem of creating and maintaining a national identity has been made considerably easier in Tanzania due to the existence of this *lingua franca*. It has fitted the purpose of national assimilation much better than English and French, since it is a language with roots on the African continent,[12] spoken by the ordinary man, and therefore not associated with an elite. The relation between the coastal and up-country tribes in Tanzania has become smoother because they have had a common means of communication.[13] This situation is almost unique in the sub-Saharan Africa.[14]

The Tanzanian authorities have been very anxious to promote the spread of Kiswahili in the country. In 1964, the government issued a statement reminding the citizens of the value of Kiswahili to the nation. In January 1967 an even stronger declaration was made by the Second Vice-President, Rashidi Kawawa. Kiswahili was to be used for all government business. "English, like Arabic, Chinese, German, Russian or French, is a language we can justifiably use when communicating with foreigners who do not understand Kiswahili."[15] In March 1967 an announcement was made by the Ministry of Education that Kiswahili was to be the medium of instruction throughout primary school courses in Tanzania.[16] These steps followed a crisis in the socialization process, which had culminated in a students' demonstration in October 1966 against a proposed national service scheme.[17] At that occasion it became obvious that the educational system was not preparing young members of the society for their various roles in the country; they acquired habits of speaking English, because it had a higher prestige in the social environment in which they were brought up; they were prepared by the educational system for roles in the urban rather than in the rural context, although only a small percentage of those who had begun primary school were ever able to move into urban roles. This weakness in the socialization function tended to have repercussions on the assimilative capability

[12] Kiswahili is an Arabized Bantu language.

[13] Linguists tend to make a distinction between coastal, or original, Kiswahili, and up-country Kiswahili. The latter is often more mixed with influences from the local tribal languages. These different Kiswahili dialects are also distinguished by the local population, but this has no political or social implications.

[14] The only two other sub-Saharan countries, where one African language is spoken by the vast majority of the population are Rwanda and Burundi. In these two countries, however, the local language, *Kinyarwanda* in Rwanda, and *Kirundi* in Burundi, has to compete with Kiswahili and French, which have equal status. In The Central African Republic, *sango* has recently been made the national language.

[15] *The Nationalist,* (Dar es Salaam), January 5, 1967.

[16] *Ibid.,* March 18, 1967.

[17] This demonstration caused the anger of the President, who decided to dismiss from the university and a few other educational institutions in Dar es Salaam 392 students, all participants in the demonstration. The President in an address to the nation at that occasion, entitled "Tanzania itajengwa na wenye moyo", gives the background of the crisis, as well as his own view on the behavior of the students. The speech has been translated into Swedish: Julius K. Nyerere, *Tanzania skall byggas med hängivelse,* (Uppsala 1967).

and the government authorities felt obliged to take these steps to combat the disintegrative tendencies.

The aims of Tanganyika African National Union have, ever since its birth, been to fight tribalism and isolationist tendencies among Africans, oppose racial discrimination of any kind, and build up a united nation. These aims are clearly stated in the TANU constitution.[18] A mobilization of mass support was achieved all over the country in the late 1950s and the opposition parties gave up or were defeated at the polls before independence 1961. The United Tanganyika Party, set up by the unofficial members of the Legislative Council in February 1956 and sponsored by the colonial administration[19] was severely defeated in the first election in the country in 1958. By the end of that year the UTP had ceased to function as an effective political organization.[20]

The other challenge to TANU came from the Tanganyika African National Congress, which was formed in 1958 following an internal dispute over TANU participation in the forthcoming election to the Legislative Council.[21] A former acting Organizing Secretary of TANU, Zuberi Mtemvu, became the chairman of the new party, the aim of which was independence for Africans only; its official slogan was "Africa for the Africans".[22] The new party posed even less of a threat to TANU than UTP. At three consecutive elections, 1959, 1960, and 1962, Mtemvu and TANC were completely outvoted.[23]

Because TANU soon developed into a genuine nationalist movement, consisting of urban workers and rural dwellers, educated and illiterate, traditional and modern elements, Muslims, Christians and Animists, it could more

[18] Tanganyika African National Union, *Sheria na Madhumuni ya Chama*, (Dar es Salaam), pp. 1—3.

[19] The story of UTP is told by Taylor, *op.cit.*, pp. 137—77.

[20] Colonial Office, London, *Report 1958*, pp. 35—36.

[21] The issue at stake was whether TANU should follow the path of constitutional development or boycott the 1959 election and perhaps drift into violence. The fateful decision to participate in the election was taken at the Annual Delegates Conference in January 1958 at Tabora. Some members belonging to the minority of the delegates, who opposed the decision, broke away from TANU and formed TANC. For an account of the Tabora Conference, see Listowel, *op.cit.*, Ch 29.

[22] *Ibid.*, p. 308.

[23] In 1959, Mtemvu standing in the Tanga constituency received only 53 votes against 1854 for the UTP candidate and 3455 for the TANU candidate (cf., Taylor, *op.cit.*, p. 173).
In the 1960 election TANC could only field three candidates. Together they collected only 337 votes. See *Tanganyika Gazette*, (Dar es Salaam 1960, Vol XLI, No 52). Mtemvu's last attempt was in the 1962 presidential election, when he ran against Nyerere and was heavily defeated: 1.123.535 for Nyerere and 21.279 for Mtemvu. See *Tanganyika Gazette*, (1962, Vol XLIII, No 64).

easily direct the new sense of nationhood into practical outlets. One step was the promotion of Kiswahili, as referred to above.

Another step was the reshaping of the provincial and district administration. The heads now became political appointees instead of civil servants.[24] The latter were organized into a unified service, providing for the circulation of these functionaries from place to place. The idea behind these reforms was that, mobilizing people into the same structures, all imbued with the same spirit of creating national unity, would facilitate the integration of the many local cultures into one national community.[25]

A positive experience of TANU as an assimilative body was gained at the local level in the early years of its struggle for independence. Particularly important in many parts of the country was the fact that, for the first time, people of different religious backgrounds had been brought together to discuss common problems. Already before independence the first steps were taken to create a unifed educational system, which, unlike before, was not divided along racial and religious lines. All schools are nowadays non-denominational.[26] The Tanzanian government has remained very alert to the danger of racial, tribal or religious feeling in politics. Significant therefore is that, according to the electoral law of the country, it is an offense to make any statement intended to exploit tribal, racial or religious issues.[27]

The racial minorities have always been small in Tanzania.[28] It has been an explicit policy of TANU to open its doors to members of any racial group. There are Tanzanian citizens of both Asian and European origin in the government and in the parliament. The assimilation of these two minority groups has on the whole, however, proceeded very slowly, mainly due to lack of interest by members of these minority groups in accepting the values for which the Tanzanian society and its leaders stand. All the same it should be pointed out that among the 2000 people granted Tanzanian citizenship in 1965—66, a considerable number were Asians.[29]

[24] William Tordoff, "Regional Administration in Tanganyika", *EAISR Conference Paper*, (December 1964).

[25] The completely opposite approach was used by the *Parti Démocratique de la Côte d'Ivoire*, in the Ivory Coast, where tribal associations were used as the nuclei for the organization of party committees in the sous-section of Treichville in Abidjan (cf., Aristide Zolberg "Ivory Coast" in Coleman and Rosberg, *op.cit.*, p. 79).

[26] See, e.g., B. Morrison, "Educating Citizens for Tanzania", *UEASS Conference Paper*, (December 1966).

[27] The United Republic of Tanzania, *Report on Rules for the Nomination Process and Conduct of Election Campaigns for the National Assembly*, (Government Printer, Dar es Salaam 1965), p. 5. Recommendations in this report were later implemented in the Electoral Law and in the Constitution. Cf., also *The Nationalist*, June 9, 1965.

[28] East African Statistical Department, *op.cit.*, Table 1.

[29] Statement in the National Assembly by the Minister for Home Affairs, Mr Lawi Sijaona, quoted by *The Nationalist*, April 21, 1966.

No doubt the more pronounced socialist policy, following the adoption of the so-called Arusha Declaration in January 1967,[30] has to some extent strained the relations between, the Africans on the one hand, the European and Asian minorities on the other — who since colonial times had represented the upper class. The President has reassured, however, that this socialist policy is not racialist in its objectives; nor have there been any signs that his followers deliberately would interpret it in another way. As the President is reported to have said:[31]

Where the majority of the people are black, there most of those who benefit from socialism will be black. But it has nothing to do with their blackness; only with their humanity.

There has been a rapprochement between mainland Tanzania (Tanganyika) and Zanzibar in the three years the union between the two countries has existed. The reasons are, among other, greater ideological unanimity between the political leaders of the two countries and a growing sense of security of the new Zanzibar government. The Zanzibar Revolutionary Council is represented both in government and parliament in Dar es Salaam and there has been an increased exchange of officers between the island and the mainland. Restrictions to enter the island, which used to be very hard even for Tanzanian citizens residing on the mainland, have recently been eased.[32] Still, however, the relations are not as close as many people would like them to be.

The problem of legitimacy

The question of how to create a legitimate political order is another challenge to the political leaders of the new states. Several governments have failed because their rule has not gained the confidence of the people, or at least, some important sectors of the population. Thanks to the fact that Tanzania achieved a high degree of national unity and unanimity on certain basic principles already before independence stresses caused by post-independence political changes have been reduced. Cases in point are the reaction to the establishment of constitutional one-party state in 1965, and the introduction in the same year of a new electoral system.[33] Both these major changes were met with insignificant opposition.

[30] Julius K. Nyerere "Socialism is not Racialism", *ibid.*, February 14, 1967.
[31] *Ibid., loc. cit.*
[32] *Ibid.*, April 21, 1967, The special office for Union affairs was dissolved in June 1967, by some considered as another indication of more "normal" relations between the island and the mainland; also *ibid.*, July 5, 1967.
[33] For a detailed account of this, see Lionel Cliffe (ed), *One-Party Democracy*, (Nairobi 1967).

The structural reorganization in the direction of a one-party state has not, however, created a guarantee that everybody is prepared to follow "the rules of the game". Opposition within a party may in certain situations pose an even more serious threat to the stability of the system than an outside opposition.[34] The dialogue, which has been pursued by various groups within TANU has, however, in most cases, been perceived as constructive, or at least, not wholly detrimental. Criticism of the government and various other institutions in the society has not been regarded as a threat to the stability of the system.

Opposition to the government authorities in Tanzania has so far been less directed at the fundamental values on which the system rests than at the fact that many individual representatives of the regime have not practised the ideology, for which their government stands. In other words, it has been a kind of spontaneous self-criticism, and directed primarily at two phenomena: the tendencies towards officialdom within the party and the government; and the lack of skilled persons in charge of government.

The complaints about the tendencies towards officialdom or bureaucratization have been frequent. Much of the criticism has come from the MPs who have complained of lack of cooperation on part of the functionaries in the party and the civil service. On one occasion a Member of Parliament went as far as claiming that the behavior of some Regional and Area Commissioners, the political heads of the regions and the districts, was destructive to the nation.[35] The Minister of Regional Administration at that time, Mr Oscar Kambona,[36] replied that none of these commissioners were above the law; and he added, the critics should not forget the invaluable contribution to the development of the country by these hardworking men.[37]

The degree of self-criticism within TANU has also been reflected in the strong voice raised against such habits of some functionaries as using the official car for private purposes or the appropriateness of the unofficial rule that shops and offices have to be closed in places outside Dar es Salaam whenever a high official is on visit. Particularly resented has been the custom, which originated in the traditional system, and was reinforced during the colonial period, that people should, when leaders are touring the country, contribute donations for their entertainment.[38]

[34] For a comparison with the West African situation, see Zolberg, *op.cit.*, p. 92.
[35] Mr. S. M. Kibuga, MP, quoted in *The Standard*, (Dar es Salaam) December 17, 1965.
[36] Mr Kambona resigned as a Minister in June 1967 after 13 years hard work in TANU. The official reason given was ill-health, but later doubts have been expressed publicly in Tanzania, whether this was the only factor determining Kambona's sudden resignation.
[37] Quoted in *The Nationalist*, July 15, 1967.
[38] This was particularly strongly condemned at a special national conference of

Some people have urged the government to get rid of some political leaders at the regional and district level, because they have no knowledge of economics and how to stimulate economic growth.[39] The first Regional and Area Commissioners were, with a few exceptions, politicians who were rendered this position as a reward for their contribution to the achievement of political independence. More recently, however, political record has not been the only ground on which appointments of new commissioners have been made. The most notable illustration to this point was the appointment in June 1967 of the head of the civil service, Mr Namata, as Regional Commissioner in the important Mwanza Region.[40]

Abuse of power and officialdom may well have been encouraged in Tanzania by the fact that such values as obedience and deference occupy prominent positions in the Tanzanian political culture.[41] An important step in the direction of promoting an awareness of civic rights among the citizens of the country has, besides the new electoral system and the rule of law, been the establishment of a Permanent Commission of Inquiry.[42]

As in most countries where an active mobilization policy is pursued, TANU has been anxious to gain control of other national institutions. Efforts have been made to guide the activities of the cooperative unions, the trade unions, and most recently the educational institutions. The Second Vice-President declared, in March 1967, that the educational system in the country must be appropriate to the future of the country, and not to its past. The University must produce people with socialist attitudes, who are also experts at different jobs, he continued.[43] When the first TANU Youth League branch was opened at the University College in March 1967 (and every student joined), *The Nationalist,* the official organ of TANU wrote:[44]

This is a historic event, because it crowns the programme of the Youth League to draw into its ranks youth of every intellectual calibre. The event symbolises the permeation of TANU into every walk of national life.

TANU in Dar es Salaam in March 1967. See, *The Nationalist,* March 4, 1967.

[39] Cf., *The Nationalist,* June 26, 1967.

[40] *Ibid.,* June 7, 1967.

[41] The heavy stress on "obedience" and "manners" as important values in life is reflected in two independent surveys which have been conducted among Tanzanian students at various levels. See, E. L. Klingelhofer, *Studies of Tanzanian Students* (mimeographed, University College, Dar es Salaam 1967), and David Koff and George Von der Muhll, "Political Socialization in Kenya and Tanzania—A Comparative Analysis", *UEASS Conference Paper,* (December 1966). The latter paper is only a preliminary report of a much more extensive study, to be published later.

[42] The Commission is comparable to the office of the *Ombudsman* in the Scandinavian countries. Cf., *The Standard,* February 23, 1966; see also J. O. W. McAuslan and Yash Ghai, "Innovation and Stability in Tanzania", *Journal of Modern African Studies,* (Vol 4, No 4), pp. 479—516.

[43] *The Nationalist,* March 13, 1967.

[44] *Ibid.,* March 18, 1967.

From the government point of view the most important implication of this "historic event" has been to increase the mechanisms for social control.

A step in the similar direction, taken recently, requires workers of all categories in Tanzania to have identity cards from their employers and to be in possession of these cards wherever they may go. These cards which are the property of the employers must be returned to them whenever an employee ceases to work. The aim of this policy has been to cope with the problem of unemployed people and loiters in the larger towns. All those without identity cards are sent back to their respective home districts to start farming.[45] Due to these measures the process of urbanization has been deliberately retarded and is under full government control. Action has also been taken against all non-citizens living in Tanzania pursuing petty business, that can be done by Tanzanians; their work permits have not been renewed.[46]

These have also been considered as a means to reduce crimes in the country. Complaints have constantly been raised, in the streets as well as in the National Assembly, about the attempts by the government to reduce criminal activities. The majority of the people feel the government is doing much too little. Calls for stronger action have therefore been raised. Members of Parliament applauded when one of them suggested to the government that it should consider hanging murderers and giving corporal punishment to thieves in public.[47] The demand was raised again later during the same session,[48] but in an answer on behalf of the government, Mr Kawawa replied that Tanzania does not favor public hanging, because history has shown that such ways of punishment do not reduce crimes.[49] Despite popular demands for public hanging, etc., the government has not yielded.

The problem of penetration

The Arusha Declaration on "Socialism and Self-reliance" is probably the most important document in Tanzania with reference to the problem of how resources for development can be mobilized. Resource extraction is considered a pre-condition for a more equalizing allocation of material benefits in the country. Before steps were taken to implement the new policy, the activities of the social and economic systems were more or less "out of tune" with the political goals. The educational system as well as the economy of the country were not coordinated with the objectives of the political system.

[45] *The Nationalist,* March 30, 1967.
[46] *Ibid.,* editorial, January 26, 1967.
[47] *The Standard,* June 25, 1966.
[48] *The Nationalist,* July 15, 1966.
[49] *Ibid., loc. cit.*

The policy introduced in 1967 can be viewed as an attempt to rectify this imbalance. It should be emphasized that the policy as such was not new in Tanzania;[50] new was the intensification of the extractive effort of the system. Tanzania changed its extractive policies from being "balanced" to being "unbalanced".[51]

If "socialism" in the Declaration refers specifically to the problem of allocation, "self-reliance" refers to that of penetration. In practical terms it is the concern with the twin problem of creating a self-sustaining economy (a "national" instead of a "colonial" economy) and an educational system which prepares individuals for roles in a society with such aims. The reasons for laying so much stress on these two problems was the growing difficulty in extracting material and human resources to meet the needs for a distribution along socialist lines within the framework of a "free" economy. The private capital stayed in the hands of those already wealthy and was only reinvested in the industrial sector, not in the agricultural sector, although over 90 per cent of the population depended on money obtained in the latter.

A change in emphasis from reliance on capital to reliance on human energies is one of the key principles of the Arusha Declaration. One sentence reads:[52]

... The energies of the millions of men in the villages and thousands of women in the towns which are at present wasted in gossip, dancing and drinking, are a great treasure which could contribute more towards the development of our country than anything we could get from rich nations.

This is a recognition of the theory that incentives to economic development are not only, or even primarily, material, but psychological; an acknowledgement of the principle that it is not better to be "a wealthy slave" than "a poorer free man".[53]

Tanzania's capacity of extracting financial assistance in Western countries became more and more limited in 1965 and 1966 as a result of its strong stand on the issue of establishing diplomatic links with East Germany and on the Rhodesian UDI issue. At least one loan from Britain of £ 7,5 m. was frozen as a result of Tanzania's break of diplomatic relations with Britain over the Rhodesian UDI.[54] Some compensation was obtained from Canada in starting an air force, a responsibility which Western Germany originally had resumed, but which it refused to carry out as a result of the establishment of an East German Consulate-General in Dar es Salaam.[55]

[50] Calls for steps in this direction had been raised earlier; cf., *The Nationalist,* January 8, 1966.
[51] Cf., p. 27.
[52] *The Nationalist,* February 6, 1967.
[53] Cf., Julius K. Nyerere, *Principles and Development,* (Dar es Salaam 1966), p. 9.
[54] *Ibid.,* p. 11.
[55] *The Standard,* June 18, 1965.

While Tanzania had a trade surplus both 1965 and 1966,[56] it had a large deficit for the trade with Kenya.[57] Tanzania could not continue to provide an ever-increasing market for Kenyan and Ugandan goods without achieving market outlets in these two countries for its own manufactured products.[58] This problem is, to a large extent, the result of the fact that Tanzania has been the economically least developed of the three countries forming the East African Common Market. On top of all these financial difficulties, Tanzania had signed loan agreements with various countries totalling £ 39 m. in 1964—65.[59]

At the same time it became obvious to the government that the targets set in the Five Year Development Plan, launched in 1964 were not going to be achieved as intended. The First Year Progress Report, published early 1966[60] revealed severe financial bottlenecks, chiefly due to withdrawal of foreign aid and insufficient domestic savings. The Tanzanian government was not able to extract enough financial resources, neither abroad nor at home. It is partly in the face of this situation that the Arusha Declaration shall be seen.

A first important change in emphasis away from reliance on capital was the government's decision in April 1966, to abandon its plan to establish 66

---

[56] 1965 the surplus was £ 3,3 million; 1966 £ 8,5 million. Cotton was during 1966 the country's major export product followed by coffee and sisal. Commonwealth countries were that year the largest market for Tanzanian products, 52,5 % of the grand total domestic exports, as compared to 54,9 % in 1965, were sent to these countries. The value of the exports to the countries of the European Economic Community declined from 18,9 % in 1965 to 16,6 % in 1966, although there was an increase in absolute terms. EFTA countries imported only 2,9 % of Tanzania's domestic exports, and the COMECON countries 3,2 %. Exports increased considerably to countries like Japan and the United States. The figures have been put together by the Central Statistical Bureau, Dar es Salaam, and these were disclosed in an article in *The Nationalist,* April 18, 1967.

[57] 1965 the deficit was £ 10 million.

[58] See Nyerere's address to the National Assembly, on June 13, 1966, reprinted in *The Standard,* June 14, 1966. A new agreement concerning East African economic cooperation was signed in June 1967 between the three Heads of State. The objective of the new agreement has been to rectify the imbalance in trade between Uganda, Tanzania and Kenya. See *The Nationalist,* June 7, 1967. The inauguration of the new cooperation took place in November 1967 at Arusha, the new centre for the common administration.

[59] Disclosed in a statement by the Junior Minister in the Ministry of Finance, Mr Sayid Rashid, quoted by *The Standard,* June 15, 1966. Loans had been signed with the World Bank (three loans) and countries like Canada, China, Sweden, The United States, The Soviet Union and Western Germany.

[60] The United Republic of Tanzania; *First Year Progress Report on the Implementation of the Five-Year Development Plan (Public Sector) 1st July 1964 to 30th June, 1965,* (Ministry of Economic Affairs and Development Planning, Dar es Salaam 1966).

new village settlement schemes and redirecting its policy "in the light of experience".[61] Mr Kawawa, who disclosed this at a Rural Development Seminar, declared that instead of establishing highly capitalized schemes and moving people to them, emphasis will be on modernizing existing traditional villages.[62]

To some extent Tanzania had already been relying on development through so-called self-help projects, in which the people have been involved without any financial rewards. Estimations made by the Commissioner for Community Development show that in the first five years of independence the value of work done through these projects was almost 77 m. shs; the amount of money saved by the government this way was roughly 68,7 m. shs.[63]

The government assumption has been that since all this work could be done while the masses were not mobilized to the maximum, much more could be achieved by rightly employing human resources. After the Arusha Declaration emphasis has been put on calls for harder work, educating the leadership at all levels, and improving the organizational set-up. Government leaders, including the President himself, have toured the country calling for hard work, discarding of old habits and the building of a state where there is no exploitation of man by man. Special appeals have been directed to the women—"the mothers of the nation"—the youth and the workers.[64]

[61] *The Standard,* April 5, 1966.
[62] *Ibid., loc. cit.;* see also J. Nyerere, *Socialism and Rural Development,* (Dar es Salaam 1967), in which he explains the idea of *juamaa* (brotherhood) villages, the basis for the new policy of rural development.
[63] Disclosed in an article in *The Nationalist,* March 8, 1967. Mr Byalugaba, the Commissioner for Community Development, revealed that the people had among other things achieved:
24.493 miles of new roads;
 3.765 old roads cleared and re-done;
  540 dispensaries;
 2.523 school blocks, classrooms and other school buildings;
  557 community centres;
  754 wells and water kiosks;
1.096 canals;
  394 dams;
  152 bridges;
 5.856 fish ponds;
65.350 acres farmed on cooperative basis.
These figures do not include projects which were constructed by voluntary agencies, such as missions.
[64] *The Nationalist* reported on March 21, 1967, that 200 women, all but eight from Bukoba, living in Dar es Salaam, had opened a 200 acre farm a few miles outside the capital. This was done in response to the policy of socialism and self-reliance, one of the leaders declared.

The leaders have been asked to go out in the villages to talk to people and make them work harder. In order to extract more resources, leaders have to help people transform their country to a higher level. This persuasion, however, can only be successful, it is emphasized, if the "expert" plays his role "diligently, devotedly, and selflessly".[65]

Village Development Committees were introduced in the country in 1962 —63 as a means of improving the communications between the government and the people. The VDCs were to become two-way channels of information.[66] In early 1965 new party cells each consisting of ten households, were introduced all over the country as still another means of ensuring easy communication between party members and between the government and the people.[67] To a large extent, parochial attitudes have always prevailed among the leaders of the VDCs and the party cells and there were calls in 1967 from the Secretary General of the Party, Oscar Kambona, to reorganize the whole party to make it "a perfect revolutionary vanguard of the people in implementing the Arusha Declaration."[68]

The dissemination of government information into the periphery of the country has largely suffered from technical, physical and organizational problems. Distribution has been a costly matter in a country where roads often are not available or impassable. Radio broadcasts from Dar es Salaam were, at least until 1966, difficult to hear in many up-country areas.[69] The party or the government has not until recently tried—except in the schools—to organize group listening to certain key broadcasts in order to secure a wide spread of correct information from the center.[70]

To a large extent news coverage in Tanzania, like elsewhere, has been about the activities of the leaders; people's efforts have been neglected or at least reduced to a secondary matter. As one way of implementing the Arusha Declaration the government has decided to alter this practice.[71]

[65] Cf., editorial in *The Nationalist*, January 27, 1967.

[66] See e.g., René LeMarchand, "Village-by-Village Nation-Building in Tanzania", *Africa Report*, (Vol X, February 1965), pp. 11—13.

[67] See, *The Nationalist*, January 6, 1965.

[68] *Ibid.*, June 2, 1967, The implication of this statement was the creation of a more tight, monolithic, political organization. The post of Secretary-General of the party was abolished when Mr Kambona left the country only a few days after he had made this statement.

[69] Mr Joseph Kisubi, MP, in the National Assembly complained that broadcasts by Radio Tanzania were not heard clearly by upcountry listeners, particularly those in Mwanza. Reported in *The Standard*, December 22, 1965.

[70] The Cooperative Education Centre in Moshi has organized educational programs based on the idea of group listening during 1967. The response has been very satisfactory.

[71] Editorial in *The Nationalist*, January 19, 1967.

The problem of allocation

The distributive capability is closely related to the extractive one. Only when an increase in the amount of wealth, produced in Tanzania is achieved, will there be any real chances for the government to distribute services and benefits to everyone, and not just a selected few. The intentions in the Arusha Declaration with immediate implication for the distributive capability of the system are the emphasis on a more equal distribution and the re-education of people to accept new values concerning what can be expected by the government. Steps were taken immediately after the Declaration to nationalize the economy; banks, insurance companies and basic industries were taken over by the state.[72]

Africanization of all institutions in the country has always been the long-term policy of the Tanzanian government, although consideration has been given to the need for competent personnel. The principle, that only if no suitable Tanzanian African candidate is available should other candidates be considered, has been predominant with regard to appointments in the civil service. In the first two years of independence there was a wave of Africanization, following naturally the exit of many British civil servants. In the beginning of 1964, President Nyerere sent out a circular in which he criticized excessive Africanization. This circular is considered by some writers[73] to have sparked off the mutinies at Colito Barracks in January, 1964. Dissatisfaction with promotions in the army had already been expressed by that time.

In March 1966, the then Principal Secretary to the President, Mr Namata, said that two thirds of all senior and middle grade posts in the administration were occupied by Africans.[74] This he considered as an indication of the success of the government's Africanization programme. At the same time, he declared, however, that "the confidence the government had placed in the expatriate officer to help train and encourage local officers for higher posts had been fully justified by events over the past few years."[75]

The bringing to an end of the monopoly of business by foreigners and minority communities in the country was not accomplished until early 1967, although calls for a move in that direction had long been made. It is worth

[72] The Tanzanian government is welcoming private enterprises to the country. The Ministry of Commerce released in the later part of 1967 a list of industries which are open to private investors. The list includes such industries as textile mills, lumber and wood factories, painting, publishing and allied industries, chemical, rubber, stone clay, glass and machine factories. In these industries, companies may be formed with 100 % private shares or with minority shares by national organizations. See, *Tanzania News Bulletin* (Stockholm, No 31, October 1967).
[73] Cf., e.g., Listowel, *op.cit.*, Appendix III.
[74] *The Standard*, March 25, 1966.
[75] *Ibid.*, loc. cit.

emphasizing, however, that African-run cooperative unions already since before independence had been in charge of marketing products for the local farmers.

The purpose of the extensive nationalization in 1967,[76] was not merely a "take over", but also an attempt to make the major means of production become a more powerful instrument against underproduction. "Only when increased production has enlarged the national cake can the socialist government have more to divide equitably between the people",[77] wrote *The Nationalist* in an editorial after the Arusha Declaration. The President himself two months later declared that:[78]

... if the people are not involved in public ownership, and cannot control the policies followed, the public ownership can lead to fascism.

One of the central aims of the Declaration has been to extend the monetary sector to the vast areas of the country which have continued to remain on the subsistence level. In presenting the Bill establishing the National Bank of Commerce, the Minister of Finance, Mr Jamal, said it was clear that foreign banking interests would not have moved capital to rural areas, as fast as had been wished.[79]

The intention behind the take-over of the banks has been to employ the financial institutions of the country in greater conjunction with the people's efforts for developmental purposes. Another way of improving the farmer's deal has been efforts to increase the efficiency of the cooperative societies. Ever since their creation, many of the large cooperative unions have been troubled by maladministration and inefficiency. Assistance to farmer have often been delayed because of administrative problems. The unions have in some cases preferred to reinvest their money in "showpiece" projects rather than in improved agricultural production.[80] Farmers have not been satisfied with the operation of the coops.

One of the most important points of criticism raised against leaders of the coops, as well as leaders of other institutions in the country concerns their "excessive" way of life. This has been perceived as an indignity by the masses. In line with the policy of the Arusha Declaration, a call for frugality has therefore been raised. Examples were set in late 1966 after the students' crisis by the President, ministers, civil servants and employees of other national institutions who slashed their salary by some per cents.

[76] See e.g., an editorial in *The Nationalist*, February 10, 1967.
[77] *Ibid., loc. cit.*
[78] Julius K. Nyerere in an address to the students of Cairo University, reprinted in *The Nationalist*, April 12, 1967.
[79] *Ibid.*, February 15, 1967.
[80] For a review of the problems of the coops in Tanzania, see The United Republic of Tanzania, *The Report of the Presidential Special Committee of Inquiry into the Cooperative Movement*, (Government Printer, Dar es Salaam, 1966).

As everywhere, the problem of allocation has become intensified by the continuous rise of expectations. People were, during the struggle for independence, promised things which, almost certainly could not be granted to them. Some politicians and government officials have kept doing this after independence. At a seminar for Area Commissioners the Minister for Housing told the audience, however, that "what we told people in 1954, we cannot tell them now".[81] Particularly in the field of education many people in Tanzania—as in other African countries—feel deceived. One letter to the Editor of *The Standard* sums up many of the feelings with regard to the educational policy of the government during the first years of independence:[82]

Although I would not like to labour on past promises, I still remember how we used to be told, and often too, that our children would have free primary education and that every child in this country would be afforded every opportunity to develop his talents to the full. What do we have now? School fees have risen considerably and the government has put tough hurdles for children in Classes IV and VIII to jump before they can be assured of their future education . . .

There has been, of course, ever since independence a growing awareness among the leaders of the shortcomings of the educational system, in particular since it has perpetuated the weaknesses of the colonial educational system; it has not been possible to provide primary education for all Africans; furthermore, the schools prepared the pupils for a life in urban occupations.

All these problems have, on various occasions, been discussed in the Parliament. The most notable occasion was the discussion of a private motion in February 1966.[83] Then, Mr Kawawa, speaking on behalf of the government, declared that the problem of education was one which could not be solved in the near future.[84]

It is worth noting that the many difficulties in solving these problems are not mentioned in the new approach which was adopted after the Arusha Declaration. Since early 1967 an almost completely new educational policy has been introduced. The previous shortcomings are going to be eliminated by the more comprehensive "education for self-reliance"-approach. It consists of three major changes.[85]

The government is as far as possible going to put more emphasis on primary education rather than secondary education. In a speech on one of his up-country tours after the Arusha Declaration, the President declared that

[81] *The Nationalist,* March 4, 1966.
[82] A letter signed by Mr Emmanuel K. Lwamgira, Bukoba, *The Standard,* March 21, 1966.
[83] See e.g., *ibid.,* February 24, 1966.
[84] *Ibid.,* February 25, 1966.
[85] Editorial in *The Nationalist,* March 10, 1967.

primary education should not aim at preparing students for secondary schools, but rather at enabling them to lead decent lives in the villages, where they are destined to live. "Those who are going on to secondary schools are being prepared to serve the many who remain behind."[86]

The second change is the higher priority given to intelligence and practical ability rather than to pure book knowledge. Instead of making the study for examinations the primary aim in the class-room, teachers shall give the pupils greater opportunities to develop their own intelligence and practical handling of problems.

The third change is closely related to the second one. The traditional glorification of education for white collar jobs is replaced by the emphasis on making education more and more geared to the development of agriculture.

The result of this revision of educational objectives has led to intensive changes in the curriculum as well as in the school organization in Tanzania. The specific changes considered by the Ministry of Education were presented soon after the Arusha Declaration.[87] Another result of the major changes in educational policies may be that primary education in the future is made free of charge.[88]

The problem of participation

A dilemma for most governments in less developed countries is to strike a balance between responding to pressures and changing circumstances as the political elite itself sees fit and responding to demands from individual citizens and groups. In a country where the demand for universal suffrage precedes the development of a strong economy, popular representation can lead to an "overloading" of the system. There is a tendency for the system to feel incapable of managing all demands. In many African countries popular participation has been allowed only under very strict control. In several countries it is the party that determines who is going to stand in the election; all nominations are made centrally. Since often only one party is allowed, the opportunities for people to participate, except on the conditions of the rulers, are few, if any. That demands are almost exclusively generated and controlled by the political elite does not exclude the possibility of high system responsiveness. It presupposes, however, a very strong commitment to the interests of the people on part of the ruling elite. The majority of the

[86] *Ibid.*, May 5, 1967.
[87] See *ibid.*, March 14, 1967.
[88] The idea of making primary education compulsory was raised in 1967 and seriously considered by the government.

African states, as well as other states, regardless of their ideological position, have, however, so far lacked such leaders. In several countries this lack of responsiveness of the elite has caused political instability.

In Tanzania the concern with the responsive capability of the system has been strong ever since Julius Nyerere gained command of TANU. Holding the view that no human being is infallible, Nyerere has always realized that the interest of the masses is best served by a political organization, in which as many people as possible can be members. In one of his many pamphlets he has stated:[89]

No party which limits its membership to a clique can ever free itself from the fear of overthrow by those it has excluded. It must be constantly on the watch for signs of opposition, and must smother "dangerous" ideas before they have time to spread.

He re-emphasized the same point in June 1965 at the time when the report of the presidential commission on the establishment of a democratic one-party state was discussed in the National Assembly. TANU should remain a "mass party through which any citizen, accepting its principles, could participate in the process of government".[90]

Tanzania is in the unique situation that within the framework of a one-party constitution voters are presented with a choice between two candidates. These candidates need the written support of 25 registered voters for nomination and have to be approved by the National Executive Committee of TANU. In the general election 1965, the N.E.C. refused to accept 16 out of 208 nominees who had been recommended by the district conferences.[91]

This electoral system undoubtedly increases the responsibility of the government authorities to pressures from the environment. Political leaders know that unless they keep in touch with popular opinion, they stand the risk of losing the next election. It was no coincidence that a large number of the political incumbents in the parliament and the TANU organization lost in the election—in many cases to quite unknown local candidates.[92] People felt that many politicians tended to be insensitive to criticism and local demands.

Naturally one of the difficulties for making the Tanzanian political system responsive enough is set by the limited resources of the country. Most of what is available for government allocation is needed for the fulfillment of the Five Year Development Plan. There has been little leeway to shift resources to projects which have been proposed independent of the develop-

[89] Julius K. Nyerere, *Democracy and the Party System,* (Dar es Salaam 1962), pp. 24—25.

[90] *The Nationalist,* June 9, 1965.

[91] See Belle Harris, "The Tanzanian Election", *Mbioni,* (The Monthly Newsletter of Kivukoni College, Dar es Salaam, Vol II, No 5). The principles for refusal by the NEC are laid down in the Electoral Law.

[92] See, *ibid.;* also, Lionel Cliffe, *op.cit.,* Chs. 13 and 14.

ment plan. For the completion of many local projects the system has had to rely on its extractive capability; it has had to encourage people to realize their own projects on a self-help basis.

The role of other voluntary associations than TANU is also of importance for the discussion of the responsive capability of the system. In most of the less developed countries the tendency has been to regard interest groups of various kinds rather as producing than consuming bodies in the system. Trade unions and cooperative unions become vital institutions for nation-building as contributors to economic development rather than consumers of the scarce resources available. The Tanzanian view is no exception to this rule. It is worth noting that unlike many other African one-party states these voluntary associations are not represented separately in the National Assembly.

The interest of the members of these voluntary associations is and cannot, however, be neglected. This certainly was the experience of the Secretary-General of NUTA, Mr Kamaliza, who, until 1967, was also the Minister of Labour. He was in a constant dilemma in choosing between response to the wishes of NUTA members or to the paramount national economic interests. A Presidential Commission was appointed in 1966 to investigate more closely how NUTA could be made to fulfill its purposes more effectively.[93]

Conclusions

Some people would answer the question, of whether Tanzania belongs to the "pragmatic-pluralistic" or "revolutionary-centralizing" pattern of one-party states in Africa, by saying that it has in its first years of independence slowly but steadily moved from the former to the latter pattern. Without even looking into the conditions prevailing outside the political center, however, this answer has to be qualified. Looking at the qualities attributed to the "revolutionary-centralizing" type of states one finds that Tanzania

[93] See, editorial in The Standard, May 11, 1966. According to the 1962 Trade Disputes (settlement) Act, strikes are illegal in Tanzania. A few attempts have been made to contravene this act. In May, 1967, the Dar es Salaam Motor Transport workers made a one day strike, which stranded more than 50.000 employees and students in the capital. 10 persons were arrested following this incident, among others a NUTA assistant branch secretary; he was singled out as the "main inspirer". The reason behind the strike was dissatisfaction among the DMT workers with three senior officials, whom they wanted removed, but the government had refused to act against. See, The Nationalist, May 30, 1967.
In June the same year the Secretary General of NUTA was relieved from his ministerial duties to devote himself wholly to the labor movement. See, The Nationalist, June 8, 1967.

recently has moved more closely to the "ideal" type in certain respects, but not in others. The rate of political mobilization has increased. Preoccupation with ideology has also increased, but it is a different use of ideology than in most "revolutionary-centralizing" states in which the Tanzanian leaders have engaged. With regard to the political organization, it has, after the constitutional change in 1965, become less monolithic than before.

The intensified mobilization policy has been best expressed in the Arusha Declaration where it clearly says that Tanzania has to rely primarily on the domestic, human resources. Only the full employment of these will, in the long run, make the country better off, economically, socially and politically.

A number of policy alternatives based on "conventional" economic and political thinking has, ever since independence, been employed with little success. The purpose of the Arusha Declaration has been to connect the neglected problem of how to increase the extraction of domestic resources with the more specialized problem of how to achieve a more equalizing distribution of goods, services, honors, and so forth. By forging a plausible link between these two distinct problems, an attempt has been made to extend the spectrum of possible policy actions. The constant application of this idea is perhaps the most important aspect of the Arusha Declaration.[94]

The Tanzanian approach to problem-solving, as illustrated in the policy of socialism and self-reliance is characterized by giving motivation a new preponderant position. This does not mean, however, that understanding and knowledge are disregarded, as often happens in revolutionary situations. Many political leaders, who put primary emphasis on motivation are only too ready to believe that they thereby have achieved also full understanding of how the problems should be solved. There is no evidence in Tanzania, however, that the government is inclined to disregard the importance of competence and understanding of the many facts underlying the particular problems concerned. Nor is it prepared to discard past efforts and experiences containing useful information.

In this respect Tanzania differs from "genuinely revolutionary" states where ideology is used as a pseudo-science in trying to solve developmental problems. One of President Nyerere's greatest difficulties after the Arusha Declaration has been to convince his own subjects as well as the outside world that the function of ideology in Tanzania is rather "instrumental" than "consummatory".[95] It is not a head-long rush away from the need for

[94] Calls for self-reliance had been made before, but it had not officially been part of the government policy to the same extent.
[95] These two concepts have been borrowed from David Apter's book on "The Politics...", *op. cit.* The effect of the "consummatory" function of ideology is to relate as many actions by individuals as possible to the ultimate ends of the system. The effects of the "instrumental" function is to leave untouched by the ultimate ends a number of intermediate aims of the system. In a system with the first type of func-

knowledge and understanding, but a means to increase possible alternatives of actions by improving political communications, developing new policy instruments and changing power relationships between social groups in the country.[96] The increased preoccupation with ideology in Tanzania is primarily a recognition of the fact that motivation is as important a part of the process of cultural secularization as increased knowledge and technical skill.

Both the 1965 constitution and the Arusha Declaration point, in some important respects, in a direction away from centralization. First of all, the new constitution legitimizes a higher degree of pluralism than ever existed before, by allowing for competition within the framework of the one-party system. The competition is not only between people appealing for the support of the people, but also, as indicated above, between centrally appointed political leaders, on the one hand, and popularly elected leaders, on the other. It was a deliberate intention of the President to move the system in this direction, once opposition from other political organizations had disappeared.[97]

Bienen has pointed out the difficulties for a one-party system to operate effectively under a high degree of centralization when the country suffers from a low rate of economic development.[98] In a sense, this is also realized in the Arusha Declaration. One of its purposes is to bring the party closer to the people. A consequence therefore has been to decentralize planning and implementation of policies to a larger extent to the regional and district levels. This is illustrated in the fact that the former district development committees are now called "development and planning committees". The regional development committees are now called "regional rural development committees".[99]

---

tion, the ideology is regarded as exclusive; there is only one way that the system goals can be achieved and this way is all lined out in the ideology. In a system with the second type, however, a higher degree of flexibility is allowed in achieving the system goals.

[96] Nyerere's own view of a revolutionary is quite unconventional: "The true revolutionary in Africa has to do two things at one and the same time. He has to keep his eyes and his attention on the road ahead, and use all the pragmatism of which he is capable so as to negotiate a passage. But at the same time he must keep the goal clearly in his sights, and let it govern his direction at all times. He must, in other words, be a realistic idealist!"

This quotation is from an address to the National Assembly of the United Arab Republic on April 12, 1967; reprinted in *The Nationalist,* May 4, 1967.

[97] In an address to the National Assembly, on June 8, 1965, the President said: "Most candidates (to the N. A.) ... are elected by a Party Committee ... (and) if we can encourage freedom of expression at National Executive meetings (of TANU), why do we discourage it in Parliament." Reprinted in *The Nationalist,* June 9, 1965.

[98] Cf., p. 37.

[99] These new titles got generally accepted in the course of 1967.

All this calls into question the usefulness of the typologies referred to in this chapter. Certainly the case of Tanzania shows that they are not immediately relevant to the understanding of the political development in that country. Something more is needed, for instance, in order to understand the differences between Tanzania on the one hand, and Ghana on the other. The political system of Tanzania has been able to persist, whilst post-independent Ghana, formerly under Nkrumah, underwent major changes after the military coup in February 1966.

Another introductory remark of immediate relevance to this study should be made. Some of the most important phases of development of the Tanzanian political system has occured *after* the material for this study was collected in Buhaya in 1965—66. One objective therefore, is trying to view the last phase, including the launching of the Arusha Declaration, in the light of the conditions existing in the rural areas, like Buhaya, a few years after independence.

Buhaya: Background and pre-independence developments II

Chapter 3

The geographical background

Bukoba and Karagwe Districts form the extreme northwestern corner of Tanzania, bordering on Rwanda in the west, Uganda in the north, and the world's second largest fresh water basin, Lake Victoria, in the east. The Kagera River, by many considered to be the uppermost part of the White Nile, makes a natural border between Tanzania and Rwanda, and for a short distance between the former territory and Uganda. After that the river turns slightly south and runs through the northern parts of the districts before it makes a northern turn and joins Lake Victoria on the Ugandan side of the border.

Bukoba and Karagwe Districts are, together with Ngara and Biharamulo, the two districts to the immediate south, parts of West Lake Region, one of the 17 administrative regions in Tanzania (cf., Fig. 1, p. 12).

The only town in the area is Bukoba, which is the center of both regional and district administration. Until 1958 Bukoba and Karagwe were one administrative unit, but were then divided into two districts. The administrative district headquarters in Karagwe is located near Bugene, a minor trading settlement about 75 miles west of Bukoba.

The physical distance between Dar es Salaam, the capital of Tanzania and Bukoba is considerable, around 920 miles by road. Mwanza at the southern end of the Lake is 275 miles away.[1] The nearest major town to Bukoba is across the Uganda border; Masaka in the former kingdom of Buganda[2] is 110 miles away; Kampala, the capital of Uganda is 194 miles from Bukoba.

The area can be approached both from north and south by road.[3] Bukoba is situated on the main trunk road from Kampala south towards Mwanza and Kigoma on Lake Tanganyika. There are at least a couple of daily bus connections with both Mwanza and Kampala. Bukoba, due to its location on the lakeshore, has weekly boat services with other major ports on the lake, Kisumu, Port Bell (Kampala), Mwanza and Musoma, thereby connecting the area with the railroads running from Kisumu to Nairobi-Mombasa and from Mwanza to Tabora-Dar es Salaam.

[1] All figures mentioned refer to shortest distance by road.
[2] The kingdom was *de facto* abolished in 1966 after the flight of the king, Fredrik Mutesa II, from the country. In the constitutional proposals of 1967, the kingdom were to be also formally abolished and divided into three administrative districts.
[3] The main road to Kampala can for some weeks in April and May be impassable due to heavy rain.

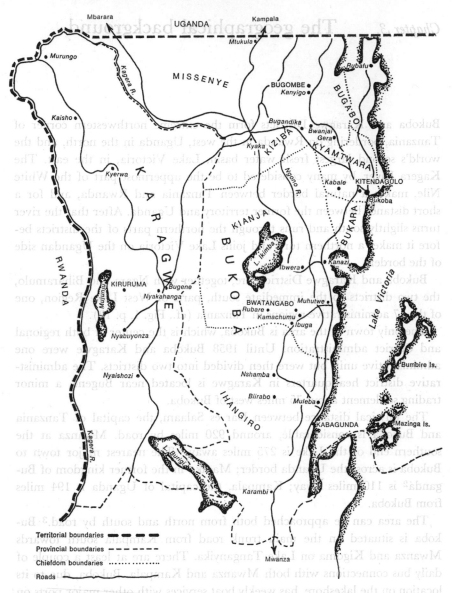

Figure 4. Geographical map of Bukoba and Karagwe Districts, Buhaya.

Bukoba has an airstrip. A private company has for some years run services six times a week, Entebbe—Bukoba—Mwanza and back. Only light planes can, however, operate from Bukoba.

The two districts have a very good public transport system, connecting distant parts of the area with the major centres, and particularly Bukoba. District roads, although sometimes in quite bad condition, are usually open for traffic the year around.

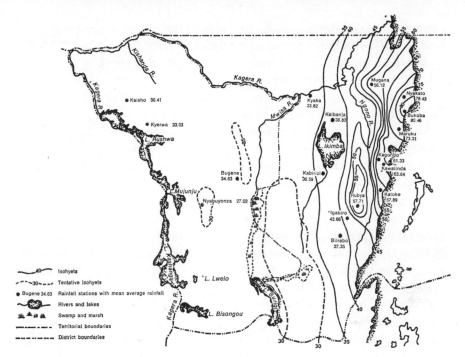

Figure 5. Rainfall and hydrography of Buhaya.[5]

The land

Physically, the area can be divided into four major zones.[4] First, there are
the costal ridges to the east, running in a north-south direction and over-
looking Lake Victoria. One can easily trace three main linear ridges: 1)
Bumbiri islands and nearby islands to the north, and particularly to the
south; 2) the coastal ridge, rising above 400 feet straight from the water
level; 3) the ridge west of Ngono River, stretching from Ibwera in the north
to Karambi in the south. On this ridge are situated a few important settlements such as Kamachumu and Nshamba. The coastal ridges all consist of
quartzitic sandstones of pre-Cambrian origin.

The second zone might be called the central depression, and is an erosio-
nal corridor of relatively subdued relief. In this zone two lakes, Ikimba and
Burigi, are found.

The third consists of the Karagwe ridges, which are developed on hard
bands of quartzite and also of pre-Cambrian origin. It is an impressive

---

[4] For a good account of the physical structure of the area, see D. N. McMaster,
"Change of Regional Balance in Bukoba District of Tanganyika", *Tanganyika Notes
and Records,* (No 56, March 1961), pp. 79—92, and W. A. Hance, *The Geography
of Modern Africa,* (New York 1964).

[5] This map is borrowed from McMaster, *op.cit.,* and reproduced with the permission
of the author.

65

escarpment, about 1000 feet high, that defines the eastern edge of this high-land. In the northwestern corner of the district around Kyerwa and Murongo there are mineralized granite basins bearing reins and stringers of tin, the only mineral depostit in the area.

The last zone consists of the Lower Kagera basin, which has later sediments. The river in its lower part is rapid and free-flowing.

Most of the coastal zone receives abundant rainfall, which is well distributed through the year. Bukoba township has one of the highest rainfalls in the country and scores an average of about 80 inches (2000 mm) a year. The highest figure ever recorded in Bukoba township was in 1947 when 105.38 inches fell; the lowest was in 1922, 61.16 inches.[6] There are no real "wet" and "dry" seasons, although April and November generally reflect peak rainfall periods, July being the driest month of the year. The rest of Bukoba District and the whole of Karagwe District suffers from the rain-shadow effect of the coastal ridges. Not even the high Karagwe escarpments can squeeze further moisture from the prevailing winds. High Karagwe is also shielded from Atlantic influences by higher ridges to the west in Rwanda. While the area around Bukoba, therefore, has a high average, the rainfall in the central depression and Karagwe is less than half the Bukoba township average (Bugene 34.63 inches).[7]

The temperature of the area is moderate. It varies only slightly from month to month, the annual average being 20°C (68°Fahr).[8]

It is likely that the coastal ridges in early times were covered by a rich climax forest, of which only small fragments can be found today. Karagwe with its higher elevation probably carried a mixed savanna vegetation. The valley floors and the central depression still display vast stretches of grassland, and woodland strips can be found along the more marked watercourses.

Haya soils differ from those found in, for instance, the areas inhabited by the Chagga and the Nyakyusa peoples. There the country is situated on, or below, volcanoes and the soils derived from these flows are fertile. The soils of Bukoba and Karagwe on the whole, in contrast, are non-fossiliferous, and generally deficient in nutrients, because they are derived from pre-Cambrian soils.[9] G. Milne, in his analysis of Haya soils,[10] arrives at the conclusion that the eastern, coastal, areas have patches of relatively fertile soil surrounded by stretches of open land, which are remarkable for their infertility. In

[6] McMaster, op.cit., p. 82.
[7] See diagram on p. 65.
[8] G. Milne, "Essays in Applied Pedology III: Bukoba: High and Low Fertility on a Laterised Soil", East African Agricultural Journal, (Vol. IV, 1938), p. 16.
[9] Milne, op.cit., p. 18; also P. Copeland Reining, "Haya Land Tenure: Landholding and Tenancy", Anthropological Quarterly, (Vol. 35, April 1962), p. 60.
[10] Milne, op. cit., p. 18.

the coastal area there is generally a scarcity of valuable land due to this soil distribution. The difference in fertility between soil under tree crop cultivation and grass land has been further accentuated by cropping techniques.[11]

Large parts of Karagwe, are generally considered to have a higher soil fertility,[12] even if soil there is also of pre-Cambrian origin. The reasons have never been fully explained; one possible reason is lower population density, a different land tenure system and tree crop cultivation being shifted from one place to another. This has led to a different management of the soil. A second factor might be that soil erosion has been less serious in Karagwe thanks to more moderate rainfalls.

The people

The total area of Bukoba and Karagwe Districts amounts to 5.950 square miles, the former being somewhat larger. According to the 1957 census the total population was 367.962 for the two districts combined.[13] Of these 175.488 were male, 192.474 female. The total increase compared with the 1948 census was 68.102, or 22.7 % It was estimated in 1966 that the population in Bukoba District well exceeded 350.000 and that another 85.000 lived in Karagwe.

The indigenous population is known as the *Bahaya*, although the people of Karagwe like to call themselves *Banyambo*.[14] The Haya-Nyambo group was the fourth largest tribe in Tanganyika in 1957, next to the Sukuma, Nyamwezi, and Makonde.[15]

The population density per square mile by district in the area around Lake Victoria in 1957 was as follows:[16]

Table 3. Population density in selected Lake districts.

District	Density per sq.mile
Biharamulo	9.9
Bukoba (=Karagwe included)	61.8
Ngara	92.9
Mwanza	153.3
Ukerewe	229.3

[11] Reining, *op. cit.*, p. 60.
[12] Information obtained at the Regional Agricultural Office, Bukoba, December 1964.
[13] The Republic of Tanganyika, *African Census Report 1957*, (Dar es Salaam, 1963), p. 21.
[14] Cf., p. 16, footnote 9.
[15] For a tribal map of Tanzania, see p. 40.
[16] "African Census . . ." *op. cit.*, p. 21.

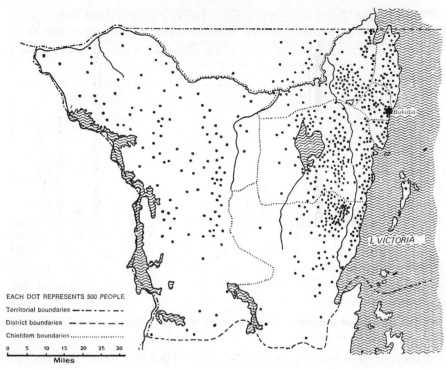

EACH DOT REPRESENTS 500 PEOPLE
Territorial boundaries — · — · — · —
District boundaries — — — — —
Chiefdom boundaries ....

0   5   10   15   20   25   30
Miles

Figure 6. Distribution of the African population in Buhaya, 1957.

The Bukoba figure is a bit misleading, however. Population density within the area varies considerably. In 1957 the density in the eastern coastal area was 270 per square mile.[17] A rough estimation of population distribution in Buhaya gives the following pattern:[18]

Table 4. Estimated distribution of population in the four major physical zones of Buhaya 1965.

Area	per cent of population
coastal ridges	67 %
Karagwe	20 %
central depression	8 %
Lower Kagera basin	5 %
total:	100 %

It is clear that the coastal area is comparatively overpopulated, while the others relatively underpopulated.

[17] Reining, *op. cit.*, p. 60.
[18] These figures are based on statistics presented in McMaster's article quoted above; added are considerations of recent migrations in the area. Cf., Fig. 6.

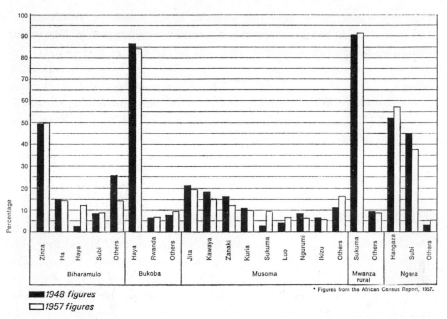

* Figures from the African Census Report, 1957.

■ 1948 figures
☐ 1957 figures

Figure 7. Percentage composition of population by tribe in selected Lake Districts.

Buhaya is very much a single-tribe area. There is a heavy majority of Bahaya-Banyambo; other tribal groups to be found in the area are Rwanda, Rundi, Zinza, and Ganda. In addition to these settlers of other tribal origin, quite a number of Banyarwanda, Barundi, Bazinza (from Biharamulo), Bahangaza (from Ngara), Bashubi (from Ngara), and Baha (from Kibondo) have taken temporary employment, especially in Bukoba District.

Percentage composition of population by tribe in five Lake districts in 1948 and 1957 is shown in Fig. 7.[19]

Both Mwanza and Bukoba Districts are dominated by one tribe. The former as well as the latter, excluding Karagwe, are densely populated and there is little room for immigrants. As a result of the overpopulation Sukuma and Haya people are nowadays settling in Biharamulo District.

A breakdown of the census shows that the minority tribes in Buhaya are found in all parts. The Banyarwanda are particularly numerous in Karagwe; the Bazinza are found mainly in the southern part of Bukoba District; and, the Ganda immigrants live in the coastal area.

The Bahaya did not constitute a majority of the population in Bukoba township, according to the 1957 census. Of the total town population, Asians and Europeans included, they made up only about one third. Some thousand Haya people, approximately 2—3 % of the total population of the

[19] The 1967 census figures were unfortunately not available by the time this chapter was written.

69

tribe, live outside their two home districts. Quite a few live in the neighboring districts in the Lake area. A substantial number live in Dar es Salaam. The percentage of female emigrants to the capital from Buhaya has been high compared with other areas. The 1957 figures show that of 1.123 Bahaya living in Dar es Salaam 798, (71 %), were women. No other tribal group represented in the figures from Dar es Salaam showed a similar distribution by sex.[20] It is alleged that a large number of these women have made their living by prostitution.

Agriculture and commerce

The Haya people have always practiced mixed husbandry, that is, they have always been sedentary cultivators, who also keep domestic animals. The main cash crop in the area is coffee. Robusta is most common along the lakeshore while Arabica is predominant on the inland escarpments, including the most western of the three coastal ridges (Ibwera—Karambi). In an area west and northwest of Bukoba the two types grow parallel. Most of the coffee is taken to Mombasa and sold at regular coffee auctions, but a new factory for processing instant coffee was opened in Bukoba 1967. Tea has recently been introduced in the coastal area. Another product, cotton is also on its way into the area, more specifically, in the southern part. Successful cotton growing in Biharamulo District has been the example. In high Karagwe, beans and Irish potatoes are commonly grown for sale. Sugar is grown on a large estate in the Kagera Valley.

The staple food in the area is the plaintain, or unripe banana, which is eaten cooked. Maize, sorghum, millet, groundnuts and cassawa, are also grown for consumption.

Fishing is practised at certain places along Lake Victoria, but still in a very primitive fashion. There is no fishing industry; smoked fish is, however, sold all over the area, where fresh fish is not available.

A large cattle ranch has recently been started by the government together with the Bukoba Cooperative Union in the eastern part of Karagwe. The aim is to provide in a few years enough meet and milk products for the whole West Lake Region.

The Indians and the Arabs have for years dominated the trading activities, although a more balanced situation has been achieved after independence, due to the emergence of a strong cooperative movement in the area. Quite a substantial number of individual Haya traders are also found in the area.

[20] "African Census . . ." *op.cit.*, p. 48.

Religion and education

The Christian and Muslim religions are well dispersed in Bukoba/Karagwe. Compared with some other major tribes in the country, the percentage distribution by sex and religion in 1957 was as follows:[21]

Table 5. Population distribution among four larger tribes in Tanzania 1957; by sex and religion.

Tribe	Male					Female				
	Prot.	Cath.	Islam	Pagan	N/S	Prot.	Cath.	Islam	Pagan	N/S
Chagga	2,1	72,6	2,2	23,0	0,1	2,5	71,0	1,8	24,6	0,1
Haya	11,2	46,7	12,8	28,1	1,2	9,4	40,2	15,6	32,9	1,9
Nyakyusa	23,0	3,5	0,7	72,8	—	24,6	3,8	0,4	71,2	—
Sukuma	3,9	7,5	2,3	85,9	0,4	2,7	6,1	2,2	88,6	0,4

Of particular interest here is that the Muslims are better represented among the Bahaya than among any of the other up-country tribes referred to in the table. The number of Muslims have always exceeded, and still does, the number of Protestants. According to unofficial figures, obtained in 1965 the religious distribution among the Haya/Nyambo is estimated as follows:[22]

Table 6. Estimated distribution of population in Buhaya 1965; by religion.

Roman Catholics	190.000
Muslims	80.000
Pagans	80.000
Protestants	75.000
total	425.000

The spread of education in East Africa has fairly closely followed the expansion of Christianity. Even today, the majority of the schools in the country are run by Christian agencies. It is not a mere coincidence that the Chagga and the Haya are among the most educated peoples in the country, as mission activities have been extensive among members of these two tribes. Comparative educational statistics of reliable character is fairly difficult to obtain, but the following figures concerning the educational facilities in

[21] *Ibid.,* p. 63.
[22] These figures were obtained from religious officials, Christians as well as Muslims. The figures show a total population slightly lower than the estimated figure for Bukoba and Karagwe Districts mentioned on p. 67. This may indicate that the number of "pagans" or animists is a bit higher than 80.000.

Bukoba (not Karagwe) District from June 1964 will give an idea of the educational achievement in one of the more developed parts of the country:[23]

Total number of school children enrolled in St. I—VIII: 33.524.
Number of school children enrolled in St. I—IV only: 27.566.

It is estimated that children in the age group 6—14 make up around 20 per cent of the total population in the area.[24] With an approximate population of 350.000 in the district, it means 9,5 % of the total population, or little less than half the total number of children in the relevant age group are enrolled in primary schools. Many children, particularly girls, have so far been forced to stop their education after St. IV owing to lack of opportunities in upper primary schools, or for other reasons. The percentage of those attending lower primary schools (St I—IV) is therefore higher. Using the estimation that this age group roughly constitutes 10 per cent of the total population, the percentage attending school of this age group is 78 %. It should be underlined that educational facilities are unevenly distributed in the district. The figures for the area around Bukoba township are higher, while they are lower in the southern and western parts of the district.

[23] The figures were obtained at the District Education Office, Bukoba, December 1964.
[24] Personal communication with the Regional Education Officer, Mr Mazula, Bukoba, December 11, 1964.

Chapter 4.   The traditional systems

Early history

The present distribution of population in Buhaya is a fairly recent phenomenon, mainly owing to the expansion of coffee cultivation, easy communications, and so forth. In early times other parts of the area seem to have been
more important.

Archaeological excavations along the Kagera River (the Karagwe section) have revealed very early human settlements. These pre-historic people
were hunters, and depended on the existence of game, wild animals of
various kinds being attracted by the water. The river basin, therefore, provided men with a plentiful food reserve. Men also held to the river since it
offered water sustenance, settlement sites on the terraces, and an avenue of
intercourse. There is no need to elaborate on the life of these pre-historic
people, but it should be emphasized that this area was inhabited already
during the Stone Age. People clustered in small settlements on the terraces
in the Kagera Valley.

With the development of agriculture, people however, turned their backs
to the river, where there is little rain and the river banks very often steep,
hence making water difficult to obtain for cultivation purposes. The agri-
culturists migrated into areas with more abundant rainfall. Both high Karagwe, and particularly the ridges on what are now the present shores of Lake
Victoria, then still covered by climax forests, became inhabited. The forests
receded and through human activities, mainly the use of fire, wide ranges of
open grassland were created. These people, all Bantu, seem to have lived
organized in small clan settlements.

Of particular interest in this area are the many rock painting sites. Those
found in the Bukoba area seem to form a link with a whole series of fairly
uniform rock paintings existing north-south through Tanzania. Rock paintings are still being discovered and the full analysis of these paintings are
not yet completed. They might reflect, however, a series of migrations of
people, most likely southwards, but there is still a large degree of uncertainty concerning this.[1]

[1] Much of the traditional history of the Interlacustrine kingdoms is still under
dispute. For summaries of differing opinion, see: K. Ingham, *A History of East
Africa*, (London 1965), pp. 41—46; G. P. Murdock, *Africa: Its Peoples and Their
Culture History*, (New York 1959), pp. 40—47; R. Oliver and G. Mathew (eds),
History of East Africa, (New York 1963), Vol I, Ch. III; B. K. Taylor, *The Western
Lacustrine Bantu*, (London 1962).

What we know, however, is that a series of migrations of Hamitic tribes took place at the end of the 16th and in the beginning of the 17th centuries. These migrations had a decisive impact on the Bukoba and Karagwe areas. These migratory peoples were all nomadic herdsmen, who migrated southwards with their longhorned cattle searching for new pastures. It is not clear whether these immigrants came all at one time or whether they entered the area in successive waves. They seem to have come in family bands, and the country in which they settled was comparatively sparsely populated. The indigenous agricultural population yielded to the invaders and accepted their rule over the area. The immigrants were known as *Bahinda,* after their leader Ruhinda. Even if the Hamitic invaders came in separate groups at different times, they all seem to have recognized the leadership of one chief.

Ruhinda is said to have come from Bunyoro. He was the son of Igaba, a member of the ruling Bito clan and the king of Bunyoro at the end of the 16th century. Ruhinda, according to one widely accepted tradition, settled in Karagwe[2] and from there extended his rule to include large areas to the east and south. His sons eventually became independent rulers of Karagwe, Kyamtwara and Ihangiro (Bukoba District), and Rusubi chiefdom (Biharamulo). Ruhinda's brother, Kibi, who is also said to have left Bunyoro, settled in Kiziba, the northern part of what is today Bukoba District.[3] A number of separate chiefdoms then crystallized in the area.

The Bito clan became rulers in Bunyoro probably during the beginning of the 16th century, when they succeeded the Chwezi clan. Traditionally the Bachwezi are said to have ruled the kingdom of Kitara, which at its peak probably covered an area from present day Bunyoro into northwestern Tanzania.[4] Academics still dispute whether the Bahinda, who possibly went south were descendants of the Bachwezi rather than the Babito. Cory reports[5] that during his field work in Bukoba, he found no informant who mentioned that the Bahinda were an offshoot of the Chwezi clan. The present author during field work in Kiziba was told by clan elders the whole story of the Bachwezi; about Isimbwa the founder of the dynasty, and Wamala, their greatest king. Other interesting information obtained was

[2] An elder from Kafuro, near the traditional site of the Karagwe chiefs (see Ch. 5, p. 90), had the following story to tell: "The first King to rule over Karagwe was Nonno, a man of Bantu origin. During his reign there was a great famine, causing many to die. Now at this time, the Bahinda came from Bunyoro with much millet and other food. These people had, too, magical powers. When they ordered it to rain, it rained. The people now had abundant food, supplied by the Bahinda, and they requested the immigrants to rule them instead of Nonno. Thus it was that the Bahinda began their reign in Karagwe."
This story was recorded in November 1965 by Mr Dominic Rutabingwa.
[3] Cf., map on p. 64.
[4] Cf., map on p. 76.
[5] H. Cory, *The History of Bukoba District,* (Mwanza 1957), p. 7.

that Kibi was the son of the ninth king of Bunyoro, known as Ishengoma, himself a member of the Chwezi clan.

What is of greatest importance to note here, however, is that traditions in the Bukoba area are all familiar with the legend of Wamala, the Chwezi king; Cory and Hartnoll[6] point out that Wamala has been the most common clan spirit among the Bahaya. Moreover, some people still call themselves Bachwezi. C. J. Hellberg points to the sociological implication of the relationship between the Bahinda and these early rulers in Bunyoro.[7] The Bachwezi were linked with the creator-god, Ruhanga/Katonda. The Bahinda, when settling in foreign areas took advantage of this and founded a social system based on the assumption that their ancestors were linked with the creator of the world, and that they hence must be superior to other people. The establishment of such a system and the acceptance of this myth was facilitated by the fact that the Bahinda were united under one chief, while the indigenous Bantu population on whose land they intruded seem to have lived together only through loose clan organizations.

The traditional systems

The Haya[8], similar for instance to the Sukuma and the Ankole people in Uganda in early days, has always been a multi-kingdom tribe. Since the arrival of the Bahinda the area has been divided into a number of small chiefdoms—varying from four to eight—with constantly changing boundaries. The original ones were Karagwe in the west (largest of them all), Ihangiro in the south, Kiziba in the north and Kyamtwara in the east; Kyamtwara later split up into four smaller units known as Kianja, Bugabo, Bukara, and Kyamtwara. To these seven should be added Missenye, north of the Kagera River. That area was once part of Ankole, later Buganda, but finally included in Bukoba District through a British-German border agreement at the turn of this century. The people of these eight petty chiefdoms can be called "sub-tribes". It would lead too far to relate the history of each of these people.[9] The main concern is with the social, economic and political features of Buhaya, which have had bearing on modern developments.

As has already been indicated, the history and tradition of Buhaya is clo-

---

[6] H. Cory and M. M. Hartnoll, *The Customary Law of the Haya Tribe*, (London 1945), Appendix V.

[7] C. J. Hellberg, *Missions on a Colonial Frontier West of Lake Victoria*, (Lund 1965), p. 31.

[8] The word "Buhaya" was originally given to the coastal area of Lake Victoria, where fishermen lived. It had for long time a derogatory meaning, because a Muhaya, a fisherman, was a person without property.

[9] For a full history, see Cory, *op. cit.*

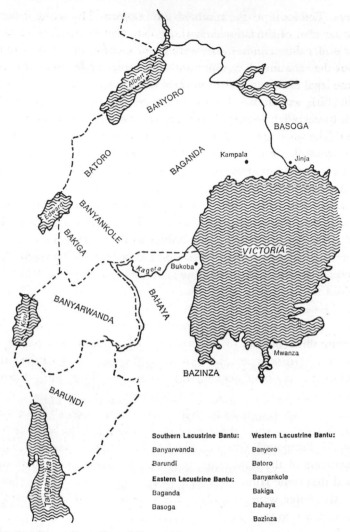

Figure 8. Interlacustrine tribes of East Africa.

The following labels appear on the map:

Southern Lacustrine Bantu:
Banyarwanda
Barundi

Eastern Lacustrine Bantu:
Baganda
Basoga

Western Lacustrine Bantu:
Banyoro
Batoro
Banyankole
Bakiga
Bahaya
Bazinza

sely related to that of Bunyoro and other Interlacustrine tribes. It should be noted, that Luhaya, the language of the Bahaya, is very similar to Lunyoro, Lutoro, and Lunyankole, the languages of the three Western Lacustrine tribes in Uganda. It differs, however, from the language of the Baganda to the immediate north.

a) *The Social System.*[10] According to tradition the Bahinda met with little resistance from the indigenous agricultural population when they came

[10] The information presented in the rest of this chapter is partly based on oral information obtained during the present author's field work in Buhaya 1964—66. To the extent possible the information has been checked with other material written on Buhaya.

to Buhaya. The local people accepted the invaders. The latter incorporated the existing clan organization into their own, thereby binding all the clans together under their chiefs. Clans were given specific functions at the chief's court, but they continued as important social units, and clan heads remained with some legal and fiscal power in their villages.

A strict line was drawn, however, between the *Hima* or *Nfura*[11] clans, to which the invaders belonged, and the *Iru* clans to which all other people belonged. The latter group of clans numbered about one hundred. At least three recognizable status groups, based on lineage, crystallized in traditional Buhaya: (1) the ruling dynasties, the Hinda, Bito, or Nkango clan; (2) the remaining Hima or Nfura clans; (3) all the Iru clans.

The Bairu were at the bottom. They were all cultivators, but with special duties assigned to them at the chief's court. The Bahima were originally pastoralists, depending exclusively on cattle, which they herded on the pastures. Members of the Hima clans were descendants of the Hamitic invaders. There was little social contact between the Hima and the Iru (Bantu) clans. They could not eat together. A Mwiru could never marry a Muhima, while the opposite was possible.

As time passed, however, lineage descent ceased to be the only factor determining status in Buhaya, particularly in the eastern part. Social conduct of individual clan members, as well as performance and services rendered the chief or the chiefdom, became important. The Haya chiefs deposed clan heads and formed new clans. If some members of a clan showed cowardice in a battle it could happen that the whole clan was degraded. Similarly if a member of a Hima clan broke the taboo and had fish, his clan could be degraded.[12] Promotion was usually due to favors accorded the chief by some members of the clan, courage in war battles, and so forth. Hence it happened that some Hima clans were degraded to ordinary Iru clans, while some of the latter were upgraded. These were known as "bastard" Hima clans, in contrast to the "pure" ones.[13]

Like the Kabaka of Buganda the Haya chief was the symbolic head of all clans; he symbolized unity, and was automatically a representative of the whole people. The principal source of legitimacy for his generally undisputed rule was the myth that he had a special relationship to the creator-god, and to the source of all life. As Hellberg has pointed out:[14]

[11] *Nfuru* means fish in Luhaya; it was the taboo of the Hima or Nfura clans. The members of these clans were strictly forbidden to eat fish.

[12] Some members of the *Zigu* clan in Kibuye village, which is part of Kitendagulo are said to have run away instead of joining the acclamations for Rugomora Mahe, the Chief of Kianja, when he passed their village. The chief got angry and decided to call them *Bahuge*—the lost ones. It has ever since been the name of their clan.

[13] Cory and Hartnoll, *op.cit.*, Appendix V.

[14] Hellberg, *op. cit.*, p. 33.

The chief was the guarantor of the continued existence of all things living and for the cosmic order. His link with the source of life meant that he was the possessor of life-force, *magara*.

To be in possession of *magara* was of greatest importance to all human beings, according to the Haya conception of life. It had however, nothing to do with physical strength. *Magara* could be held by both living and dead people. The greatest tragedy that could happen to a human being was that he or she died without having brought any children to the world, because this implied that the life-force has been extinguished.[15] It was also believed that *magara* changed with the phases of the moon. It was particularly strong at full moon. At these occasions people gathered at the chief's palace and by appearing to the public the *Mukama*,[16] reinforced his position as holder of the key to well-being and order in the chiefdom. This regular ceremony served a legitimizing purpose.

Because of their special relationship to the divine powers, the Bahinda held the highest rank in society.[17] In order to allow for the perpetuation of a "pure" Hinda dynasty, it was the only endogamous clan. It happened however, that the chiefs took wives even from Iru clans. The situation could become particularly critical, when a Mukama as his heir appointed a son, whose mother was of Iru origin, since the mythical belief, and in fact the source of legitimacy for the whole social and political organization, was that the Bahinda were destined to rule. A disparity developed between prescribed rules and the real situation, which in the long run would be one of the factors undermining the Hinda supremacy in Buhaya.[18]

The particular position of the chief determined the organization of the social, economic and political systems, which were closely intertwined. As the superior representative of the community he had the ultimate right to ownership of property. All cattle and land formally belonged to the chiefs. Cattle were "borrowed" from them according to a complicated system and all Hima cattle-herders depended on the chief for their living.

When a man died without heirs his land reverted to the chief, who could re-allocate it as he wished. The Mukama, however, had even more extensive

[15] Cf., H. Benettsson, *Östafrikansk verklighetsuppfattning och människosyn*, (Uppsala 1966).

[16] The chief in Buhaya as well as in Ankole, Toro and Bunyoro was known as *Mukama*, which literally translated means the "chief milker".

[17] Kyamtwara and Bugabo chiefdoms were since the beginning of the 18th century ruled by the Nkango clan, which is of Hima stock and closely related to the Bahinda. The clan came from Buzinza (Biharamulo) and its members married into the Hinda clan. They were never fully recognized by other Hinda chiefs, but gained full recognition in their respective chiefdoms. In Kiziba chiefdom the ruling clan was the Bito clan. In Buhaya all members of the royal clans, the Hinda, Bito, and Nkango, were known as Bahinda.

[18] Cf., Chapter 6, pp. 113—14.

rights over the land of his subjects. He could, for instance, give a number of plantations or farms to his favorites. The latter then automatically became the real owners of the land, while the original occupants remained as tenants. Farmers, affected by this system had no right to dispose of their land; they could not absent themselves from the *shamba*[19] for a long time without the permission from the landholder; they were liable to punishment if they did not pay their tribute to the holder, and so forth.

This feudal land tenure system was known as the *nyarubanja*[20] system. It developed in all the chiefdoms of eastern Buhaya, but never in Karagwe. The main reason for this can be found in the differences in the physical environment. Karagwe had a sparse population and there were plenty of pastures, on which the Hima herdsmen could graze their cattle, separated from the Iru population. Land never became a scarce resource and hence cattle remained the only valuable asset for the local Hima population. The custom in Karagwe, as well as in Ankole north of the Kagera River, was that the Hima aristocracy was given a share of the tribute that was collected from the Iru population by the chief. This way they were guaranteed supplies for their subsistence without having to mix with the rest of the population.

In eastern Buhaya, what is now Bukoba District, the situation was the opposite. Land soon became scarce and the pastures fewer. The scarcity of land in the coastal part, reinforced by the fact that the central depression and the Kagera Valley were not good cattle-herding areas, made the Bahima settle and become cultivators. Soon land became more valuable than cattle. The chief began to give compensation to his favorites in terms of control over specific land plots, from which they could collect their own tribute, rather than in terms of cattle.

Buhaya offers an interesting example of how differences in the physical environment between Karagwe, on the one hand, and the coastal area, on the other, affected the development of the social system. Karagwe remained much closer to the patterns found in Ankole, while the eastern part developed a social system, not so different from that of Buganda.

In Karagwe the social—and physical—boundaries between Bahima and Bairu remained almost as strict as in Ankole. In the latter chiefdom a Muhima could not marry a Mwiru, because it was illegal to give the latter cattle. A Mwiru was never allowed to enter military service. A Mwiru could never reach any position of influence in society; he could only become an assistant to the Muhima.[21] In Karagwe a similar pattern prevailed. The Bahima lived in secluded communities; their settlements were unstable since

[19] Kiswahili for "a cultivated land plot".
[20] The word means the big *kibanja, or* "the big land holding".
[21] K. Oberg, "The Kingdom of Ankole in Uganda", in M. Fortes and E. E. Evans-Pritchard (eds), *African Political Systems,* (New York 1940), pp. 121—162.

they were not cultivators and had no roots in the soil. A Muhima could not marry a Mwiru. The chief owned all cattle and he handed them out to the Bahima to herd. Should a Muhima wish to marry he could use the chief's cattle to pay the bride-price. Similarly, if he wished to slaughter a cow, it was possible. Since the driving force in the life of the Bahima was cattle, the chief was insured against any malversation of his cattle. To be without cattle was the same as losing interest in existence, for a Muhima of the old days. It has been related that many Bahima at the time of rinderpest, committed suicide rather than suffer the shame of having no cattle.[22] The Bahima of Karagwe never became sedentary cultivators, like members of the Hima clans in the coastal area. Rules similar to those of Karagwe were never inforced in any of the Bukoba chiefdoms.

The landholder in eastern Buhaya had according to the *nyarubanja* system great social power over the tenants on his land. The majority of the Haya farmers were, however, owners of their own land. The nuclear family lived on a plantation known as a *kibanja*. The ownership of it was invested in one member of the family. Inheritance was patrilineal and ideally from father to eldest son. This direct succession, however, was not always assured in the cases of polygynous marriages.

The general rule that the *kibanja* was transferred from the father to a single son did not mean that this son could do as he wished with the land. His brothers and other relatives kept an eye on him, and he could not sell or give away any land without the consent of the members of his family. On the whole, selling of land occurred very rarely. Priscilla Copeland Reining has shown the considerable consistency in the position of land holdings in one Haya village between 1911 and 1953.[23]

The reason for the consistency in the position and size of the holdings in eastern Buhaya was primarily land scarcity. Grassland was impossible for cultivation of bananas or coffee trees. The Bahaya developed the notion that the *kibanja* had a continuity transcending the development cycle of a single family. Hence unoccupied land could not be transferred to others, unless contested for several generations. The land plot of one family was not only a cropping unit, but also the location for a social unit. A land holding under tree crop cultivation supplied most of the subsistense, offered location for the physical residence and determined the social orientation of the occupants in the sense that they thereby were members of the smallest territorial unit, the village. This helps to explain why the Bahaya in the coastal area have always valued land so highly.

[22] R. de Z. Hall, "The Social Organisation in Karagwe", *Bukoba District Book*, (Bukoba 1928).
[23] P. Copeland Reining, "Land Resources of the Haya", in D. Brokensha (ed), *Ecology and Economic Development in Tropical Africa*, (Berkeley 1965), pp. 217——244.

The transfer of property from father to son implied that other sons had to find land in other places. There were two immediate consequences of this system. First, clan members were scattered all over Buhaya,[24] a factor that tended to increase the degree of geographical mobility in the area. Secondly, considerable uniformity of custom and behavior was achieved throughout Buhaya. In this respect, Buhaya was similar to Buganda.[25]

Child rearing in traditional Buhaya was aimed at enhancing the authoritarian pattern of society. Strong emphasis was put on obedience and deference towards parents, particularly the father. Respect for elders was another rule children had to learn at an early age. There is an old Haya proverb saying that "those who do not consult the elders will never construct a house".[26] Independent innovations made without consulting the elders were discouraged. These innovations reflected refusal to take advice from more experienced members of the community, and hence they were considered examples of pride, a characteristic which was disliked.

The Bahaya had a very well organized educational system, which was explicitly aimed at perpetuating the values of the community. All boys at the age of twelve got engaged in a kind of "national service". The training was partly done at the chief's residence, partly in the sub-chiefdom from which the boys originally came. The young boys were taught both military and civil matters. In the daily training program was included sports, games, dancing and the fostering of skills in warfare as well as cleaning of the Mukama's huts and the teaching of good manners.

The training at the chief's palace continued for two months; after that they were sent back to their sub-chiefdom, where instruction went on until the boys were married. Each group of boys, generally known as a *muteko,* had its special symbol and was clearly distinguished by the male Bahaya. It was estimated that approximately 50 per cent of those who were taken to the service were dismissed in the course of the training period. Those who passed with credit were marked down for future honors.[27]

The younger generations in traditional Buhaya, therefore, were socialized into accepting a common code of behavior by institutions under central political control. The educational system also served as a basis of recruitment to more specific roles in society of young qualified persons. Finally, it promoted the process of assimilation. Members of different lineage descent and

[24] Cf., *ibid.,* p. 235.
[25] For a sociological analysis of Buganda, see, Apter, "The Political Kingdom..", *op.cit.,* Apter, "The Politics..", *op.cit.* and Fallers (ed), *op.cit.*
[26] White Fathers' Mission, "Enquete sur les moeurs et coutumes indigenes", (Kashozi, Bukoba, undated and unpublished).
[27] "The Primitive Native Education System 'Muteko' ", *Bukoba District Book,* (Bukoba 1928).

from various sub-chiefdoms were drawn together, and this considerably helped fostering a common identity.

b) *The Economic System.* Most people in Bukoba and Karagwe have always been small-scale hoe-cultivators, working independently in family and household units on the land plot surrounding their homes. The introduction of cattle on a large scale by the Bahinda and their fellow immigrants meant an economic change since it brought many peasants manure. Cory and Hartnoll[28] argue that the Bahinda needed food stores for their courts, soldiers, etc., and therefore, in exchange for the manure produced by their cattle, and the consequent increased fertility of the soil, asked for a share in the harvest. The two authors claim that this might have been the origin of the tribute system.

As it is today, the plaintain was the main food crop in old times. The Bahaya had a perennial crop which besides yielding fruit all the year around did little to exhaust the soil. Robusta coffee has been grown in the area for a long time. Some people claim it is indigenous to the area, while others[29] maintain it was first introduced by the Bahinda. Whatever its origin, the hierarchical organization of society was reflected also in the way coffee was cultivated, used and marketed. Every coffee tree used to belong to the chief. This system was tied to the belief that the first coffee tree had been brought there by Wamala, the Chwezi king, who was the greatest spirit in the Hinda pantheon. The planting of coffee was rigorously controlled. Only the chief and his closest followers were allowed to do it. Being in possession of coffee trees not only implied an economic privilege but also social status. All planting was therefore under strict supervision and witnesses were used, etc. Jervis[30] maintains that to be found in possession of coffee without evidence as to its source and proof of permission to plant it entailed very severe penalties, since the offender had trodden on royal preserves. Hellberg has pointed to the relationship between the *magara* of a man and his coffee trees. Should one tree die, the owner would also die.[31]

The coffee seed with its twin halves was symbolically used to establish blood-brotherhood.[32] People in all positions seem to have practised this institution. The chief sought the relation with another chief; nobles sought it among themselves; while the Bairu sought the honor of this relationship with those in the social scale above them. It was a way of seeking protection

---

[28] Cory and Hartnoll, *op.cit.,* Appendix III.

[29] T. S. Jervis, "A History of Robusta Coffee in Bukoba", *Tanganyika Notes and Records,* (No 8, December 1939), pp. 47—58. Jervis claims that the Hamitic migrants in the area brought the coffee down from Ethiopia. It is worth noting that coffee trees still grow wild in an area 15 miles northwest of Bukoba.

[30] Jervis, *op. cit.,* pp. 54—55.

[31] Hellberg, *op. cit.,* p. 71.

[32] Jervis, *op.cit.,* and H. Rehse, *Kiziba—Land und Leute,* (Stuttgart 1910), p. 97.

for those humbler members of society, who did not benefit from ordinary social and economic privileges.

As seen from this account coffee was closely related to the social and political tradition of the tribe. The control of the chief includes also the trading of coffee. The coffee was exported particularly to the kingdoms in the north. Cattle and bark-cloth were the goods obtained for the coffee. That coffee could be sold in Buganda where it was also grown at that time, is partly explained by the fact that the Bahaya had learned from Arabs how to prepare coffee with spices, a method that proved successful. This is also an indication that the Bahaya were involved in trade with the Arabs at an early time. Rehse[33] mentions that people from Kiziba used to trade ivory with the Arabs. The ivory was obtained in Ankole and then taken to Unyamwezi (Tabora) and resold there.

There were naturally very few places to market products, a fact that always put a limit to trading. Not until the first Arabs in the middle of the 19th century went to settle at Kafuro in Karagwe did any differentiation of trade take place. Cowry shells and trade beads were probably introduced at that time.[34] Some trade took place between the chiefdoms in Buhaya, but their economic structure was too similar to make exchange of products a necessity.

In traditional Haya society inequality in wealth and social status was accepted as a rule of nature; it could not be changed. Nor did there exist any sense of "right" to participate in the riches of other people. If a man did not have enough to eat and drink, it was supposed to be his own fault. He was either lazy or the gods had punished him. Such people were rather sneered at than pitied.

The masculine contribution to cultivation was minimal partly because of the permanent character of the banana plants. Men were responsible for the condition of the house, hunting and herding. The only publicly recognized cooperation between men in the villages seems to have taken place in these fields of activity. No organized common labor, as among the Sukuma people ever existed, although there were special herding and fishing guilds.[35]

c) *The Political System.* The chief was the natural centre of political authority. His power was divine; he was the highest judge and the absolute ruler of his subjects. He was responsible for what the Bahaya call *emilembe n'omugisha,* the peace and well-being of the people. A chief's performance was judged from his capacity to make rain and avoid famine in the chief-

---

[33] Rehse, *op.cit.,* p. 5.

[34] Taylor, *op.cit.,* p. 139. The traditional site of the Karagwe chiefs at Bweranyange, that burnt down in the early 1950s at a grass-fire, contained remnants of a variety of goods that the "great" Rumanyika (1850—80) got as gifts from the Arabs at Kafuro or had exchanged with them for slaves.

[35] Cory and Hartnoll, *op.cit.,* pp. 181—87.

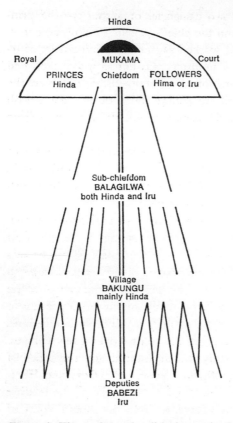

Figure 9. The traditional political organization in Buhaya.

dom. Moreover, the Mukama was the focus of identity. Through him the individual member of a clan could feel solidarity beyond his own little community; to feel that he was a member of *eihanga*—a country (read chiefdom). Even though a common language and culture was dispersed throughout Buhaya, because of the high degree of geographical mobility within the area, the loyalty was to the chiefdom. A "Haya-consciousness" never developed in old times.

In the Haya chiefdoms political power was associated with social status and economic wealth. Possession of many heads of cattle was an indication not only of wealth and social status, but also of political power. Being a *nyarubanja* holder had a similar implication. In fact, the political power was often acquired first and determined the obtaining of social status and economic wealth.[36]

[36] For an interesting discussion of the role of politics in traditional and contemporary Africa, see L. A. Fallers, "Social Stratification and Economic Processes" in M. J. Herskovits and M. Harwitz (eds), *Economic Transition in Africa,* (New York 1964).

Political power was delegated to two categories of authority—the princes, *balangira,* all of royal descent, and the chief's personal followers, *batekwa,* who were of non-royal clans and worked as ministers, sub-chiefs, courtiers or messengers. The institution of ministers was not so well established as in certain other Interlacustrine kingdoms.[37] There existed, however, the position of Prime Minister, *omukuru we kibuga,* later during the British colonial period renamed with the Ganda term, *katikiro.* He was always from a commoner clan.

At the court, the corps of officials consisted of princes and the chief's own followers, both Hima and Iru. At the sub-chiefdom level, authority was in the hands of both princes and members of the *tekwa* group.[38] At the parish or village level, the majority of the rulers were *balangira.*[39]

A few words should be said about how the village organization developed. Once village boundaries were drawn up, mainly according to the sphere of influence of various clans, in each village, the clan of the first settler was recognized as the leading clan.[40] When newcomers of other clans came to settle within the village boundaries, quarrels often broke out between the clans. The chief found it necessary to appoint an impartial arbitrator to settle these disputes. He usually chose for this office a prince, but sometimes one of his personal followers, who was given the control over a few villages. This is how the parish level of authority was introduced and the office of the parish chief, or *mukungu* was established. According to Cory and Hartnoll, in course of time the mukungu took over from the head of the leading clan the right to allocate land in his village.[41] From the chief's point of view, this new institution meant that he could remove some competitors for power from the immediate political centre, and thereby reduce the risk for a power struggle between the many potential heirs.

The chief at the parish level ideally combined three distinct roles; as political authority (*mukungu*); as prince of the ruling dynasty (*mulangira*); and, as landholder of *nyarubanja* (*mutwazi*).[42] The parish chiefs held in

---

[37] See A. I. Richards, *East African Chiefs,* (London 1960), Ch. VII, "The Haya", pp. 180—82.

[38] Cory and Hartnoll, *op.cit.,* claim that authority at the sub-chiefdom level was in the hands of appointed chiefs chosen among the relatives of the chief. Richards, *op.cit.,* and Reining in a paper "Village Organization in Buhaya", *EAISR Conference Paper,* (June 1952), are of the opinion that the sub-chiefs were mainly of non-Hinda descent. Reining, referring to a sample she made in 1951 provides some evidence for her view. The answers which the present author obtained from Haya elders tended to confirm Richards' and Reining's point rather than that of Cory and Hartnoll.

[39] See diagram on p. 84.

[40] Cory and Hartnoll, *op.cit.,* pp. 269—71.

[41] *Ibid.,* p. 273.

[42] Reining, "Haya Land Tenure . . .", *op.cit.,* p. 66.

the beginning their office at the grace of the Mukama; later it often happened, however, that they designated their own successor, usually the eldest son, to office; the Mukama only confirmed the designation. An important step towards centralization of social and political control in the system was taken with the establishment of parish chiefs. The latter served as political representatives of the central authority, and as such collected tributes, transmitted important messages, and so forth. These duties were, however, hardly onerous, and the mukungu had his own assistants known as *babezi* to help him carry out his duties. On the whole the quantity of output in the traditional political systems in Buhaya was minimal. People in the local village communities lived a rather autonomous life. The Mukama did not interfere in their daily life unless in case of emergency, such as war. Another important function of the parish chief was settling conflicts in the villages. The different clans often quarreled over land and the mukungu served as adjudicator in these cases.

The sub-chiefdom units developed as a result of the need for a stronger internal organization. Once the chiefdoms had consolidated as separate units inter-chiefdom feuds became more frequent. The chief placed a number of parishes and their rulers under a common administrative head, *mulagirwa* (later renamed with the Ganda term, *mwami*). The sub-chiefdom became known as a *gombolola*. Every sub-chief was responsible for a local military organization, which was part of the chief's army. Being in possession of a substantial number of soldiers, many of these sub-chiefs enjoyed a powerful position. Particularly in those cases where the gombolola was given to a relative of the chief, the risk of a power struggle was imminent. Many of the battles in the old times were fought between the chief and his followers against a powerful sub-chief, supported by his local army. In most cases the Mukama was successful in curbing the dissidents; yet, the disintegration of Kyamtwara chiefdom during the 19th century, for instance, was caused by lack of central control over strong sub-chiefs in Bugabo, Kianja, and Bukara.[43]

No chief in Buhaya ever managed to achieve control over the whole area. There was a continuous power struggle between and within chiefdoms. Major reasons for war were desire for cattle, or internal rivalry within the ruling dynasties.[44] It was very common to ask for help from the Kabaka of Buganda; Ganda warriors seem to have played a decisive role in many battles fought in Buhaya.

[43] Cory, *op.cit.*, pp. 51—68.

[44] Kakoko, a son of the "great" Rumanyika of Karagwe, who was left-handed and by tradition therefore ruled out as a chief, during the late 19th century, when he acted as a regent for his younger brother, killed seventeen of his nearest relatives and took out the eyes of his step-brother.

War and trade brought the Bahaya in contact with other tribes. The Baganda were alternatively looked upon as friends or enemies, but always with respect. When Stanley visited Karagwe for the second time in 1889, he reported that Karagwe depended to a certain degree on Buganda.[45] The chief of Kiziba regularly paid tribute to the Kabaka of Buganda. Contacts to the south were limited. Ihangiro and Karagwe chiefdoms sometimes fought the chiefs of Rusubi, but except for a few traders, it seems as if the Bahaya never travelled to the southern shores of Lake Victoria. The Sukuma-Nyamwezi peoples and others from the east and the south were known in Buhaya as *banyamahanga*—foreigners—because of their different way of life.

Conclusions

Because of, among other things, the land tenure and inheritance system in Buhaya, the cultural assimilation of people in the area, like in neighboring Buganda, proceeded quite far in the pre-colonial times; a common language and similar customs were adopted in all Haya chiefdoms. The social integration of Bahima and Bairu, however, proceeded much further in eastern Buhaya than it did in Karagwe.

Moves were made through the introduction of new political offices at the parish and sub-chiefdom level to increase the rate of assimilation within each chiefdom. This, however, made the amalgamation of the different chiefdoms into one political unit much more difficult. The reason why the development in Buganda took another direction—towards a strongly centralized political organization—was the emergence of a new system of legitimizing political roles.

The constant conflict between persons wielding authority because they belonged to the royal dynasty, on grounds of *ascription,* and those who performed services to the chief, on grounds of *achievement,* was in Buganda resolved in favor of the latter. As Apter[46] has pointed out, performance in serving the Kabaka, and thereby the state, became the sole basis of chieftaincy. Princes of no direct descent from the Kabaka himself were all placed in the same position as most commoners. These princes were usually given estates, but never political authority. According to one source all the princes of direct descent were killed on the accession of a new Kabaka in Buganda.[47]

[45] H. M. Stanley, *In Darkest Africa,* (London 1890), quoted in Cory, *op.cit.,* pp. 116—17.
[46] Apter, "The Politics . . .", *op.cit.,* pp. 107—116.
[47] Richards, *op.cit.,* p. 47.

In Buhaya the ruling clan always formed a caste of its own. There was a stigma attached to being a Muhinda. Although the Haya chiefs also used to promote certain people because they had rendered the chiefdom a service, the problem of whether ascription or achievement was the true basis of authority was never solved in Buhaya. The danger of disintegration and political disorder always remained imminent in the Haya chiefdoms. There were always princes prepared to lay claim to the throne, even if they were not designated heirs.

The political structures in pre-colonial Buhaya were *diffuse,* although a certain degree of differentiation of roles existed. The need for an elaborate political organization was non-existing in the traditional society. The chiefs had the ultimate control of all important resources in society, people, cattle, land, and coffee trees. The regular collection of tributes was duly carried out by the parish chiefs. Penetration by the central authority down to the village level was however, *intermittent;*[48] interference from above was rather sparse. Moves to enhance the strength of the political authority in the Haya chiefdoms were generally made, not by increasing the tributes, but rather by waging a war against a neighboring people.

Unequal distribution of wealth, status and power was accepted as a divine rule in traditional Buhaya. The inequality was less visible in Karagwe where Bahima and Bairu lived physically more excluded from each other than in the eastern part; there the *nyarubanja* system made the hierarchical structures of society highly noticeable to the commoner. This feudal land tenure system made several people depending on the grace of a few privileged persons in society. Personal attachment to the chief or one of his relatives was the best way for a Mwiru to secure some benefits and some protection in society.

The material needs of the ordinary men in the traditional society remained more or less constant, and were usually satisfied by existing resources. Hence there were few, if any "input" demands on the political authorities. The members of the traditional society had limited expectations of their rulers and there is no evidence that they tried to convert these into political actions. By and large the political culture of pre-colonial Haya society was, what Almond and Verba call, *parochial.*[49]

Individual political participation or cooperation in organized groups, such as age grade associations or secret societies, were unknown in Buhaya. There was nothing whatsoever like the leaders of the age grade associations in Sukumaland, the *basumba batale,* whose main responsibility was to organize collective work among the men of their age groups, but who in their capa-

[48] *Intermittent* is used by Almond and Powell *op.cit.,* p. 218, to describe the political structures in undifferentiated political systems.
[49] Almond and Verba, *op.cit.,* p. 16.

city of community leaders wielded considerable political power.[50] Malcolm writes that the *nsumba ntale* could say to the chief: "My people, whom I represent, refuse to comply as they do not consider your instruction either just or reasonable."[51] Infallability was however, unthinkable in Buhaya, where the myth claimed that the political rulers were related to the creator-god. This system of belief fostered the idea that only the chiefs had the responsibility to care for the state of the chiefdom; people remained passive subjects.

The Bahaya had, in pre-colonial times, few means of showing their dissatisfaction with the rule of the chiefs. Individual members of the system holding a position of power, particularly those of the ruling dynasty, did sometimes conspire against the Bakama, but did so because of individual ambitions rather than common grievances. Generally, acts of oppression and violence could be committed by a chief without his authority being seriously questioned.[52] The only way the commoner could show withdrawal of support for his superior was by migrating to another area. This was quite common in Buganda; Cory and Hartnoll mention the existence of the same phenomenon in Buhaya,[53] but to what extent it was used, nobody knows with any accuracy.

[50] See e.g., J. G. Liebenow, "Responses to Planned Change in a Tanganyika Tribal Group", *American Political Science Review*, (Vol. L, June 1956), pp. 442—61; and D. W. Malcolm, "Sukumaland—An African People and Their Country", *Mwanza District Book*, (Mwanza 1938).
[51] Malcolm, *op.cit.*,
[52] There is a story about Chief Kalemera I of Kyamtwara that he killed all his male children. He was advised to do so by his followers, who feared that he would have the same experience as his father, Nyarubamba, under whose rule all his heirs had started to quarrel with him and each other.
He also is renowned for having had the blood of all his cattle flowing down a hillside for the fun of seeing blood. When it turned out that the blood from the slaughtered cows was not enough to flow down the whole slope and into the Mulelezi River, he ordered his own people to be killed. He is known in the local tradition as a bad king, but no attempts were ever made to dethrone him.
[53] Cory and Hartnoll, *op.cit.*, Appendix III.

The first non-Africans to arrive in Buhaya were a number of Arab slave and ivory traders. One does not know exactly when they first came to the area. There is information that the first Arab to visit Buganda was Ahmed bin Ibrahim, who came in 1844.[1] He also went to Karagwe, then the greatest of the Haya chiefdoms, where he and some of his companions built their residence at Kafuro, a few miles east of Bweranyange, the site of the chief.[2] The Arabs brought a number of new articles into the area, such as the *kanzu* — the long gown generally worn by male Arab traders and beads as already mentioned. It is also interesting that they presented the chief at Bweranyange with such things as Chinese porcelain.[3]

Ahmed bin Ibrahim was not simply a merchant; he was also seriously interested in spreading his own religion. When in Buganda, he took the opportunity to teach the then Kabaka, Suna, the doctrines of Islam.[4] Both Suna, and his successor, Mutesa I, kept contact with the Arab merchants, not only for religious and economic reasons, however. Mutesa, particularly, the founder of the "great" Buganda, who was eager to extend his influence over an area as wide as possible, saw in his Arab contacts, valuable allies. His close contact, particularly with the Sultan of Zanzibar, had its importance for him, considering the Anglo-Egyptian expansion towards the south, which aimed at placing the whole Nile basin under Egyptian rule.

Mutesa's friendship with the Arabs, however, came to a sudden end in 1874, when he had all the Muslim converts in Buganda imprisoned and killed.[5] The Sultan of Zanzibar was too far away to retaliate. The Kabaka

---

[1] J. M. Gray, "Ahmed bin Ibrahim—the first Arab to reach Buganda", *Uganda Journal*, (Vol 11, September 1947).

[2] Cf., p. 74, footnote 2.

[3] Pieces of Chinese porcelain have been found at excavations in Bweranyange. A total evaluation of what Bweranyange contained at the time of Rumanyika has, however, not yet been made, although steps in that direction have been taken both from Makerere University College (Dr M. Posnansky) and the Office of the Conservator of Antiquities in Dar es Salaam.

[4] Cf., "Extracts from Mengo Notes", *Uganda Journal*, (Vol 11, September 1947), p. 110. There is also a story about Suna's reaction to Ahmed bin Ibrahim's complaint that the Kabaka was killing people, who had been created by a God, and that both the Kabaka's own life and his kingdom had been given him by that same God. To this Suna is said to have answered: "Where is there a God greater than me?"

[5] Gray, *op.cit.*, p. 87. The reason is said to have been that certain Muslims had refused to eat meat slaughtered by the Kabaka's "pagan" butcher.

was later also saved from Egyptian expansion thanks to the Mahdi rebellion in the Sudan.

The Arabs who settled at Kafuro never came to exert the same influence as in Buganda. Despite the fact that Ahmed bin Ibrahim spent a large part of his life at Kafuro, his missionary activities never seem to have been very extensive, or at least, successful. Rumanyika enjoyed having foreign visitors, and was always gentle-mannered towards them, but he never went as far as accepting any foreign religion. Ahmed bin Ibrahim, however, faced a tragic death at Kafuro. Unwillingly he got himself involved in the internal power struggle following the death of the great Rumanyika. After this incident all Arabs at Kafuro seem to have deserted the place.[6]

The Arab presence at Kafuro was hence a short interlude but it reflected the greatness of Karagwe during Rumanyika's reign. It coincided with the arrival of the first European explorers in the area. Speke and Grant visited Karagwe in 1861; Stanley the first time in 1876. The latter stayed at Kafuro. To these European explorers the other Haya chiefdoms were of marginal interest. The location of Karagwe on the main Arab slave route, the reputation of Karagwe, and the intelligence of its ruler, Rumanyika, attracted the Europeans.

Karagwe's greatness, however, came to a sudden end. There are two main reasons for this: the internal struggle for power after Rumanyika's death; and, a severe rinderpest. After Rumanyika's death all his successors were killed young or died a natural death at an early age; the regents responsible for the country behaved very harshly and without any insight into the problems of the chiefdom. The rinderpest hit the whole area west of Lake Victoria in 1890, but was particularly damaging in Karagwe, where about 90 per cent of all cattle in the chiefdom died. Many Bahima killed themselves or migrated to Ankole, Rwanda and Urundi. Around 1890 a small-pox epidemic also took a severe toll of the population in Buhaya.

The decline of Karagwe coincided with the advent of the first Germans in the area. Europe's interest in East Africa was not awakened until the 1880s, following the reports of the first explorers. The German government, despite its new imperial outlook, showed, however, little interest in extending its influence to East Africa. A privately sponsored colonialist company, the Society for German Colonization, founded in 1885 by a man called Carl Peters, became the chief competitor with the British in the struggle to gain control of East Africa. The people in the area around Lake Victoria had a strong impression in 1889 of what "the scramble for Africa" meant. One German and one British expedition were penetrating inland towards the big

[6] *Ibid*. Gray quotes Major Gaetano Casati, who was with Carl Peters' expedition that reached the area in 1889 as saying that when they passed Kafuro it was completely abandoned. Today, only a mango tree reminds of the former Arab settlement.

lake from the Indian Ocean. The main points of interest were the source of the Nile and the acquisition of the strong kingdom of Buganda.[7] In 1889 the situation in Buganda had changed. Mutesa was dead and succeeded by Mwanga. The former had invited Christian missionaries to come to his country before he died. Mwanga, however, had them persecuted in 1886. The result of this was almost a civil war, in which representatives of all the three monotheistic religions, Catholics, Muslims, and Protestants, joined forces and deposed Mwanga in 1888. Mwanga, who had earlier refused to become a Christian agreed to be baptized at a Catholic mission station, while living as a refugee in southern Buganda. In 1889 he was back on the political scene as the commander of the Christian forces in the kingdom. Just before the German expedition reached the Ganda capital, Mwanga had gained control of the kingdom.

Carl Peters, who led the German expedition offered the Kabaka far more generous terms than the English, and the Ganda Catholics, who were afraid that in the event of a British take-over the Protestants would benefit, seem to have talked him into accepting Peters' offer. When Mwanga did so, it was feared that the latent hostility between Protestants and Catholics in Buganda would come out in the open. Behind the former stood the British, behind the latter the Germans.

Fortunately, the focus on Buganda was not so strong in government circles in Europe as it was among the leaders of these two expeditions. At a conference in Berlin 1890, an Anglo-German agreement was signed, in which Peters' treaty with Mwanga was cancelled. A boundary was drawn between British and German territories on the west side of Lake Victoria following the first parallel south of the Equator from the lake to the Congolese border.[8]

As a result of this agreement the whole of Buganda was placed under British influence. Later in 1902 a southern portion of Buganda, Missenye,

[7] The German expedition was led by Carl Peters and the official objective of the expedition was to relieve Emin Pasha, the Governor of the Equatoria province in the southern Sudan, who was cut off from contacts with Egypt and London because of the Mahdi rebellion. Pasha was a former German scientist, whose original name was Eduard Schneitzer. While still young he converted to Islam and later entered Egyptian service. He became Governor of Equatoria in 1878. In 1890 he decided to switch his allegiance to the German Emperor.
The British expedition, which was also interested in the fate of Pasha was led by a man called Fredrik Jackson, and sponsored by British East Africa Company.

[8] This historical account has deliberately been made short. It is only a summary of the wide and complicated drama that was staged in and around Buganda in the late 19th century. The following sources are credited: Ingham, *op.cit.,* Hellberg, *op.cit.,* D. A. Low, *Religion and Society in Buganda 1875—1900,* (East African Studies Material, Kampala 1956), and J. V. Wild, *The Story of the Uganda Agreement,* (London 1965).

was ceded and became a separate chiefdom under German rule.[9] The Germans decided to establish a post at Bukoba just south of the new border.

The events in Buganda did not pass unnoticed in Buhaya. Many refugees from the civil wars that took place in Buganda during the 1880s and 90s came to settle in Buhaya.[10] A number of them stayed at Buyekera, today part of Bukoba township. Others went to settle in Kianja on the invitation of Chief Kahigi II. Many Baganda settled in what is now Kamachumu and soon turned this place into a major trading center, encouraging Indians, Arabs and other Africans to set up their shops in the area. Kamachumu has ever since remained one of the most important trading centers in Buhaya.[11] The events in Buganda were also to influence German policy towards missionaries, as shown below.[12]

The Germans in Buhaya

Emin Pasha, who in 1890 shifted his allegiance from the British to the Germans, arrived towards the end of that year at Bukoba where he established a post. Before coming to Bukoba he had laid Tabora, the main Arab trading center among the Nyamwezi people, under German administration. He had only lately on his expedition been informed about the Anglo-German border agreement. He himself did not like it. From his own letters there is no doubt that Emin Pasha regarded Bukoba as a stepping stone for further expansion, strategically situated just south of the newly established border.[13] His wider colonial ambitions made his visit to Bukoba short, however.[14] He soon left the area and travelled towards the north, possibly in the direction of his old province, Equatoria in the Sudan. In 1892, while on his way, he was killed in the Congo.

A combination of imperialist policies, personal ambitions, and simply unusual coincidencies determined the new borders in the area west of Lake Victoria. Emin Pasha's followers, who became responsible for the colonial administration, faced a large problem in trying to convince people about the

[9] Cf., p. 94.

[10] Mwanga himself sought refuge in Kiziba in 1892, when new disturbances broke out in Buganda.

[11] This information was mainly obtained during an interview with Haji Suleiman Hamadu, a businessman in Kamachumu, and son of one of the original Ganda immigrants in the area.

[12] Cf., pp. 95—98.

[13] F. Stuhlmann in his work, *Mit Emin Pasha ins Herz von Afrika*, (Berlin 1894), p. 116, quotes a section of a letter by Pasha to Stuhlmann written in November 1890, in which the former expresses that the new station in Bukoba will serve as his *pied-a-terre*.

[14] Cory, *op.cit.*, p. 143.

importance of the new borderline between Buganda and Buhaya. The close relationship that existed between Buhaya and the kingdoms to the north was not easily broken. The chief of Kiziba, in particular, who usually looked to the Baganda for help against his enemies in the rest of Buhaya, was not inclined to obey the new agreement. Several punitive expeditions were hence pursued by the Germans against Mutatembwa, ruler of Kiziba from 1870 to 1903. Although the first south parallel had been recognized as the official border, the Kagera River remained de facto the border between the two colonial territories, Uganda and Tanganyika, until 1902, when Missenye, as mentioned above, came under German administration.

In the first years of German rule little effort was made to stop the trade between Buhaya and the kingdoms in Uganda: Buganda, Ankole, Toro, and Bunyoro. Only when a severe epidemic of sleeping sickness broke out, were more serious steps taken to stop the crossing of the border. The traffic of people and goods across the border was however, never completely cut off.

The German government took over the administration of the whole of the Tanganyika Territory in 1891. The highest official in the country was the Governor; under his command stood civil administrators and, the so-called, *Schutztruppen*. The Germans did not follow any one particular policy in establishing an administrative apparatus in Tanganyika. In large parts of the country the traditional African authorities were forced to surrender and replaced by German officials, and at the lower levels, by coastal Swahili people who were sent out in the country to act as agents of the new colonial administration.[15] The Germans lacked competent staff, however, and this seems to have been the main reason why in certain up-country areas, Buhaya, Buzinza, Buha, Rwanda and Burundi,[16] the colonial govern-ment decided to adapt the traditional system for administrative purposes. From the German point-of-view, it was basically a good idea since all these areas had systems with strong central authorities. Another reason for using this system of "indirect rule" was probably the distance of the area from Dar es Salaam, the capital of the new colony.

The features of the German administration in Buhaya have been well summarized by D. L. Baines, the first British political officer to arrive at Bukoba after the German defeat in 1916:[17]

Except when German interests were concerned the Administration interfered as little as possible in the internal affairs of the various Sultanates. Implicit obedience was required and undoubtedly obtained to all orders issued by the Government or the Sultans. Complaints against the Sultans were discouraged, presumably in accordance

[15] See, e.g., Clagett Taylor, *op.cit.*, p. 21.

[16] Rwanda and Burundi (Urundi) were part of German East Africa and after the First World War designated League of Nations Mandatory Territories to be administered by Belgium.

[17] D. L. Baines, "The Anglo-German War", *Bukoba District Book,* (Bukoba 1919).

with true Prussian spirit that authority must be maintained right or wrong. Authority was entirely concentrated in the Sultans and they appointed, reappointed or removed chiefs at all grades at will, a slavish subservience to themselves being the sole qualification for office.[18]

The reaction to the German occupation by the Haya chiefs varied. The chief of Ihangiro accepted the new rulers at once. Mukotani of Kyamtwara became involved in fierce battles with the Germans. Mutatembwa of Kiziba, as already mentioned,[19] caused the Germans to send military expeditions into his chiefdom several times. Kahigi II of Kianja was in many respects the cleverest of them all. He soon realized the strength of the foreigners and made certain political moves to please the Germans. They, on their side, regarded him as their favorite chief and trusted him in all situations. Kahigi took advantage of the internal splits in Kyamtwara, Bugabo, and Bukara. He accused the chiefs of these areas for plotting against the new rulers. These accusations, whether true or not, rendered him material benefits, and certain parts of neighboring chiefdoms were given to him. The Germans seem to have unofficially made him the "Paramount Chief of Buhaya". Karagwe, which at this time had seriously declined,[20] was deprived of its own chief, and placed under Kahigi. He appointed one of his uncles, Kyobya, to rule on his behalf. Kyobya was an efficient ruler, but highly unpopular with the local Banyambo. These people, with a proud tradition and strong focus on their own chiefs, could not consider being ruled by a man from Kianja, one of the smaller chiefdoms in Buhaya. But times were changing. Kyobya's rule over Karagwe was the first indication to the Banyambo that from now on the chiefdoms in the coastal part were to become more important, and Karagwe placed in a backwater.

One of the important things that took place during the early colonial period, was the establishment of Christian churches in Buhaya. The first Roman Catholic missionary landed near Kanazi in Kianja chiefdom in 1880. Because the local rulers suspected that this man was an agent of the Kabaka of Buganda, he was refused permission to settle.[21] Twelve years later another group of Catholic missionaries arrived in Buhaya and this time, with the help of the German administration, they were allowed to begin activities from a station built at Kashozi in Bugabo chiefdom.

Many of the first Catholic catechumens in Buhaya were Ganda refugees. The Haya chiefs were very reluctant to permit the establishment of mission stations on their territory. Particularly stubborn was Kahigi, and because of his special position, it is likely that the Germans did not want to put strong pressures on him to change his attitude. In the case of Mutahangarwa, the

[18] The Germans used the term "Sultan" for chief, and "Sultanate" for chiefdom.
[19] Cf., p. 94.
[20] Cf., p. 91.
[21] Hellberg, *op.cit.*, p. 73.

chief of Kiziba, who had some of the new Catholic stations burnt, the Germans forced him to build new ones.[22]

To the position of the chiefs the spread of monotheistic religions was probably more detrimental than their subordination to the German administration. They realized that conversion to Christianity, or even Islam, would mean commitment to other values, which in the long run tended to undermine the religious basis for the Hinda rule. Their suspicion was also directed towards the new schools. The Bahaya had their own educational system which was aimed at perpetuating the prevailing values of the society.[23] The introduction of another school system was therefore regarded as a serious threat.

As time passed however, some of the chiefs realized that they could derive personal advantages from sponsoring missions in their chiefdom. Others only gave in after external pressures. It is worth noting that none of the chiefs were personally converted to Christianity or Islam during the German period.

The Haya chiefs were never faced with a competition for influence between the three monotheistic religions at the same time as Mutesa and Mwanga had been in Buganda. Ever since 1892 the Catholics were given more or less official status. As has been pointed out by a Haya observer:[24] "to be a true friend of the Germans you had to be a Catholic".

The missionaries themselves in Buhaya had not the same urgency to gain access to the Bakama and put political pressure on them, as they had in the more strategical kingdom of Buganda. The courts of the Haya chiefs were to the Europeans in the political periphery and this probably saved Buhaya from some of the more serious problems that occurred in Buganda as a result of the mixing of religion and politics at an early stage of development.[25] The Catholic missionaries in Buhaya, once established in the area, concentrated their efforts rather on the common man than on the political authorities.

The Germans and the Catholics could not prevent the Protestant creed from being spread in Buhaya, but advocates of the latter faith had to fight "underground" for a long time. A number of Kiziba traders were converted by Ganda evangelists during their frequent visits to Buganda, and they brought the new creed back to Buhaya. In Kiziba they formed a small group of believers that used to meet secretly in a cave on the shores of

---

[22] F. X. Lwamgira, *Amakuru ga Kiziba n'Abakama Bamu,* (Bukoba 1949), p. 459. For an extensive account of early Christian mission activities in Buhaya, see Hellberg, *op.cit.,* and *Edini omuli Buhaya,* (published to celebrate fifty years of Roman Catholic mission activities in Bukoba, 1941).
[23] Cf., p. 81.
[24] J. Kibira, *Aus einer afrikanischen Kirche,* (Bielefeld 1960), p. 20.
[25] See, Low, *op.cit.*

Lake Victoria.[26] The first Haya Protestants had been in contact with the revivalist group within the Protestant-Anglican Church of Buganda. Accordingly, strong emphasis was put on the act of conversion itself.[27] Protestantism was associated with the British, and the Germans in Buhaya feared the influence of "British" ideas on the local population. The official German policy in the colony was not directed against any particular religious creed. Protestant missionaries had, for instance, been allowed to start a big station in the Usambara Mountains, near Tanga, as early as 1891.[28] The German officers at the post in Bukoba had watched, however, the tragic consequences in Buganda of the competition for influence between Catholics and Protestants. They were anxious to avoid similar disturbances in their own territory. The pro-Catholic policy in Buhaya was probably also determined by the personal attitude of the Commandant of the post. Both Stuhlmann and Langheld, two of the most important figures in the German colonial administration in Bukoba, were against the Protestants. Stuhlmann, for instance, was a blood-brother of Kabaka Mwanga, who had been converted to Catholicism. Langheld showed his sympathy for the Catholics, by giving them land for the resettlement of 2.000 Catholic Ganda refugees.[29]

The Protestants were refused any official recognition by the Germans until 1910, when the German Bethel Mission was allowed to open a "trading mission" in Bukoba. At this time the Catholics had already established six major stations in Buhaya. The main reason for the change in policy was that the German missionaries managed to convince the colonial authorities about the "dangers" of the spread of Islam in the area between Lake Victoria and the Congolese border. The Germans intended to set up stations in Rwanda with Bukoba as a supporting station. Important for the change in German attitude towards Protestant missionaries in Buhaya was also that the request this time came from a German society and not from the Anglican missionaries in Uganda.

Bukoba started in 1910 as a mission station and was supervised from the new main Protestant mission centre in Rwanda. The missionaries soon realized, however, that the use of Bukoba simply as a supporting station was unsatisfactory. Owing to pressures from certain individual missionaries and

[26] See, Hellberg, op.cit., Ch. III.

[27] Called the "Pilkington Revival" after George Pilkington, a priest of the Church of England and a CMS (Protestant) missionary in Buganda. He had translated the Bible into Luganda. The Bible became the main instrument in the evangelization movement which started around 1894.

[28] J. Kibira, "A Study of Christianity among the Haya Tribe; West Lake Region Tanganyika", M. A. Thesis, (Boston University School of Theology, unpublished, 1963).

[29] Ibid.

the local Haya evangelists, it was decided two years later to organize the Bukoba station on a more independent and permanent basis. Evangelization was officially to be carried out only in those areas where the Catholics were not yet established. Hence a new station was opened at Nyakahanga in Karagwe in 1914.[30]

The spread of Islam in Buhaya was carried out by individual traders, originally Arabs, who came to settle and work in the area. It spread owing to several reasons: the Muslims lived among the local people; they spread their faith along with their business; they chose wives from the local people; they achieved strong communities due to the unity of their faith; and, they practised no discrimination on grounds of race, color, class or birth.

Islam did not spread, however, as quick as the Christian faith among the Bahaya. Kibira has mentioned three main reasons.[31] The Bahaya, like the Baganda, were never taken as slaves by the Arabs; the latter only travelled through the area. The victory of the Christians in Buganda meant a strong barrier to further Muslim penetration southwards. Finally, the Bahaya were against circumcision; this practice, used by the Muslims, had traditionally been regarded with contempt by the local people.

The Catholic White Fathers and the German administration in Bukoba were not always on good terms. The German administrators kept complaining about the unsatisfactory standard of the Catholic mission schools in the beginning of this century; they even threatened to send Muslim teachers to the villages, should the mission schools not improve.[32]

Towards the end of the German rule in Buhaya school attendance rose rapidly, particularly in Kiziba. Hellberg quotes figures[33] which show that in 1912 the Catholics had 55 schools with 1.400 pupils in Buhaya; there was only one government school, located in Bukoba, with 250 pupils.

This account of changes in Buhaya during the time of the German rule will be incomplete without mentioning the growth of commercial activities on a large scale. The first Indian shop in Bukoba was founded in 1894, and a number of other Indian and Arab merchants moved up from the coast and Tabora to establish themselves in Bukoba. Similarly, Asians moved south from Kampala and Masaka in Uganda. Business remained in the hands of the foreigners during the period before the First World War. Bahaya could get employment in minor positions with the Indians and the Arabs. New employment opportunities were also opened up at the missions, where bearers and servants were badly needed. On the whole, the changes

[30] Hellberg, op.cit., p. 117.
[31] Kibira, "A Study of Christianity . . .", op.cit., pp. 38—39; also J. S. Trimingham, Islam in East Africa, (London 1962), p. 35.
[32] R. Austen, "Political Generations in Bukoba, 1890—1939", EAISR Conference Paper, (June 1963), p. 8.
[33] Hellberg, op.cit., p. 114.

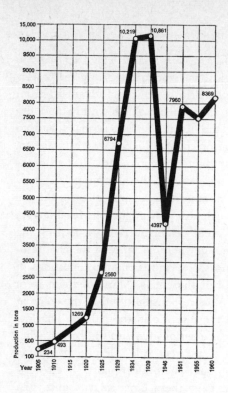

* Figures originally compiled by Mr Carl Friedrich, IFO-Institut, München, Germany.

Figure 10. Coffee production in Buhaya, 1905—60.

which took place in the economic sector in these years, however, affected the local Bahaya only to a little extent.

One major innovation that the Germans carried into effect was the cultivation of coffee on a commercial basis. This met with resistance, however, because the religious and social taboos[34] were still strongly supported by the local population. Lwamgira tells how Mutahangarwa, one of the first chiefs to accept the idea, did so despite strong warnings from the old people.[35] The monopoly of the chiefs to plant coffee was also brought to an end during the German period. In addition to the Robusta coffee, Arabica was introduced on the high ridges in the area. The first figures for African produced coffee (both Robusta and Arabica) in Buhaya were very modest; in 1905, 234 tons were produced. Five years later it had increased to 493 tons. From then on, as the diagram above, indicates, production of coffee shows a rapid increase every year, until the peak was reached in 1939.[36]

[34] Cf., pp. 82—83.
[35] Lwamgira, op.cit., p. 466.
[36] The figures shown in the diagram above were obtained from Mr Carl Fried-

99

The British take over

The First World War did not affect Buhaya very much. The area was too far away from places of greater strategical interest to the European powers involved. Towards the end of the war, the British, however, advancing from the north, made a major amphibious raid on Bukoba township and destroyed vital German installations in the town.[37] The Germans had to retreat southwards. British administration over Buhaya was established, following this raid, in 1916, with Major Baines in command. He had great difficulty in convincing the Bahaya of the value of the change, particularly as the coffee price fell in 1917, and a number of epidemic diseases hit the area. Moreover, the two strong chiefs of the area, Kahigi and Mutahangarwa, had just died. They were the last "great" chiefs in Buhaya. During the British period there was a gradual decline in the importance of the chieftainship. The main reason was the changing social and economic conditions in the chiefdoms, but also the lack of skill of the chiefs. Many of them were not qualified to carry out the administrative responsibilities that the colonial rulers assigned to them, and preferred the idle life in the palace. The low qualifications of the chiefs in Buhaya was a serious blow to the British who, like the Germans, practised a system of indirect rule. Despite the many shortcomings of the Bakama, the British gave them all support. Their position was enhanced by the British, who gave them large salaries and cars. This is not the place to review British colonial policy in Tanganyika, but a general impression from Buhaya is that the policy of indirect rule became increasingly difficult to pursue as social and economic conditions began changing.

German and British administration in Buhaya, although not in the whole of the colony, resembled each other in that both relied on the traditional authorities for the implementation of administrative and political decisions. It was believed this system was the safest way of maintaining law and order; there was also the vague idea at least among the British that it benefitted the Africans. Political participation by the local population in governmental institutions was a completely foreign idea to the Germans, and did not occur as an alternative in British policy until the 1950s.

The type of political system that the Germans and later the British tried to set up was aimed at enforcing law and order, and promoting increased production of agricultural primary products, in Buhaya, coffee. On the whole the colonial administration worked through the traditional authori-

---

rich, a German agricultural economist, who pursued research on coffee cultivation in Bukoba during 1964—65. Cory, *op.cit.*, p. 163, mentions that in 1906 Bukoba produced 214 tons African and 526 tons European planted coffee.

[37] *Ibid.*, pp. 173—88.

ties, but new important institutions set up were the Ministry of Agriculture and the Police Force.

Despite these new government structures the integration of the many local cultures in the territory with the colonial "elite" culture was a complicated process. The British paid little attention to the values and norms prevailing in the traditional societies. The Africans disliked the disintegration of their communities, which was the effect of the British attempt to gain control of the country. Their reaction to colonial rule will be discussed in the two following chapters.

The Germans had introduced taxation in 1904, and special employees were sent out to collect this tax from each household; originally the rate was 1 rupee, later increased to 4½ rupees.[38] One third of this went to the chiefs. The poll tax was kept by the British, and increased as the administrative organization expanded. Unlike the Germans, the British used the parish chiefs for the purpose of tax collection. The financial burden of many Bahaya became very heavy as a result of the tax.[39] Particularly the nyarubanja tenants were struck hard; they had to pay an annual tribute also to their landlord. Cory and Hartnoll claim that in the colonial period the patriarchal land tenure system turned into one of serfdom,[40] owing to the increased dependence of many tenants on a monetary economy. The British showed little interest in changing the nyarubanja system, although it is true some legal steps were taken, the most important being the abrogation in 1936 of the power to create new nyarubanja holdings.[41]

The British built up a legal system which was partly new to the Bahaya. Many more acts were defined as criminal. They also made it possible for women to plead in court.[42] This and similar changes had effects on the social system.[43] Traditional patterns of relationship in the villages were breaking down, and the absence of a strong visible central authority in the rural communities created among many people a sense of insecurity. Arson, fighting between villagers, members of different sub-tribes and so forth, were not uncommon in the colonial period.

The British formed a Council of Chiefs in Buhaya in 1926. For the first time in Haya history the rulers of the eight chiefdoms were brought together to discuss common problems.[44] This policy was also applied in other multi-

[38] The Indian monetary terms were used in the first decades of colonial rule, mainly due to the monopoly of the Indian immigrants in the commercial sector.

[39] Lwamgira writes: "The Europeans made us suffer a great deal by this tax" op.cit., p. 473.

[40] Cory and Hartnoll, op.cit., note to paragraph 553 b.

[41] Richards, op.cit., p. 180.

[42] Cory, op.cit., p. 157.

[43] Cory and Hartnoll, op.cit., par. 1255.

[44] "The Buhaya District Council—Historical Background", special paper prepared by the District Executive Officer, Mr. A. E. Kaombwe, (February 1965).

chiefdom areas, such as Chagga- and Sukumaland, the main purpose being to improve local government. The relation of the political authorities and the people at the local level was, however, hardly improved with this new local government institution. It was not until 1951 that the Chiefs' Council was turned into a real local government authority with wider power and wider popular representation.[45] Another major reorganization carried out by the British affected the traditional courts, which were organized and named according to the Ganda model.[46]

It would be wrong not to mention the name of Francis X. Lwamgira. More than any other individual Muhaya he put his stamp on the development in Buhaya during the British period. He started his career as liaison officer of the chief of Kiziba at the German *boma* (district headquarters) in Bukoba. He continued in this position during the first years of British rule. From 1926—45 he was secretary to the Council of Chiefs. Due to his intelligence and strong personality he soon became one of the most powerful persons in Bukoba. In fact, he was referred to as "the King of Buhaya". He personally worked to improve the relationship between the local Haya chiefs. If there was any tendency during this period towards a common "Haya" identity, it was largely thanks to Lwamgira's work.[47]

During the British period, the Protestants could get on better terms with the administration. An Anglican mission was asked to come and help the Haya Protestants in 1917; these missionaries continued until 1924. Then a South African Wesleyan society was called in, but its members failed to cooperate with .the local Protestant group. Eventually the German Bethel Mission was allowed to return, on the special request of the Haya priests. During the Second World War, when the Germans were detained or had to leave the country, the American Augustana Church and the Church of Sweden took over the missionary responsibilities for the Protestant church in Buhaya.[48]

In 1924 the group of Protestants had grown from a few hundred to about 2.000,[49] but this was still much below the estimated figure for the Catholics. Even Muslims exceeded the number of Protestants.

British attempts to change the Haya society were also highly noticeable in the field of agriculture and education. They wanted to improve coffee cultivation by making the local farmers adopt more scientific methods. Old coffee trees had to be uprooted, banana stems used for mulching. The first efforts were made through the extension service of the Ministry of Agricul-

[45] See below, Ch 6, p. 122.
[46] Cf., p. 85 and p. 86.
[47] Lwamgira put a great deal of effort in to getting the tribal history of Buhaya recorded. His own books were a result of this.
[48] Hellberg, *op.cit.*, gives a full account of this development.
[49] Austen, *op.cit.*, p. 11.

ture, but failed. Even when it became by law compulsory, the results were minimal.[50] The British experts did not seriously consider the effects on the local population of their hierarchical political structures, and the economic stress under which many Bahaya lived owing to lack of fertile land and their particular land tenure system.

Educational experiments were carried out in Buhaya by the British during the 1920s and early 30s. The principal aim was to mix traditional with modern education.[51] W. B. Mumford, the first British education officer posted at Bukoba, was the man behind these experiments.[52] Yet, no major results were ever achieved. Efforts to bring more agriculture into the school curriculum failed because the colonial educational and agricultural departments never reached an agreement as to how this could be effected. Moreover, there was, as will be shown in the next chapter, a widespread opposition among the Africans against any step in that direction. The result was, however, that the Nyakato middle school outside Bukoba was turned into an agricultural training centre.[53] Two years of this type of activity made the British realize that graduates were reluctant to enter farming. The principal of the school refused, however, to change the curriculum back to the type of education which was contained "within four walls". It became a community training centre, but eventually it was established as a secondary school.

The presence of both Catholic and Protestant missionaries had the effect in the educational field of stimulating the construction of new schools. Although this was not so pronounced before the Second World War as after, the competition between Protestants and Catholics helped the Bahaya to obtain educational facilities at an early stage. The distribution of schools was very uneven, however, and mission schools were concentrated in the eastern part of Buhaya, particularly in Kiziba and around the town of Bukoba. The people in Kiziba tended to be most receptive to modern education; hence it turned out that a large portion of the new local elite, that emerged in early years, came from this chiefdom.

The condition for enrollment in the mission schools was adherence to the "right" faith. Therefore, Protestants could only send their children to Protestant schools, and Catholics to Catholic schools. The Muslims had no schools of their own, and gained access to Christian schools only in exceptional cases. Most of the Muslims, however, at least before the Second World

---

[50] For African reactions to these campaigns, see Ch. 6, pp. 115—16.

[51] Compare with the current educational aims in Tanzania, Ch. 2, pp. 54—55.

[52] Mumford later became an international authority on education in colonial territories.

[53] R. Austen, "The Study of Indirect Rule in a Tanganyika Province", *EAISR Conference Paper*, (December 1963) p. 13.

War, were not interested in modern education; they were quite satisfied with the knowledge of the Koran.[54]

Conclusions [55]

For the ordinary Muhaya the most important changes during the first years of colonial rule were created by religious and educational activities. Being a Protestant or a Catholic meant a new identity. Bonds of solidarity were established within the church communities which affected the stable, traditional patterns of human interaction in the villages. Local village communities were divided according to religious affiliation. At certain places where religious identities were particularly emphasized, relationship between members of the two Christian communities was very strained, and sometimes became the reason for disputes.[56] The rivalry between the different Christian creeds never became, however, as tense as in Buganda, where they were a major determinant of political allegiances in later years.[57]

With the establishment of the colonial administration the traditional Haya authorities were forced to give up responsibility for their subjects; the chiefs were no longer allowed to pass death sentences; the ultimate decision in all administrative matters lay with the colonial representatives.[58] The attitude of the local people toward their chiefs began to undergo a change, mainly due to the fact that the Bakama became associated with the new regime. It is clear also, however, that other factors, social and economic, contributed to a new evaluation of the chiefs. Modern education, for instance, tended to undermine the religious myth that served as the justification of the Hinda

[54] Cf., Ch. 6, p. 117.
[55] Many of the conclusions concerning the impact of colonial rule on the Bahaya will be drawn at the end of Chapter 6 and 7.
[56] From the old files of the Evangelical-Lutheran Church of Northwestern Tanganyika, the following incident can be used to illustrate how emotions in the local communities could sometimes run high. It is reported in a letter from the Superintendent of the Bethel Mission, Bukoba, to the Father Superior, White Fathers' Mission, Kashozi, and dated September 7, 1936:
"I have to notify you of the following occurrence, which has repeatedly happened at our Native Church of Kishanje, gombolola Rubafu. On three occasions during divine services conducted ... at Kishanje in the course of the last months a group of Roman Catholics, wearing medallions entered the Church building and disturbed the peace and sanctity of the proceedings. In each case they were ordered to keep the peace, but refused or very noisily and ostentatiously left the Church continuing their disturbances outside the building ..."
[57] See Low, op.cit.; also, F. B. Welbourn, Religion and Politics in Uganda 1952—62, (Nairobi 1965).
[58] Hellberg, op.cit., p. 70.

rule. The internal struggle within the ruling dynasty was tearing on the validity of existing political structures. One of the best illustrations of the reluctance to support the traditional regime and its representatives was the high speed with which many Bahaya accepted the new monotheistic religions. Particularly notable was the Protestant willingness to fight "underground" for the spread of their new faith.

The major problems created by colonial policies will be dealt with more specifically in Chapter 6 and 7. A few remarks about the most prominent features of the colonial political system should, however, be made. A certain degree of structural differentiation took place, but the set-up remained hierarchial as in the pre-colonial period. The policies of penetration were *exploitative;* people were forced to follow new government directives, aimed primarily at benefitting the colonial rulers; the local Bahaya had no direct opportunities to participate in the government structures. The majority of the Haya population could no longer live a secluded life in their village communities. Although the "downward" flow of government output was by no means intense, the daily life of the rural inhabitants was considerably affected by the new regulations of the colonial rulers.

The process of allocating material benefits and rewards to members of the society was colored by the general ideological outlook of the colonial elite. The latter developed autonomous political goals, by and large indifferent to the interest of the rural African population. Only very few opportunities for advancement in society were available to the local Bahaya, of which many were withdrawing their support for the old system and looked for new chances in commerce, education, and the civil service. Although Buhaya soon became one of the most developed parts of Tanganyika, social and economic development was much quicker in Buganda. Many more opportunities developed in Kampala, because it was the main town in Uganda. The quick changes in Buganda was further enhanced by the railway link between Kampala and Mombasa, and the introduction of cotton as a complementary crop to coffee and a new source of income. In Buhaya, the new railway connection with Dar es Salaam from Mwanza, or the regular boat services on the lake which were opened, had little impact on the occupational structure of the area. Moreover, coffee remained during the whole colonial period the sole major cash crop. Buhaya was only benefitting from the "spill" of modernization in Buganda; this would have clear political implications.

Chapter 6.　　Early reactions to colonial rule

The previous chapter was an attempt to describe the new socio-economic and political structures which developed during the colonial period. The intention is now to deal more specifically with the Haya reaction to various aspects of the colonial rule.

By way of introduction it is worth noting that the relationship between the Bahaya and the many Christian missionaries in the area was never, with one exception—the South African Wesleyans—really bad; in fact, in most cases they were very good. The missionaries helped develop Luhaya into a written language; the Bible and other religious documents were translated into the vernacular.

The contact with the European missionaries generally created envy, but not necessarily resentment among the Bahaya. The relative absence of European settlers in the area helped to maintain this rather uncomplicated relationship. Another factor that definitely contributed to the Haya acceptance of new cultural values was the inadequate capacity of the traditional authorities to sustain the religious myth underlying their rule. People's confidence in the traditional myth had been shaken already in pre-colonial times, following the struggle for power between heirs with Hinda and non-Hinda mothers.

The withdrawal of support for certain traditional values was therefore quite easy for many Bahaya, and it did not take long time until they accepted a new belief system. This was particularly striking with reference to the religious system. Any magico-religious separatist movement like in the Congo, Kenya, or Central and South Africa never emerged in Buhaya.[1] Kibira credits this to the striking similarity of many conceptions in traditional Haya religion and in Christianity.[2] It is also likely that the weakness of the indigenous religion facilitated the conversion to one of the new monotheistic, and particularly the Christian, religion.

Owing to its contact with the Pilkington revival, the Protestant church

[1] See e.g., F. B. Welbourn, *East African Rebels*, (London 1961); J. W. Fernandez, "African Religious Movements", *Journal of Modern African Studies*, (Vol 2, No 4); G. Balandier, "Messianisme et Nationalisme en Afrique Noire", *Cahiers Internationaux de Sociologie*, (Vol XIV, pp. 41—65); G. Shepperson, "The Politics of African Church Separatist Movements in British Central Africa", *Africa*, (Vol XXIV, No 3); B. G. M. Sundkler, *Bantu Prophets in South Africa*, (London 1948).
[2] Kibira, "A Study of Christianity . . .", *op.cit.*, pp. 70—71.

in Buhaya has always been strongly fundamentalist-revivalist. The representatives of this faith are known in East Africa as *balokoke*. Their movement was particularly strong in Buganda, Ankole and Buhaya. It is based on puritanism and orthodoxy. The aim is to save people from decadence and wordliness. The strong undertone of individualism in this movement has stimulated its members to higher aspirations, not only in the moral, but also in the material field of activity. The *balokoke* movement within the Protestant church is one of the more radical reactions to the traditional system. It repelled many of the most pertinent features of the old Haya society, polygamy, communalism and the drinking of *pombe*—the local alcoholic drinks.

A similar movement never emerged within the local Catholic church, partly because its leaders placed less emphasis in such moral principles as monogamy, abstention from alcoholic drinks, and so forth. The conversion to Catholicism generally implied less of a change from traditional cultural values than did conversion to Protestantism.

In summing up Haya reaction to mission activities in the area, it is clear that the religious sphere was no place where a major confrontation between Africans and Europeans would occur. This was reinforced by the fact that the missions absorbed quite a few Bahaya as their employees at various levels. There was in the colonial period more room for social mobility in the religious and educational institutions of the missions than in any other walk of life. This fact cannot be disregarded when discussing the Haya attitude to the missions.[3]

The new churches and schools, however, could not absorb everyone, and a permanent problem during almost the whole colonial period was that demands for education rose more rapidly in Buhaya than the available school facilities.

Bahaya Union—African Association

It is against this background that the formation, in 1924, of the first political organization in the area, the Bahaya Union, should be viewed. It was started by a number of educated Christians and an illiterate Muslim tra-

[3] I do not imply that there were not many points of dissatisfaction with the missionaries. Several Bahaya can tell about how they were expelled from school for very minor reasons; also how they were forced to accept modes of behavior, which were exact copies of the European pattern. On the whole, however, there is no evidence that these grievances were politicized.

der.[4] Only people of Bukoba District (then still including Karagwe) were eligible for membership, which made the organization purely tribal in character. The Bahaya Union cut across religious lines, however; in the leadership were representatives of all three monotheistic religions. The emphasis in the activities of the association was rather on the tribe than on any particular religion or chiefdom. The Union was not restricted to educated people only. Its aim was to advise people, "to civilize them", as it was explicity said in the programme. It was not going to involve itself in "governmental affairs", but claimed it would approach the government in case union members faced difficulties in their activities.[5]

In 1927 the name of the organization was officially changed from Bahaya Union to African Association, although in the correspondence of the organization both names were used parallel for some years. The change of name did not come about without dispute. Many argued that as the organization was primarily concerned with the problems of Buhaya, the old name should be kept. Others were of the opinion that any African should have access to membership, not only Bahaya. The latter group was successful in its argument, particularly as there had been some attempts at this time to form a similar association in Dar es Salaam and at other places in Tanganyika; this enhanced their position.[6]

It was now officially called "an association for mutual aid among Africans." Its objectives was to "guide people in obeying the rules of the government and the chiefs, to follow these in every respect, that is right".[7] It would bring peace to the people, and give all Africans equal rights. Emphasis was put on the fact that this association was opened to everyone, not just young people.[8]

The African Association theoretically abolished the tribal identity, that its predecessor, the Bahaya Union, wanted to establish. In the constitution of

[4] The first leaders of the Bahaya Union were Herbert Rugizibwa, who also acted as secretary, Clemens Kiiza, Suedi Kagasheki, and Ludovic Kaitaba. According to a letter, dated March 15, 1924, contact had been made from Bukoba with the Tanganyika African Civil Service Association in Tanga. The letter said: "Here in Bukoba are many youths who are enthusiastic to accompany us to be members of your beloved association." This was the seed of the Bahaya Union; it was registered in August the same year.

[5] For the information about the Bahaya Union and the African Association I am indebted to Messrs. Suedi Kagasheki and Herbert Rugizibwa. The former was kind enough to give me access to his personal files. The above information is all compiled from the constitution of the Bahaya Union.

[6] The Tanganyika African Association in Dar es Salaam was formed in 1929. Among those who most strongly advocated the change of name was Mr Kagasheki, the most prominent Muslim member of the Bahaya Union.

[7] Quotation from the *Constitution of the African Association*, Bukoba, 1932.

[8] There was one qualification for membership: everyone had to write a personal letter of application.

the former organization, Buhaya or Bukoba was never mentioned. However, in practice, partly owing to lack of communications with other areas in Tanganyika, activities and membership were restricted to Buhaya.

A new, and politically important, factor that was introduced with the emergence of the Bahaya Union and the African Association was the election of office-holders. This idea was readily accepted by its members. In the long run, the acceptance of this principle would have a wider impact on the political system.

Typical of these early political activities in Buhaya was the acceptance of the existing social and political structures of society. The African Association talked in general terms of equal rights for all Africans. It did not mention anything, however, about the discrepancy in opportunities between the European and Asian communities, on the one hand, and the Africans, on the other. There was a high degree of deference towards government authorities, including the chiefs.[9] In the early activities there was no open disagreement with the Bakama, although it is clear from the issues raised that the members of the African Association had values, and priorities different from those of the chiefs. The new political association was reflecting the demands of people who had developed a new way of life; who did not think that the chiefs, or even the colonial government, alone could guide the development of the Haya society. Both the Bahaya Union and the African Association wanted improvement in the field of public health, education and of the rights of women in society. All these issues showed the acceptance of European influences among the Bahaya and their willingness to reject basic values of the traditional system. In a letter to the Council of Chiefs in 1933, the African Association wrote:[10]

The Europeans have taught us a different way of life. In Europe a woman has the same rights—she can even become a queen. Also religion has taught us that women are equally recognized before God. We realize that this law (that only male heirs are allowed to inherit) originated in the time of our great great grandfathers, but this does not mean that we should not adapt ourselves to new customs.

The above letter which was signed by forty members of the Association was a clear indication that a new elite prepared to compete with the traditional one had emerged in Buhaya. Their continuous claims for equal rights of inheritance for women, however, did not create any immediate response in government circles.

The Haya community in these years became concerned about the increasing number of prostitutes. This problem was also taken up by the new poli-

[9] Letters to the chiefs were, for instance, opened by the traditional greeting: *Kamerere Lugaba;* they continued: "We all fall before your feet and kindly ask you to listen to our request".

[10] Letter to the Council of Chiefs from the African Association (September 12, 1933).

tical association. Buhaya had already become renowned in East Africa for its export of prostitutes[11] and this issue stirred discontent among the male Bahaya. Many found their wives leaving them for the big towns. "In former times", the African Association complained in a letter to the chiefs in 1932 "a Chief used to exile such girls from his chiefdom, but nowadays he has not the same power."[12] Nowadays a woman can leave her husband at any time, and since she is "supported" by government laws, the husbands have no way of channeling their complaints, the members said. They were sure that prostitution would come to an end in ten years, if the government would make prostitutes pay tax on their incomes.[13]

The main theme around which many of the activities of the African Association centered was education. In fact, as will be seen, it became a major issue in local politics in Buhaya throughout the colonial period.

When the colonial government decided to make Nyakato Central School[14] an agricultural training centre in 1934, the Association sent a number of complaints to the provincial administration and even to the Governor himself. The decision was made at a time when the poll tax had been raised and promises about more schools and dispensaries were made by the colonial administration. The prevailing opinion among members of the Association was that the change of Nyakato School to an agricultural training centre was highly inappropriate. To them it was a step backwards. "The School" was the most important means of development. What was the use of an agricultural training centre, they asked.

There was another factor that aroused strong feelings among the local people. The result of the closing of Nyakato as an ordinary school meant that Haya school boys had to be sent to other parts of the country for education above St. IV.[15] This, they thought, would have the effect of alienating the pupils from their home society.

[11] Cf., P. Reining, "Progress Report on Research among the Haya", paper presented to a conference arranged by the "Centre de Recherches Scientifiques du Ruanda-Urundi de l'Institut pour la Recherche Scientifique en Afrique Centrale", Astrida 1952.

[12] Letter to the Council of Chiefs from the African Association (November 4, 1932).

[13] Prostitutes nowadays do pay tax—but the problem has remained. Many of the Haya women who practise prostitution invest their money in land back home in Buhaya. In the last three years the Tanzanian government has taken steps to reduce prostitution in the main urban centers.

[14] Cf., p. 103.

[15] In a letter to the Government Inspector of Schools, Bukoba, the African Association wrote January 27, 1935:

"Our Bukoba boys under the age of 15 or 16 years who now have to be sent abroad, to Mwanza or Tabora or somewhere else lose the advantage of home education; they come home to their fatherland and enter into the School of the third teacher, the World. They are very grown up people with School education, but do not know

In all its activities, the Bahaya Union-African Association showed a great interest in the advancement of the people. Its focus was, however, almost exclusively on Buhaya. The association was not affiliated with organizations with similar purposes in other parts of the country. The members were not interested in perpetuating a political system based on values similar to those of traditional Buhaya, but they were still concerned with the dangers of disintegration of the social system. Illustrations of this anxiety was their reaction against prostitution and their feeling that the governmental authorities could not do anything about it; similarly, they were afraid that sending their children to other parts of Tanganyika would cause the alienation of the children from certain features of the Haya sub-culture.

In the late 1930s communications with other political groups in the country were established. In 1936 the full name of the organization in Buhaya became Tanganyika African Association; it was now a branch of a territory-wide organization.[16] With a few exceptions, however, the Bukoba branch remained in its activities limited to Buhaya. The only "national" issue discussed in those years was that of a closer union in East Africa.[17] Until then the political organization in Buhaya had been mainly an "improvement association"; it was the only legitimate channel through which the newly emerged elite in the area could forward their developmental demands and participate in local politics. So far their activities had remained quite moderate, and the British had not intervened to stop them.

Towards the end of the 1930s, however, another issue arose that seriously affected the relations between the Bahaya and the administration. In this matter the Bukoba branch of TAA played an important part. As mentioned in the previous chapter, the British began at this time campaigns to increase the coffee production in the Bukoba area. For this reason, regulations concerning inspection and scientific methods of improvement had to be implemented. According to the principle of indirect rule, the chiefs were first approached. If the British could get the authority of the chiefs behind the scheme, certainly people would accept it. On this issue, however, the chiefs themselves were reluctant. They feared farreaching changes in land tenure —the British had passed the law abolishing the right to create new *nyaru-*

---

some times how to speak properly their mother language; they do not understand how to live in community with their family and cannot even build a native hut for themselves; moreover, they are quite alienated from the traditional histories of their country and do not know the geography of their local divisions of the District they live in. In short, they come back building castles in Spain. A long stay away from home makes them denaturalized natives and useless for home life as true Africans . . ."

[16] Edward Barongo, *Hotuba ya Bwana Mheshimiwa Nyerere*, (TANU Western Lake Branch, Bukoba 1958).

[17] For an account of the discussion of closer cooperation in East Africa in the colonial period, see B. Chidzero, *Tanganyika and International Trusteeship*, (London 1961).

banja holdings in 1936. It would also imply much more careful work with the coffee trees. With no real support from the chiefs and without any consultation of the local people, the project was doomed to fail. The situation became very serious in 1937 when riots broke out in different parts of Buhaya following British attempts to implement more modern agricultural methods. Lwamgira had formed, what he called, the Agricultural Association together with a group of "progressive farmers", a few months earlier. Even their attempts, however, to convince the Bahaya about the benefits of the new rules failed completely. In fact, Lwamgira himself at one time got stoned by a mob.[18]

The coffee riots marked a dramatic end to a period in which people had become more extensively involved in political activities in Buhaya. The time was gone when only the chiefs and their selected representatives decided the fate of Buhaya. No real clashes had occurred between the chiefs and the members of the new political organization in the area, but, as Austen has pointed out, the former tended to regard the leaders of the African Association as "unrepresentative and semi-educated".[19] The chiefs probably felt the competition from members of the new local elite; the latter, however, were not only interested in breaking down the old system. This came out in their reaction on such issues as the closing of Nyakato and the introduction of new methods of cultivation. The emergence of these issues also revealed the lack of contact and understanding between the Bahaya and the colonial authorities. Buhaya as a sub-system in colonial Tanganyika was not integrated with the goals of the colonial system, and attempts in that direction caused constantly increasing resistance from the local Haya population.

The Bahaya Union-African Association to some extent, at least in its initial stages, served as a bridge between the old and new systems. Its aim was to integrate a larger number of people into the modern culture represented by the Europeans. The new political leadership in Buhaya, however, lacked the support of the colonial elite. In the long run, therefore, the main aims of political activities changed and became opposition to the colonial rule. This did not become fully evident in the period before the Second World War, although the coffee riots was a serious indication of this change. The war brought a decline in political activities. Many leading Bahaya were taken to serve in the *King's African Rifles*. The majority were sent to Madagascar; some, however, fought as far away as South East Asia. The impact on the Africans, when confronted in the army service by new values and impressions, is hard to assess. In Tanganyika the political atmosphere definitely changed after the Second World War; this also had its effect on Buhaya, where political activity increased again.

[18] Austen, "Political Generations . . .", *op.cit.*, p. 14.
[19] *Ibid.*, p. 15.

Kianja Labour Association.[20]

A new organization known as the Kianja Labour Association was founded in Kianja chiefdom immediately after the war. It was a strange mixture of traditional and modern elements. Its focus was narrow, limited entirely to the problems of Kianja. At the same time, however, it was anti-traditional. Its main objectives were to put an end to Hinda privileges and, as implied in the name, to persuade people to work for their advancement. It was an exhortation, in some way, for self-reliance.

KLA came about as a result of long disputes in Kianja concerning the right of succession to the throne in the chiefdom. When Kahigi II died in 1916[21] he left among others, three sons, who all claimed the right to succeed their father. They were Kalemera, Mutembei, and Bwogi. Kalemera was the eldest and was appointed by the British to succeed Kahigi.[22] Kalemera reigned till 1943 but during his reign conflicting groups emerged over the issue whether Kalemera had the right to rule, since he, like Bwogi, we're born by women of Iru descent; only Mutembei was a "pure" Muhinda. Leaders of these two groups were mainly Bahinda, but they had supporters from among the ordinary people. The group that opposed Kalemera was known as the *Bakimala,* the other as the *Babinga.* One of the leaders of the former group, Mr Selemani Bukende, was imprisoned for eight years in 1929 after having been accused of creating disturbances. These were so serious that the Governor himself at one occasion had to visit the area in order to bring the situation under control.

When Kalemera died in 1943, Mutembei succeeded him. He had reigned less than a year, however, when he died. The District Commissioner then appointed Bwogi as his successor. Many people believed that Mutembei had been poisoned to death and that certain people of the *binga* group were responsible. Feelings again ran high. Leading Bahinda complained that since the Bairu were the traditional servants, it was a disgrace to have a man with Bwogi's origin as a chief.

The two groups in Kianja were organized around a chairman and a secretary, but no membership registration was kept. All the same, mobilization of wide support was obtained. The *Bakimala,* for instance, at one time raised several thousand shillings to pay a lawyer who was pleading their right in a legal case.

[20] My main sources of information concerning KLA are ex-chief, Bwogi, and former leading members of the association. Most of the information was obtained orally, but I also had access to the personal files of the ex-chief. Most of the written documents belonging to the KLA leaders had been deliberately burnt, because they feared retaliatory measures by the British if they were found with such documents.
[21] Cf., p. 100.
[22] For a full story, see Cory, *op.cit.,* pp. 131—32.

It was against this background that the Labour Association was founded. The issue of Bwogi's origin was combined with a general attack on the privileges of the ruling dynasty which Bwogi symbolized. The internal dispute within the Hinda clan in Kianja was now brought out in the open. This, no doubt, tended to accelerate the undermining of the chiefs' authority in Buhaya. Attempts to reconcile the chief with the KLA failed. Between 1947 and 1953 several meetings were held, but at every one of these it was clear that the chief was not prepared to share power with the KLA in his chiefdom. In the first years the attacks from the new political organization were moderate, but as time passed, they increased. The latter complained about the extravagant living of the chief and his failure to take into account the wishes of the people. They even demanded Bwogi's resignation, but they were not to see the fruits of their efforts in this direction until 1958, when their organization had already been dissolved. The British supported the chief to the very last years, when pressures finally became too strong. The British attitude to the incidents in Kianja extended the range of the conflict and gave rise to considerable anti-colonialist feelings in many parts of the chiefdom. At one stage the British burnt all documents belonging to the organization and confiscated all financial assets, totaling 7.000 shs. In 1954 KLA activities were finally curbed.

KLA differed from the African Association in that it was the first political organization in Buhaya to make outright claims for the abolition of the rule of the chiefs. The latter should not continue enjoying their traditional power and privileges. They should no longer be allowed to confiscate the land holdings of ordinary people or demand tribute from the people to pay for visiting officials.[23] Connected with these demands was also the abolition of the *nyarubanja* system.

In its official attitude KLA put great emphasis on the need for hard work as a means to achieve development. At one occasion, a leading KLA member, when arguing with Bwogi, said: "A man who does not work is useless. Theft is a result of laziness, and can therefore only be abolished by hard work"[24] This demand was certainly radical in the Haya context. One illustration of the willingness among KLA members to work was the erection of a private school at Kakono in Kamachumu. It was built purely on a self-help basis. The school was deliberately located near a Catholic mission as a protest against the low intake of pupils at the Catholic school.

It is dubious whether the Labour Association achieved its goals. It was

[23] At this time the chief could order his subjects to build camps for visiting officials, mainly Europeans. They could, according to some informants, be forced to give these officials their bananas. Moreover, none of those who were ordered to work for the visitors got paid. This custom created wide dissatisfaction.

[24] Minutes of a meeting held at Kanazi, January 11, 1947, between members of KLA and Chief Bwogi.

so much involved in disputes with the chief that little time was left for hard work. It is, however, wrong to underestimate the political importance of KLA. It served as a training ground for many of those who later were to attain leading positions in the nationalist movement. It also helped increasing the sense of dissatisfaction with the colonial regime and the traditional political authorities in Buhaya.

KLA:s organizational network was not very elaborate and membership never reached a very high level. During its last year of activity, 1954, it had 1372 members, two thirds of these being in Kamachumu, the main trading center in the chiefdom.[25] This does not mean, however, that its support was as small as that. Many more people were favoring the objectives of KLA, but were not due-paying.

Tanganyika African Association revives [26]

The Tanganyika African Association branch in Bukoba which had been inactivated because of the war had a strong revival in the late 1940s, when Mr Ali Migeyo took over the leadership of the organization. Again, one of the main reasons for its new strength was the Haya reaction against British plans for agricultural improvement. This time the colonial administrators wanted to stop the spread of the banana weevil by uprooting old stems of the banana plant; the old stems were also to be used for mulching the coffee. The damage caused by the weevil was serious, and the British took strong action to combat it. Fines were introduced as punishment for those who did not comply with the new orders. This made many people simply take the first opportunity to uproot their coffee trees, rather than risk being found without having mulched the *shamba*.

Traditionally it was considered an action of madness to uproot the stems of the banana. The Bahaya could not understand, why this had to be done now. Several people believed it was a "trick" directed against them.[27] Consequently, the reaction was spontaneous. First it was more or less unorganized. In Bukara chiefdom, a movement known as the *Twayanga* (We refuse), was one illustration of the Haya reaction to the new agricultural schemes.[28]

[25] Report by the Deputy-Chief of Kianja on a KLA meeting held at Kamachumu, June 14, 1954.
[26] For material presented in this part of the chapter I am very much indebted to Mr Edward Barongo, Regional Commissioner, MP, and Mr Samuel Kassano, MP, Bukoba.
[27] This came out also in interviews with local TAA leaders in Kiziba and Kyamtwara chiefdoms.
[28] Personal letter from Mr Barongo, April 5, 1966.

Soon the main burden of carrying the propaganda against the British was taken over by TAA. Migeyo, an illiterate Muslim trader, was a forceful speaker, and he soon got the Bahaya to react strongly against the new orders, and in particular, the way they were introduced and implemented. He had been in contact with politicians in Mwanza, and they advised him that, if he wished to achieve success in his plans to oppose the administration, he had to have a strong political organization.[29] As chairman of TAA he travelled extensively in Buhaya, spreading the word that the methods suggested by the British were bad and a colonial artifice. The British had little success in fighting back. They could not get their message across, that this new policy in the long run would benefit the Haya farmers themselves. The confidence in the colonial system had been shaken already before and the Bahaya were sceptical against any attempt to impose on them new regulations.[30]

Ali Migeyo was also helped in his campaign against the British by the general sense of economic insecurity among the Haya farmers. The intensification of agricultural production that the British advocated tended to shake the traditional Haya view of cultivation. Several people simply believed they were not going to produce enough for subsistence. This feeling was naturally enhanced by the fact that the British paid little attention to how the Haya farmers lived.

The revival of TAA was mainly due to the widespread primary resistance to the agricultural improvement schemes of the British. Local politics in Buhaya ran, to a large extent, into neo-traditional channels. Other issues also contributed, however, to the growing strength of the organization after the Second World War. The lack of educational facilities was still acute, despite efforts by the colonial authorities in the late 40s to step up educational development in the country. A number of new government schools were built in these years. Also the missions began to concentrate more on education.

The general dissatisfaction with lack of educational facilities was, however, not only channeled through TAA. Leading Protestants started, immediately after the war, an association aimed at promoting education. The new organization, Bahaya Union, collected money, and a primary school was built at Rubale. Although it has continued running its school, this new Bahaya Union never developed as a mass organization.[31]

[29] One of his main contacts in Mwanza was Mr Abdu Kandoro later one of the founders of TANU.

[30] Cf., R. E. S. Tanner, "Conflict within Small European Communities in Tanganyika", *EAISR Conference Paper,* (July 1962).

[31] Information obtained from Mr Sospater Zahoro, one of the founders of the Bahaya Union.

At this time, also the Muslims requested schools of their own. The main problem was that no Muslim teachers could be recruited. All the same, efforts were made by local Muslims all over Buhaya to collect money for building their schools. Some were built, for instance, in Kamachumu and Kanyigo, supported mainly by the richer section of the Muslim population. In the 50s, the schools obtained official support from the East African Muslim Welfare Association.[32]

An educational association was formed in Karagwe in these years by Mr Gressim Kazimoto, also a member of TAA.[33] Its main aim was to stimulate education in Karagwe, where, partly due to lack of mission stations, only a small number of schools existed and many people had still not realized the importance of modern education.

This trend is also documented in the minutes of the Council of Chiefs, later the Buhaya District Council. The District Council itself got more involved in supporting higher education in the early 1950s. An upper primary school for girls was built, and scholarships for higher education at Makerere University College, Kampala, Uganda, or overseas, were provided.

In 1949 the first cooperative societies in the area were registered and the following year a central body, The Bukoba Native Cooperative Union, was created. The number of primary societies grew rapidly, eventually amounting to fifty.[34] BNCU—or Bukoba Cooperative Union, as it was later to be called—succeeded the Bukoba Native Coffee Board, which for years had purchased coffee from local zonal agents, mainly Indian merchants. The reason for starting the cooperative union was firstly to secure for the African a higher annual income for their coffee; by avoiding the "middleman" —the zonal agent—it was argued that a higher return to the individual farmer could be secured. Secondly, the coops were looked upon as means to improve cultivation. After the British failure to encourage improvements in cultivation of coffee among the Bahaya the new coop societies were the best alternative. It was hoped that, through the democratic organization of a cooperative movement, a better social and political setting for economic change would be obtained. Another important aspect was that only through a cooperative movement could the trade monopoly of the Asians be put to an end.

BNCU faced several problems in its initial period. Misappropriation of funds was very common in the local societies, and the Union lacked staff to carry out a satisfactory supervision. This experience, however, made the

---

[32] Information obtained from Haji Suleiman Hamadu, Kamachumu and Mr Hamisi Mukwangu, Kanyigo.
[33] Information obtained from Mr Kazimoto, August 28, 1965.
[34] M. Wamala, "The Cooperative Movement in Tanganyika", paper published by the Publicity and Education Department, Bukoba Cooperative Union (Bukoba undated).

leaders realize the importance of qualified staff members. Consequently, much money has been invested in education of leaders, both at the union and the society level. Partly as a result of this, many of the political leaders and prominent civil servants in Tanzania have taken their first steps in the BNCU.[35]

The fact that so many farmers immediately joined the local societies made BNCU the first mass organization in the area, but not even within this movement could local rivalries be avoided. Tribal considerations had to be made at appointments to more prominent positions. Many members of BNCU feared that too many Baziba, people from Kiziba chiefdom, would get into the union leadership. As time passed, however, the BNCU managed itself quite well to overcome these parochial feelings.

Many leaders at various levels within the new cooperative movement in Buhaya combined this position with leadership in one of the political organizations. The BNCU, however, never rose to such significance in local politics as did The Victoria Federation of Cooperative Unions in Mwanza.[36]

A movement to establish a paramount chief, *Lubamba,* in Buhaya emerged in the early fifties. Discussions arose after similar steps had been taken in Chaggaland. Most of the debates were held in the new district council, but it was an issue lively discussed also in the local press and by people in general. No unanimity, however, could be obtained. The Bahaya were very deeply divided on this issue.

Some people thought that one of the eight chiefs should be elected or appointed paramount chief. The problem was however, who should be elected. Every chief believed he was the most qualified or the most popular. For this reason, and others, another group of people suggested that a commoner with good qualification should be made *Lubamba;* lineage descent should not determine who was to be appointed to this position, they argued.[37] Buhaya was divided along "modern" and "traditional" lines, but the issue eventually died out, mainly due to the emergence of a nationalist movement with a new focus.

Although Karagwe had been in a backwater ever since the establishment of colonial rule in Buhaya, there were, however, after the Second World

[35] The most prominent are: Mr George Kahama, former Minister and Ambassador; Mr Christopher Ngaiza, Ambassador; Mr Gosbart Rutabanzibwa, Ambassador and Mr Gerald Rugarabamu, Principal Secretary.

[36] See, e.g., George Bennett, "An Outline History of TANU", *Makerere Journal,* (Kampala, No 7, 1963).

[37] Candidates suggested among the commoners were Mr Kahama, Mr Rutabanzibwa and Mr E. R. Munseri, Editor of the local Haya newspaper, *Bukya na Gandi,* (Bukoba).

War, many activities to improve the situation of that chiefdom. Reference has already been made to Mr Kazimoto's Educational Association; he also started a Farmers' Association, the first seed of cooperative societies in Karagwe. These two associations formed the basis for recruitment to TAA, which grew very strong in western Buhaya. Mr Barongo estimates that about two thirds of the 7.000 members of TAA in 1954 were from Karagwe.[38] The reason for its strength there was however, not mainly as in eastern Buhaya the farmers' reaction to agricultural improvement schemes. There were other, more important, reasons. General resentment against the British had existed since 1939, when the colonial authorities exiled their chief, Rumanyika. As many people in Karagwe had great confidence in him (and particularly in his power to make rain), this action created strong feelings against the British. Secondly, the physical distance of Karagwe from the district headquarters at Bukoba was great; people had fewer opportunities to bring their complaints to official authorities than others, simply because of lack of communication. They felt generally neglected. When therefore, Ali Migeyo and others told them that TAA was going to improve the situation, many people spontaneously joined the organization. A third factor of importance was that the traditional authorities in Karagwe still kept calling on their subjects to offer food and lodging for any official visitor to the chiefdom. This, as in the case of Kianja[39] created much bitterness, and people were therefore eager to dispense with this obligation.

In 1954 Mr Migeyo was imprisoned by the colonial authorities and this meant a temporary reduction of activities by TAA. Other leaders feared that they would be jailed. There was also at this time an internal dispute, which affected the efficiency of TAA. A secretary was sent to prison because of financial irregularities. Mr Elias Lushakuzi, an African member of the Legislative Council in Dar es Salaam, became acting secretary. He suggested that a separate African Association should be formed in the West Lake Province, the aim of which should be to encourage advancement of that area only. His argument in support of this "tribal" proposal was that the West Lake area was so rich and people were more highly educated than in other parts of Tanganyika. Therefore, Lushakuzi could see no reason why the Bahaya should waste time and money in cooperating with other tribes in the country. His proposal was however, turned down by the majority of the leading members of the Bukoba branch of TAA. Soon after this incident all property and documents belonging to the Association was removed from Mr Lushakuzi's house, that also served as office. He became upset by this and left the association. This and other internal quarrels paralyzed the organization.

[38] Personal letter from Mr Barongo, March 18, 1966.
[39] Cf., p. 113.

Buhaya in a Tanganyika perspective

In order to put Buhaya in a proper perspective within Tanganyika it is worth asking how events in this area until early 1950s compared with developments in other parts of the country. There is no doubt that the Bahaya were among the first to organize themselves into associations with specifically political leanings.[40] Before the founding of Tanganyika African Association in Dar es Salaam 1929, and its extension to other parts of the country,[41] nothing similar to the Bahaya Union, except the Kilimanjaro Native Planters Association, existed in the country. There were African civil servants' associations, like the one in Tanga, referred to earlier.[42]

Like all the early political organizations in Tanganyika the ones in Buhaya focused mainly on local problems; they served as tribal improvement associations, and as a platform for the new, often more educated, elite in the area concerned.

The Haya dissatisfaction with the British plan to make Nyakato Central School an agricultural training center was probably the first organized African agitation in the country concerning education. The widespread reaction in Buhaya to agricultural improvement schemes was by no means unique. Although the coffee riots in Bukoba were the first violent reaction against the British agricultural policy, protests among Africans were elsewhere just as strong. For instance, in the 1940s local reaction to the enforcement of bench terracing was very strong in the Uluguru and the Usambara Mountains.[43] Culling of cattle, a rule introduced by the British, was strongly opposed in the same years by farmers in Sukumaland and in Mbulu District.

It is worth noting that there was comparatively little reaction to British

[40] The Kilimanjaro Native Planters Association was founded in 1925 as a result of the extension of coffee planting to the slopes of Mt Kilimanjaro.

[41] There is conflicting information as to when TAA was organized in the various parts of Tanganyika. Mr P. A. P. Semesindi, once Secretary of TAA in Zanzibar and Pemba for many years has given the following years for the establishment of branches in different places throughout the country: Dar es Salaam, 1929, Zanzibar, 1934, Pemba and Dodoma 1934, Singida, Kondoa, and Iringa 1936, and Mpwapwa and Tanga 1937. These dates were given to the present author by Mr Barongo in a personal letter, March 18, 1966. George Bennett, op.cit., quoting Lord Hailey says that TAA had only one branch outside Dar es Salaam in 1940, and that was in Dodoma. Lionel Cliffe in an EAISR Conference Paper, (December 1964), "Nationalism and the Reaction to Agricultural Improvement in Tanganyika during the Colonial Period", p. 6, maintains that the Government, by 1936—37 was aware of TAA branches outside Dar es Salaam in the following places: Bukoba, Kondoa, Singida and Mpwapwa. That the Bukoba branch was not recorded by Mr Semesindi can be understood, considering the limited nature of communications that existed between Bukoba and the capital in these years.

[42] Cf., p. 108, footnote 4.

[43] Cliffe, "Nationalism . . ." op.cit., p. 4 and p. 8.

agricultural policy in Chaggaland. There are at least two reasons for this. Firstly, coffee was a new crop in the Kilimanjaro area, introduced in the colonial period. The Chagga people unlike the Bahaya, had no traditional beliefs about the coffee and could therefore more easily adopt new methods of coffee-growing. Secondly, the Wachagga were fortunate to get organized into a cooperative movement at a very early stage, in 1932. It is likely that many of the grievances which occurred in other places, were taken care of within the cooperative movement, where the *rapport* between Africans and Europeans seems to have been exceptionally good.[44]

Generally speaking, primary resistance to agricultural improvement schemes in Tanganyika was very common during the whole colonial period. It got particularly strong where traditional beliefs were closely attached to certain agricultural activities, e.g., coffee cultivation in Buhaya, and cattle-breeding in Sukumaland and Mbulu District, and where the communications between Europeans and Africans were strikingly low. Moreover, the coercive methods often used by the British tended to increase dissatisfaction in many areas.

The Belgians managed to introduce agricultural change in Rwanda-Urundi in the 1950s by using coercive measures.[45] They used the same methods of punishment as the British, fining, when seedlings were not mulched or cared for as instructed. Resistance prevailed for some time, but attitudes changed when the growers realized the increase in cash income. That success was achieved in Rwanda-Urundi, but not in Tanganyika is due, among other things, to the fact that when the Belgian schemes were introduced in 1953 they could benefit from the general coffee boom on the world market. Coffee prices were then extraordinarily high. Secondly, the people in the Belgian territories had even less freedom to express their opinion than the people in the British territories. In the very authoritarian situation that existed in Rwanda-Urundi, farmers had no choice but accept the orders.

While the relations between the Haya chiefs and the leaders of the African Association in the first years were not strained, a clear change in these relations could be noted after the Second World War. The emergence of a stronger TAA branch in Bukoba and the KLA in Kianja chiefdom caused more widespread reactions to the chiefs. This was partly owing to their close cooperation with the colonial administration, which gave them almost unreserved support against the popular opposition. The situation in Buhaya resembles that in Sukumaland, where the activities of new political associations resulted in an open conflict with the chiefs.[46] Buhaya differed

[44] See Wamala, *op.cit.*, p. 3.
[45] M. J. Herskovits, *The Human Factor in Changing Africa*, (London 1962), p. 167.
[46] Liebenow, *op.cit.*, p. 458.

from Chaggaland on the other hand, where the formation of the Kiliman-jaro Chagga Citizens Union led to demand for a paramount chief for the whole area. Opposition to this demand, conducted by the Chagga Congress, was heavily defeated.[47] This is an indication that the function of the tradi-tional value system in Buhaya and Sukumaland was consummatory, while in Chaggaland, rather, instrumental.[48] People in Buhaya and Sukumaland were forced to withdraw from the values underlying the traditional political system, because these were inconsistent with the values and demands gene-rated in a society affected by new influences, such as commercial activities, education and monotheistic religions. People in Chaggaland were, to a much larger extent, able to combine traditional values with the new de-mands; they were capable of "traditionalizing" modernization, like the Baganda, because their society was not penetrated by a myth similar to that in Buhaya.

The first indications that the British were reconsidering their principle of ruling exclusively through the traditional authorities came in the late for-ties. Certain changes in local government, which were proposed, were first tried in Buhaya and Chaggaland, the areas which the British undoubtedly considered most advanced.[49]

The first attempt to introduce some kind of popular representation in Buhaya was made in 1947. Local councils with ex-officio representation had existed in Buhaya since the 1920s at the chiefdom and gombolola level; in addition to these there was of course, the Council of Chiefs for the whole Buhaya. Instead of having only chiefs, sub-chiefs and parish chiefs in these councils every village was now to elect two representatives each. This pro-ject did not work out well, partly because of opposition to popular represen-tation among many of the traditional authorities. A new attempt was made in 1950. It was more farreaching. Every council was going to get an elected majority with the traditional authority as chairman. It was also decided that people would be allowed to elect their own chiefs at different levels.

Although these moves by the British in Buhaya and in other areas were caused by the increased political reaction to the colonial administration they fell short of the demands put forward by local TAA branches. In Bu-koba the TAA members felt that they were not guaranteed better represen-tation. They asked for a reserved number of seats in the new Buhaya Dist-rict Council, but were told that they had to turn to the people to ask for

[47] See Bennett, *op.cit.*
[48] Cf., pp. 58—59, footnote 95.
[49] Evidence of this is found in e.g., F. A. Montague, "Some difficulties in the Demo-cratization of Native Authorities in Tanganyika", *Journal of African Administration,* (London, Vol III, January 1951), pp. 21—27; also C. C. Harris, "Development of Local Councils and Re-Organization of Local Government, Bukoba District", *EAISR Conference Paper,* (June 1952).

a mandate to represent them on the council. This was, however, a difficult move because of insufficient organization, intimidation from the traditional authorities and a general fear among people of opposition to the established authorities. The division between the traditional authorities and representatives of the political organizations, TAA and KLA, had increased considerably in these years. It is in the face of this development, that the British decision to act more strongly against some of the political leaders in Buhaya in 1954, should be seen.

Conclusions

Efforts to overcome the parochial chiefdom identities in Buhaya were difficult. TAA was the only organization that could offer a common platform for people from the different chiefdoms. Only after the Second World War, however, did it really become an organization with a considerable membership. Significant for the persistence of parochial attitudes in Buhaya was that a competing political organization, Kianja Labour Association, was formed with only a petty chiefdom as focus. Attempts to establish a paramount chief failed owing mainly to local rivalries. The British had made no serious efforts to integrate Buhaya with the rest of the country, and the African political organizations in other parts of the territory were too weak to be of any influence on the developments in Buhaya. This tended to create among certain Haya leaders a sense of self-consciousness; to them Bahaya were too good to cooperate with other tribes in the country. Many Bahaya compared themselves with the Baganda, and saw that they were doing well without any cooperation with the rest of Uganda.

The legitimacy of the colonial rule and the power of the traditional authorities was seriously questioned in Buhaya after the Second World War. To a large extent this was due to a poor performance of these political authorities on issues relating to the extractive, distributive and responsive capabilities of the system. The traditional political systems in Buhaya were now formally functioning as sub-systems of the larger Tanganyikan political system, for which the British were responsible. Much of what was done by the British and accepted by the local chiefs, therefore, tended to affect the latter as well. The reluctance or inability of the colonial rulers to take into consideration local demands concerning, for instance, education also created dissatisfaction with the traditional chiefs among members of the new elite. Sometimes, the chiefs were even more stubborn than the British. This was the case in the question of popular representation on the local councils. On the issue of agricultural improvement, however, the chiefs and the leaders of TAA were more in agreement.

In the period discussed in this chapter the shortcomings of the colonial political system became obvious. It was no longer capable of increasing the extractions of resources, in terms of increased agricultural production. Local people in various parts of Tanganyika were not prepared to accept the new rules voluntarily. The feedback of the British attempts to improve agricultural production among Africans was a withdrawal of support and increased participation in both organizations hostile to the regime.

Lack of educational facilities and the monopoly of Asians in the economic field of activities also became political issues in these years. To some extent, educational improvement could be achieved through self-help projects, but many Bahaya joined the ranks of TAA and KLA with the idea that the government was responsible for providing schools, but had shown itself incapable of doing so. The rapid growth of the cooperative movement in Buhaya reflected Haya frustrations with the lack of opportunities in business, and the low prices that were obtained for their coffee.

It is also worth noting that goods, services and benefits were not evenly distributed throughout Buhaya. The eastern part remained favored; this was one of the reasons for increased political participation in Karagwe. In the field of education, Christians were far ahead of Muslims and others. Both these trends had clear political implications.

One of the most significant contributions by the new political organizations was the change they were able to achieve in the political culture. Traditional Haya values implied that the chiefs only were responsible for the welfare of the people and the state of the chiefdom. No popular participation was allowed. Political involvement in government became a major issue, however, as new influences were spread in Buhaya. The people who had withdrawn their support from the traditional political values, and organized themselves in political associations, took the lead in disseminating these new ideas. The idea that officials and representatives of the people should be elected, was a widely recognized principle in Buhaya. This was reflected in the demands put forward to the British in the late 40s and early 50s.

The events in Buhaya in these years were not only significant to the development in the area itself, but also had wider repercussions on the rest of the country. Politically, Buhaya was one of the most active parts in Tanganyika, and events there had a great impact on the official British attitude in these years.

Chapter 7

The growth of a mass movement

About the same time as Ali Migeyo was jailed and the activities of TAA
and KLA circumscribed in Buhaya a new party, the Tanganyika African
National Union—TANU—was founded in Dar es Salaam.[1] To some
extent TANU was a continuation of TAA. Many TANU leaders, like Julius
Nyerere, Abdu Kandoro, John Rupia, Alli Sykes and Andrew Tibandebage
had had their first political training in TAA.

The formation of TANU was significant. It introduced a new period in
the history of Tanganyika. For the first time, a serious attempt had been
made to form a political movement on a nation-wide, mass basis. Coordination of effort was needed, and for this to be achieved, a strong organization had to be built. Julius Nyerere, a former secondary school teacher and
the first Tanganyika African ever to study in England for a higher degree,[2]
became its first chairman. Around him he had collected a number of Africans, most of them well educated, with whom he had been in contact at
various places. This group included friends from Tabora Government
School where Nyerere passed his secondary school degree; alumni from
Makerere University College in Kampala, at that time the only university
institution in East Africa; others were mainly friends made during his TAA
years. The special duty of organizing the party in the country-side fell
upon Oscar Kambona, another secondary school teacher. During 1954—56
he travelled extensively in the country, made contact with local political
leaders, and started one TANU branch after another.

This is not the place to write a full history of TANU. Attempts to do so
have been made by others.[3] It should only be pointed out that the leaders
of the party were a group of people very committed to the idea of making
their country independent and changing the character of the political system. Nyerere had been influenced by Nkrumah's writing and the Conven-
tion People's Party became the model on which TANU, with some local
adaptations, was built. Many of the leaders were teachers or civil servants,
and this constituted a problem since according to British colonial regula-

[1] The actual date of registration was the 7th of July. This day, known as *Saba saba*
in Kiswahili (the seventh day of the seventh month), has ever since been a day of
great celebration among Tanzanians; after independence it was made a national
holiday.
[2] For an account of Nyerere's early life, see Listowel, *op.cit.*, Ch. XVI ff.
[3] *Ibid.*, Clagett Taylor, *op.cit.*, and Bennett, *op.cit.*

tions these categories were not allowed to enroll in political organizations. Nyerere, Kambona, and others, had to make a personal choice, whether to continue teaching, or go into politics. None of them, however, seem to have hesitated in choosing the latter alternative. Another problem was that the colonial and traditional authorities in the country did everything to paint the new organization in black. To convince local people of the value of the new ideas about self-government, and the need for mass membership, therefore, became an even more difficult task. Another problem was that in many parts where people had little cash money, paying the membership fee was a heavy burden.

It seems as if the timing of the foundation of TANU in 1954 with the hearings in the country by the United Nations Visiting Mission,[4] aided the extension of TANU into certain up-country areas. The British, however, intervened in many places, and prevented the opening of TANU branches with the excuse that they could not comply with the registration rules. This way of obstructing the spread of the nationalist movement was used, for instance, in the politically active Lake Province. In the early 1950s Mwanza had turned into a political up-country center. Some of the active leaders came from TAA, others from the new cooperative movement, the Victoria Federation of Cooperative Unions.[5] By resisting British moves to make the culling of cattle compulsory, TAA had increased its popularity among the Sukuma people. While the British later managed to retard the formal registration of TANU in the Mwanza area,[6] the VFCU, as already mentioned,[7] served the purpose of channeling political demands.

TANU in Buhaya

Registration of TANU in the West Lake Province was also held up by the British, officially owing to complications with formalities, but in reality, for the same reason as in Mwanza, fear of increased political activities against the regime. To some extent the growth of TANU was aided by the very efforts of the British to complicate the registration of local party branches.

---

[4] Chidzero, op.cit., Ch V.

[5] It should be recalled that it was from this group that Ali Migeyo drew much inspiration in his effort to combat the British agricultural improvement schemes.

[6] According to Chidzero, op.cit., p. 202, the Registrar of Societies refused to register in 1954 TANU branches at Mwanza, Malampaka, and Nassa in the Lake Province. The explanation given by the Chief Secretary of the Legislative Council was that the Government was "satisfied that they were being used, for purposes prejudicial to the maintenance of peace, order and good government".

[7] Cf., p. 118, footnote 36.

Owing to this, many district secretaries turned to the central headquarters for help and this created, at an early stage, strong links between the political centre and the periphery.

Kambona visited Buhaya in 1954 to gather impressions of problems in the area, and make contacts with local politicians. He quickly won the confidence of the political veterans, like Mr Kagasheki and Mr Rugizibwa. The personal reputation of these two men facilitated the spread of the organization. Nyerere visited the Bukoba area around the same time and got a warm reception by the Bahaya. He also won the support of a Swedish missionary, Miss Barbro Johansson, then headmistress of the Kashasha Girls' School in Kiziba chiefdom.[8]

The actual registration of TANU in Bukoba District was not achieved until March 1956. Those who signed the application for registration were Herbert Rugizibwa and Edward Barongo, a former policeman, who had met Nyerere in 1954 and became an enthusiastic supporter of TANU. He now was to become a full-time politician. In that capacity he was the single most important person in the work of extending TANU throughout Buhaya and the other areas of the province, Biharamulo and Ngara.[9] Barongo was a forceful speaker, and moreover, had his speeches and pamphlets about the new movement printed for wider circulation. More than anyone else in Buhaya, he realized the importance of a strong and well coordinated communications network.[10] Another important member of the local TANU leadership was Samuel Luangisa, who, with the same enthusiasm, helped to build the new party in the district. A number of Bahaya, like Andrew Tibandebage and Vedast Kyaruzi, who had been active in TAA and TANU in Dar es Salaam, never became involved in setting up the local TANU branch in Buhaya.[11]

The members of the first TANU District Committee, who met in Bukoba in May 1956 formed an interesting mixture of old and young men. Herbert Rugizibwa was made the first chairman, and Zefrin Kashumba, a former KLA leader, vice-chairman. Barongo became the secretary and Luangisa the membership registrar.[12] The committee's first "mission" was to Karagwe, where a series of meetings were held to stimulate the spread of TANU. Karagwe, as already mentioned, was a TAA stronghold.[13] The leaders believed, therefore, that it was easiest to muster support there.

[8] She was later to become an MP in Tanzania, 1960—65.
[9] Listowel, op.cit., Ch. 27.
[10] Barongo published many articles in English and Swahili papers in Tanganyika, and provided his followers with speech notes.
[11] Their role in politics have been described by Listowel, op.cit., Chs 16, 17, 18, and 20.
[12] Personal letter from Mr Barongo, March 18, 1966.
[13] See p. 119.

In 1957 Bukoba was made a provincial centre for TANU's activities. Hence Rugizibwa was promoted to provincial chairman, Barongo to provincial secretary, and so forth. That same year Nyerere made his first official visit to Bukoba as chairman of TANU. Barongo, in a short pamphlet,[14] compiled a brief history of political development in Buhaya, and took extracts from Mr Nyerere's speeches. Even taking into consideration the propaganda purpose of the pamphlet, and Mr Barongo's own position as chief TANU advocate in the area, one understands from the content that Nyerere's visit is likely to have been a great success.[15] He visited major trading centers such as Kamachumu, Nyakahanga-Bugene, and Bwanjai, and held a large meeting at Bukoba, where, according to Barongo's estimate, around 10.000 people had gathered to listen to the TANU chairman. Barongo notes that when Nyerere quoted Nkrumah's famous slogan "Seek ye first the political kingdom and everything will be added unto it", in Kiswahili[16] there was much applause and rejoicing.[17] There is little doubt that the Bahaya were attracted by Mr Nyerere. His simple way of approaching them and his ability to put his message across opened the field for wider TANU support in the area.[18]

The first serious internal trouble in TANU, however, emerged in 1957. Mr Rugizibwa was dissatisfied with the way coffee was marketed through the BNCU. He disliked particularly the monopolistic position the cooperative movement had been rendered by the authorities. He actually accused BNCU of cheating the local coffee growers, the same accusation the BNCU had brought against the Asian businessmen. Rugizibwa had started his own organization, Buhaya Coffee Planters' Association in 1955, an organization which aimed at serving the Haya coffee farmers without deducting from their income what he called a "heavy membership fee".[19] The colonial government which supported BNCU did, however, not allow registration of his association; Rugizibwa, disappointed, went as far as writing a letter of complaints to the United Nations, but even such efforts came to nothing.

BCPA received considerable support from certain parts of Buhaya, particularly Kianja and Ihangiro chiefdoms. But as it never got registered, a fact from which it suffered, it is difficult to make an accurate assessment of its popularity. One of the reasons why Rugizibwa's association could have become a major threat to BNCU was the fall of the coffee price in

[14] Barongo, "Hotuba . . .", op.cit.
[15] This has been confirmed by independent sources in Buhaya.
[16] *Tafuteni ufalme wa nchi yenu vitu vingine vitakuja baadaye.*
[17] Barongo, "Hotuba . . ." op.cit., p. 11.
[18] This has been brought out in a number of interviews with local people in various parts of Buhaya.
[19] Information obtained in personal interview with Mr Rugizibwa; later confirmed by Mr Barongo and Mr Kassano.

the late 1950s. People tended to believe him when he claimed that the BNCU was responsible for the reduced income. At this time the BNCU was also threatened by extensive coffee smuggling. The price of Bukoba coffee remained constantly lower than that of Buganda in these years, and private businessmen, both Asians and Africans, smuggled tons of coffee across the border to Uganda annually.[20]

A majority of the TANU leaders thought that Rugizibwa's attempt to draw advantage of the fall in the price of coffee and oppose the cooperative movement was an offensive step, as it went against the official TANU policy of support for organizations, like the BNCU. In March 1958 therefore, they forced a showdown with their chairman at a meeting, held at Nyakahura in Biharamulo District. Rugizibwa was asked to make a choice: to either remain as provincial chairman of TANU, or act as managing director of his Planters' Association. He made it clear that he preferred the latter position. His decision was not only dictated by his strong interest in the BCPA, but also by the "harder" line that other leading TANU members wanted to take against the chiefs and the colonial administration. This line was particularly advocated by Ali Migeyo, who had been released from jail. Rugizibwa felt the others were going too far and "jumped off the wagon".[21]

At this time, early 1958, another of the political veterans, Zefrin Kashumba, was manoeuvered out of the TANU leadership. The Provincial Conference in 1958 signified the real victory of the more "radical" group, and the overthrow of the remnants of the "conservative" element, here meaning the more traditionally, or even tribally oriented group. It highlighted the generational conflict that existed within TANU in Buhaya, and, for that matter, in other parts of the country as well.

Following the meeting at Nyakahura, Barongo succeeded Rugizibwa as chairman; Luangisa was promoted secretary. The attack on the local administration and the insufficient degree of popular representation was sharpened. TANU demanded, for instance, a new constitution for the District Council. Major changes the party wanted to be effected were: (a) that chiefs and sub-chiefs no longer were to be ex-officio members of the council; (b) that the chairman was not to be the District Commissioner, or one of the chiefs; and (c) that all members of the council were to be elected on a TANU ticket.[22]

[20] See The Bukoba Native Cooperative Union Ltd., *Annual Reports for the Union's years 1959/60 and 1960/61*, (Bukoba, 1962).

[21] Personal letter from Mr Barongo, March 18, 1966, and interview with Mr Rugizibwa. It is worth noting that Mr Rugizibwa himself is a relative of the present chief of Kiziba.

[22] Personal letter from Mr Barongo, March 18, 1966.

At first these demands were all put down by the colonial government, but TANU continued its struggle. Probably sooner than most of the TANU leaders themselves had expected, a change in colonial policy took place. There are three main reasons for this. First of all, TANU continued to grow strong, and heavily defeated competing parties at the polls in 1959 and 1960.[23] Secondly, the old Governor, Sir Edward Twining, who had been responsible for much of the denigration of TANU was replaced by Sir Richard Turnbull, a man with a more liberal attitude towards the nationalist movement. Significant too was the third factor, the appointment of Ian MacLeod as Colonial Secretary. Unlike all his Conservative predecessors, he was prepared to grant political independence to the colonial territories.

The Buhaya District Council got a new, more liberal, constitution in 1959.[24] It was the first step in the direction TANU had instigated. The chairman was now elected. Parity between ex-officio and unofficial members was, however, retained until 1960. In 1959 the council majority decided to make the late chief, S. L. Ntare of Ihangiro, its first elected chairman, with Mr Munseri,[25] as vice-chairman. In the local district council election in 1960, following the abolition of ex-officio representation, all representatives were, for the first time, elected on a TANU ticket. Mr Luangisa became the chairman of the council. Thus in two years, the TANU leaders had achieved their goals presented at the Nyakahura conference.

In the pre-independence years, Mr Barongo and his TANU friends led the attack against the *nyarubanja* system, which they considered a "feudal relic". Propaganda against this system, dispersed through the TANU organization, was no doubt important in paving the way for its total abolition. This was not achieved, however, until 1965, when the National Assembly passed a bill doing away with one of the most typical features of the Haya society.

The relative success of TANU in Buhaya and elsewhere made the Bahaya regard politics in a more favorable light. Educational qualifications had so far for ordinary people been the most important criteria for advancement in society, but with the emergence of TANU, political involvement and leadership had rendered many more individuals—several without any educational qualifications—status and influence. Politics became a new field in which people saw an opportunity for upward mobility. Since the number of leading positions in TANU was limited and opinions split however, conflicts were almost bound to arise. At the national level this occurred at the TANU Annual Delegates Conference in Tabora early 1958. The big issue there was whether TANU should participate in the forthcoming

[23] Cf., p. 42.
[24] Kaombwe, *op.cit.*, p. 2.
[25] See p. 118, footnote 37.

elections to the Legislative Council or not. Listowel maintains[26] that the overwhelming majority of the delegates arrived at Tabora with the opinion that TANU should boycott the elections. They resented the tripartite system of voting that the colonial government, as an example of its new policy of multi-racialism, had proposed.[27] Mainly thanks to Nyerere's own eloquence and the loyalty of his closest followers the opinion of the conference was swayed in favor of participation.[28]

Not all delegates, however, were convinced by Nyerere's argument, and this resulted in the first breakaway from TANU. Zuberi Mtemvu and a few others dissatisfied with the TANU stand and other conditions in the party, decided to form the Tanganyika African National Congress, the aim of which was independence for Africans only.[29]

Local opposition

As the events at Tabora preceded the change in the TANU leadership in the West Lake Province, the new party, TANC, became a natural attraction for those local Haya politicians, who had been "ousted" at the Nyakahura meeting or soon after. A number of these, all belonging to the old generation, having worked in TAA or KLA, decided to support Mtemvu and his party. Following the first visit by Mtemvu to Buhaya, Zefrin Kashumba, the former provincial vice-chairman of TANU, became the first TANC chairman in Buhaya.

The new party was never really able to mobilize any considerable support in the area, except in certain localities, particularly Kamachumu, the home of Kashumba. Reference to the general failure of TANC to gain votes in the elections 1959 and 1960 has already been made, and does not need repetition.[30] Although Bukoba District was one of TANC's strongholds it never became a serious threat to the local TANU branch.

The general conception has been that TANC was an opposition group placed to the left of TANU. The reasons for this were that it had taken a radical stand on the race issue; it had refused to cooperate with the British in the first parliamentary election;[31] and Mr Mtemvu in 1961 had visited Communist China and other Communist countries.[32] If one looks more

[26] Listowel, op.cit., p. 304.
[27] The tripartite system meant one vote for one candidate from each racial group, Africans, Asians and Europeans.
[28] Listowel, op.cit., p. 306.
[29] Cf., p. 42.
[30] See p. 42.
[31] It fielded some candidates in the election 1959, however; all were defeated.
[32] Clagett Taylor, op.cit., p. 199.

closely at the activities of TANC at the local level in Buhaya, however, it certainly does not appear as a radical party. The race issue, for instance, was of very little relevance in Buhaya; the local people had little understanding for the motives of the Congress. The TANC branch in Buhaya was in fact a "traditionalist" party. Many of its supporters were people dissatisfied with the non-compromising stand of TANU on the question of the future position of the chiefs; TANU wanted their political authority abolished.[33] In its program, TANC came out openly in favor of the restoration of the privileges of the Bahinda. It criticized, for instance, Chief Petro Nyarubamba, who had succeeded Bwogi, because he advocated a policy of social integration between Bahinda and Bairu. TANC also rejected the TANU proposal that all land, which traditionally belonged to the chiefdoms, should be considered government-owned land.

The Tanganyika African National Congress became to the Territory what the United Party was in Ghana:[34] a party made up of a conglomeration of separate, mainly parochial interests. TANC, like this Ghanaian party, was never capable of presenting a coherent national program that could compete with that of TANU; there was simply not room for another ideology. Another shortcoming of TANC was that it lacked a strong and popular leader.

The UTP which was started in 1956 was introduced in Buhaya by Elias Lushakuzi, the member of the Legislative Council who had left TAA after an internal policy dispute.[35] Lushakuzi argued that if people supported UTP, the Bahaya would get their first secondary school for girls.[36] It is claimed that he won the support of certain groups of teachers and other educated people. Some supported him too, because they considered him an important man, and what he had to say they believed would carry weight in government circles.[37] Lushakuzi left UTP after some time, however, and the leadership was taken over by John Lujwangana. He managed to build strong support for the party in Bugabo chiefdom, but this was still not enough to ensure a seat in the 1959 election. UTP was too closely associated with the administration to gain wide popularity, a fact that TANU leaders were quick to propagandize.

The Haya material which has been available for this study clearly shows that TANU had a wide support, particularly in the villages, where it to some extent had taken over the support of those who earlier had been mobilized into politics by TAA. The two "opposition" parties before inde-

---

33 Interviews with former TANC leaders in Kamachumu.
34 See Apter, "The Politics . . ." op.cit., p. 109.
35 See p. 119.
36 The first secondary school for girls in the West Lake Region was opened in 1965.
37 Interview with Mr Kassano.

pendence, TANC and UTP, were constrained to smaller, but not unimportant groups in Buhaya. The former had a strong support from many Bahinda and their personal followers; TANC constituted the "traditionalist" opposition. UTP was most popular among the educated people, although for some time it enjoyed support among local villagers in certain pockets in Bugabo chiefdom. Its leading members, however, were the well educated sector of the population. There is also some evidence that the Catholic Church in these years supported the opposition groups; in any case, the Catholic Church feared that its strong position in Buhaya was threatened by the growth of a mass movement. Local records from Karagwe, for instance, indicate that the White Fathers there, threatened members of their church with the denial of the sacraments if they joined TANU. Teachers and other mission employees were told that they had to leave their work with the church if they became members of TANU.[38]

Independence in December 1961 did not become the turning-point that so many people had expected. The local rivalries in Buhaya continued and were even intensified. The division between the "educated" opposition and the TANU leadership in Bukoba District was to be highlighted in a series of incidents following independence. The TANU call for cooperation between all citizens regardless of race, religion, tribe or status, was difficult to implement immediately in an area like Buhaya, where role differentiation had proceeded relatively far, but social integration, despite the early efforts of TANU, was still incomplete. Religious identity remained strong, although schools after independence were put under government inspection and became non-denominational. The positions of chief, sub-chief and parish chief were abolished in the local government system in 1963. The chiefs who had the necessary qualifications were offered jobs as ordinary local government officers. In Buhaya five of the eight Bakama did this. The others preferred to remain as honorary chiefs, performing their traditional, ceremonial functions at each new moon.[39] Whatever position the Bakama chose, they remained influential among those who still believed in the validity of the traditional Haya myth.

The teachers were the first to challenge the new TANU rule in Buhaya after independence. Particularly Catholic teachers, elected members of the District Council, began to oppose the policy of the government, and declared that they wanted nothing to do with TANU. In fact, they argued, that they had been elected to the Council not thanks to TANU, but because of their own skill and competence.[40] Their attitude was partly a reflection of

[38] Interviews with TANU leaders, Nyabuyonza branch; also records from that branch office.

[39] Among those were the two young chiefs, Petro Nyarubamba of Kianja and Rukamba of Kyamtwara.

the fact that they felt pushed aside by the new TANU leadership, which had a substantial Muslim element. The Muslims had joined TANU in large numbers, partly because they saw in the new party an opportunity to channel their dissatisfaction. Many were promoted to top positions in the Bukoba branch. They were by no means in control of the local party organization, but their number was sufficient to create among certain Christians the impression that Islam was a condition for becoming a TANU leader.[41] Many leading Haya Catholics identified themselves more strongly with their church than with TANU.

The real clash came in connection with the District Council election in April 1963, when about twenty-five teachers, who were dissatisfied with TANU, decided to run as independents against officially nominated TANU candidates. Almost all the independent candidates contesting the election were returned as members of the Council, where they now controlled about half the number of the 51 seats. This created antagonism in the district. The Catholic church was accused of having financially supported the campaign of these independents, although no proof was ever presented to support this charge.[42] The independents were derogatorily labelled "Kabaka Yekka"[43] and "Tshombes" by TANU people, because of their separatist tendencies. Some of the chiefs, and the remnants of the TANC group attempted to take advantage of the situation. Relations became particularly tense between the new chief of Kyamtwara, Rukamba, and the government.[44]

At this stage, the central government decided to take steps to settle the crisis. Mr Barongo, who was then Regional Commissioner of the Northern Region (Arusha-Moshi) was sent to Bukoba to investigate the incidents. His report to the President led to the dissolution of the Council by the Minister for Local Government, who holds this power prerogative according to the constitution.[45] Twenty-six of the elected members were re-nominated to the Council, while instead of the oppositional independents, twenty-five new members were appointed.[46] Chief Rukamba and three other men were detained, but later released.[47]

[40] Personal letter from Mr Barongo, March 18, 1966.
[41] The following important posts were held by Muslims at that time: Regional chairman, Member of TANU National Executive Committee for West Lake Region, and District chairman.
[42] Interview with Mr Kassano.
[43] "Kabaka Yekka" is the name of the political organization in Uganda, which has strongly supported the interests of the kingdom of Buganda.
[44] The Regional Commissioner at this time was Mr Luangisa, a relative of Rukamba.
[45] *Tanganyika Local Government Ordinance,* Chapter 333, Suppl. 62., part III, No 16—17.
[46] Kaombwe, *op.cit.,* p. 5.
[47] Personal letter from Mr Barongo, March 18, 1966.

This crisis in Buhaya revealed two things: first of all that the TANU organization in Buhaya lacked an integrative quality. Despite Nyerere's own efforts to reorganize the party in 1962, when he had stepped down as Prime Minister, some of the locally important groups had not been fully assimilated into the ranks of the party. Secondly, the electoral success of the teachers was an indication that this category enjoyed wide respect and support among the local Bahaya. It was not surprising since the Bahaya in the colonial period had been brought up to respect the knowledge which teachers and priests represented and, moreover, the Bahaya in general had willingly accepted this. Education to the local population in the area represented *maendeleo*—development—more than anything else. For many Bahaya it was a difficult choice in the District Council election: either the teacher who associated himself with the qualities of his profession, or the politician, who associated himself with the legitimacy of TANU.

The events in Buhaya was the more serious to the central government as exactly the same situation occurred in the District Council election in Chaggaland two months later. There a quarter of the thirty-eight councillors were returned as independents.[48] After these incidents the government decided to issue a decree, prohibiting teachers from involvement in politics, unless they resigned from their professional post.[49]

After the local election in 1963 the TANU branch in Buhaya remained quite exclusive and an extensive system of local rapporteurs was created. The Regional Commissioner issued statements to all local government officers to be more careful when explaining government policies and to stop quarreling in the villages.[50]

This move coincided with the sweeping reorganization throughout the country of the political structures. The government was aware that the nation had to be built as much "from below" as "from above". In order to achieve this, the government needed a better link with the people in the rural areas. This link was established by the formation of Village Development Committees all over the country.[51] At the local level, TANU village branch chairmen also became heads of the VDCs. The old parish chiefs under the new title, Village Executive Officers were made the secretary of the VDC, besides their other executive functions, such as tax collection, implementation of government policies, and so forth.[52] The impact of this new system was hardly felt during its first year of operation. Despite

[48] Tordoff, *op.cit.*, p. 51.
[49] This was the same situation as in the colonial period; cf., pp. 125—26.
[50] Note from the Regional Commissioner to all local government and party officials, May 2, 1963, Bukoba.
[51] See Lemarchand, *op.cit.*, pp. 11—13; see also Fig. 11, p. 138.
[52] His new title was Village Executive Officer.

TANU efforts to strengthen its hold of the population in Buhaya certain pockets of opposition still remained.

Much dissatisfaction had its origin in the fall of the coffee price on the world market. This trend which started in the late 50s had not been reversed. Since many Bahaya were exclusively depending on coffee for a cash income, this was a serious blow to their economic position. Their grievance was probably reinforced, by the fact that during the coffee boom they had become used to more "extravagant" patterns of living, but now they were forced to "tighten their belts" again. The fluctuation in the coffee price affected Buhaya particularly much since so many of the farmers were still growing coffee in a very unproductive way; the opposition to the British improvement schemes had delayed the spread of more productive ways of cultivation of coffee.

Farmers tended to blame the BNCU for the reduced income and the cooperative movement in Buhaya had to go through still another serious crisis, which it however, managed to overcome. The coffee smuggling to Buganda reached a new peak after independence[53] and the confidence of individual members in the cooperative movement began to shake. Many Bahaya were prepared to support Rugizibwa's Planters' Association, but it had still not achieved—and was not to achieve—formal registration. In the local societies, the lack of confidence was reflected in a higher turnover of elected officials.[54] Generally, the economic deterioration, to a large extent owing to factors beyond the control of the central government, in the years immediately after independence, tended to increase the pressures on the political system. New opportunities in society did not keep up with the rising expectations and the increased demands on the government. This was most dramatically illustrated with the mutiny at Colito barracks north of Dar es Salaam on January 20, 1964.[55] Dissatisfaction with government performance prevailed, however, also in Buhaya. Many prominent Catholics, who were dissatisfied with the way the government had interfered in the local council election in 1963 remained hostile to the local TANU leadership. At Kamachumu, teachers and African White Fathers from Rutabo mission tried to form a "front" against local TANU leaders. They were supported in their efforts by the remnants of the local TANC group which had been particularly strong in that area.[56] The African priests publicly preached on matters concerning the state of Buhaya after independence. It

[53] BNCU, "Annual Reports", op.cit.
[54] This was found when looking through the annual reports of five local societies, Kanyigo, Kitendagulo, Ibuga, (Kamachumu area), Ilemera, and Nyabuyonza, for the period concerned.
[55] Listowel, op.cit., Appendix III.
[56] For the information about these incidents I have relied mainly on TANU files, interviews with local politicians and White Fathers who were involved.

was reported to the government which considered this an improper way of mixing religion and politics. This "opposition" group also campaigned in the villages in order to gain control over essential local institutions, such as the VDCs, the committee of the local cooperative societies, the school commmittes, and so forth.

This opposition was restricted to a small area, and had no immediate impact beyond the small number of parishes concerned. It was exclusively a local "revolt". Still it was significant for the situation in certain other parts of Buhaya as well. The reason why it came to a more open and organized expression in the Kamachumu area is probably that it has always been a politically unstable area.[57] The local crisis there was brought to an end after a personal intervention by Cardinal Rugambwa, the head of the Catholic church in Buhaya. This was in March 1964.[58] At this time, TANU again made efforts to gain better control of the situation in Buhaya, and reduce the many local tensions.

Conclusions

A principal aim of TANU policies has always been to bring the village communities in various parts of the country into the national fold. A large part of this chapter has dealt with the difficulties that emerged when politics began to increasingly affect aspects of the daily life in the local communities. The new political leaders identified themselves with the cause of the common man. At least one major reason, however, why the process of creating a common national—and social—identity became complicated in Buhaya was that, although traditional social structures were breaking down, a new system of social stratification had been fostered in the colonial period. Particularly religious identities had become deeply rooted in the minds of many Bahaya. Besides religion, education and ownership of new economic resources determined social status. The nationalist movement faced problems in its efforts to break down these social and religious identities as illustrated in the events of 1963—64.

A prominent feature of the political development after independence has been the replacement at the local level of traditional political structures with a new political machinery. Traditional roles have been replaced by

---

[57] Kamachumu was the main scene for conflicts between *babinga* and *bakimala;* it was the stronghold of KLA, and later of TANC.

[58] Rugambwa was the first African Bishop in the Catholic Church in Buhaya. In 1960 he became the first African Cardinal. He is a grandson of Chief Kahigi II.

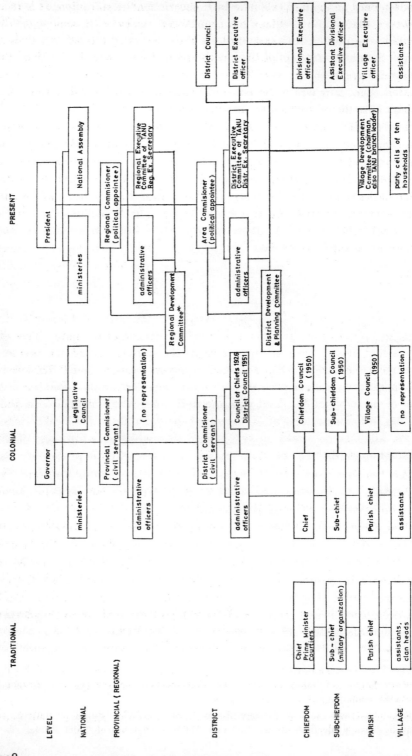

modern ones, integrated in a new local government organization. It is true, however, that although chiefly power has been abolished, in some cases the persons who perform the new roles are the same as in the old. As a result of the increased differentiation and the high degree of centralization, the villagers have been left with fewer opportunities to decide on their own matters. One problem in the post-independence period has therefore been to legitimize the new structures and the new roles.

The TANU leaders have ideologically committed themselves to work for the people—to help satisfy their needs. Ideally, what they take away from the people in terms of tax and levies should be returned to the masses as means to improve their material situation. No doubt, more schools, health dispensaries and local roads have been built after independence in Buhaya than ever before, and people have willingly contributed their own time and work. The *reciprocal* character of the government penetration has, however, to some extent been blurred. In the first years of independence cooperation between leaders at the local level in Buhaya was not good. Moreover, the coffee price remained low; tax-paying was therefore much more seriously felt by the individual villager.

A third factor that affected the relation of the political leaders to the rural inhabitants was the general political orientation of the latter. The villagers had always been oriented towards the output side of the political system. At the time of independence this pattern was reinforced. They were encouraged to look at the political system mainly for material rewards. People were understandably less anxious to listen to the call for contribution by everyone to achieve development.

The *nyarubanja* system was abolished, but that in itself did not create new opportunities for social, economic and political advancement. The Asians remained in control of much of the local business in Buhaya. The expectations of the people, reinforced in the struggle for independence were, and could not be, met by the government.

This should not, however, conceal the fact that deliberate steps were taken by the government to improve the responsiveness to local demands, the most important being the establishment of VDCs. For the majority of the Bahaya independence significantly improved the opportunities to participate in political activities. As a result of the local election crisis in 1963, however, teachers and people practising religious occupations were excluded from holding political office.

Figure 11. The organization of the centre-periphery relationship in the traditional political systems of Buhaya, in the colonial system and in the present Tanzanian political system.

*These committees were in the course of late 1967 renamed "Regional Rural Development Committees".

Rural attitudes to development:
A case study

Chapter 8

The problem of identity

The historical legacy of Buhaya, which has been presented in the earlier part of the book, makes an inquiry into the effects of the national assimilation process on the rural Haya population particularly interesting. There were already before independence indications that old loyalties and traditional social identities were breaking down and new ones were emerging. The new relation of state to village that was established by the colonial power limited the importance of the chiefdom as focus of identity. Socioeconomic and political change in the colonial period also led to a growing self-consciousness of the new Haya elite in their relation to representatives of other tribes. It was, however, never allowed to be expressed in organized political structures. The emergence of a new nationalist movement, TANU, put a halt to that.

Religious divisions grew strong in the colonial period and remained important even in the years of independence as shown in the previous chapter. Roman Catholics and Protestants lived in a constant rivalry with each other. Many Christians in Buhaya tended to look down upon the "uneducated" Muslim sector of the population. Again, TANU managed to a large extent to overcome these divisions, but in some places they remained strong.

These divisions in Haya society and their impact on the political community before and immediately after independence should be born in mind when the study now is focused on the attitudes of the local Haya population a few years after independence. To shed some light on the assimilation of the Bahaya into the new nation three main dimensions have been selected. (1) What is their affection for the new nation and why? (2) To what extent have the villagers joined TANU, the creator and the symbol of national unity? (3) How attached are the Bahaya to their own place of residence? The last question has been included on the assumption that a high degree of social security and satisfaction is necessary unless a policy of mobilization at this stage of low economic development will lead to an intensification of conflict in society.

Affection for the new nation

One assumption often made by social scientists studying Africa has been the existence of a wide discrepancy between the values prevailing at the national and the local level of politics in the new states. Robert LeVine, for instance, has raised the hypothesis that African parents socialize their children for participation in the local authority systems of the rural areas only and not for roles in the national citizenry.[1] The same point has been taken up and elaborated by others, e.g., James S. Coleman[2] and Pye and Verba,[3] more recently in their books on problems of political development.

The hypothesis has not been empirically tested against survey data. One purpose of this chapter will be to show whether the Haya material confirms the hypothesis. It is based on two questionable assumptions: (1) that only parochial values prevail among the adult population in rural Africa; (2) that there is a significant absence of socializing agencies other than the family, e.g., political parties and other voluntary associations. Moreover, the hypothesis does not state in specific terms what values African parents transmit to their children, and in what way these values are incongruent with the values of the new national elite.

The previous account has shown that the part played by modern institutions such as political organizations, schools and foreign religious agencies has been significant. The situation in Buhaya at least seems to be much more complex than the hypothesis suggests. Not only is the long presence of modern socializing agencies, but also the inherent capacity of many Bahaya to withdraw their support for various elements of the traditional system likely to have contributed to a change in the whole socialization process in rural Buhaya. An indication of the extent to which the change in the general orientation towards the political community and the various local sub-communities has taken place, was shown in the answers to the question: "For which institution do you think it is most important to teach a child to work?"

Table 7. Beliefs about for which institution it is most important to teach a child to work; by parish. Absolute number in brackets.

(in %)	Bugombe		Kitendagulo		Bwatangabo		Kabagunda		Kiruruma		Total
Family	3,5	(2)	3,5	(2)	3	(3)	7	(5)	0	(—)	3,5
Clan	7	(4)	2	(1)	3	(3)	6	(4)	2	(1)	4
Village	5,5	(3)	9	(5)	2	(2)	6	(4)	13,5	(6)	7
Religious inst.	23	(13)	9	(5)	5	(5)	14	(10)	15,5	(7)	13,5
Nation	41	(36)	77,5	(44)	87	(85)	66	(48)	69	(29)	72
No Infor.	—		—		—		1	(1)	—		—
Total	100	(58)	100	(56)	100	(98)	100	(72)	100	(44)	100

[1] Robert LeVine, "Political Socialization and Culture Change" in Geertz (ed), *Old Societies and New States*, (New York 1963), p. 282.
[2] Coleman, "Education ..." *op.cit.*, p. 222.
[3] Pye and Verba, *op.cit.*, Ch 1.

We can never know for sure whether a man in all situations will act as he believes is correct; nor do we know if what a man is teaching another man is understood by the latter in the way it was intended. Still there is very little to suggest that the conflict between loyalties to parochial institutions, such as the family, clan or village, on the one hand, and the nation on the other, is one that the Bahaya experience as very real. The nation occupies a predominant position in the minds of most respondents. Geographical distance does not make any difference. The man in the isolated Kiruruma has basically the same orientation as his fellow-tribesman in Kitendagulo, who goes to work in Bukoba every day. Nor does age, education or membership in TANU constitute a major differentiating variable. This fact needs further explanation. Before doing so, however, another interesting finding should be noted. It is not the traditional or parochial institutions that the Haya villagers regard as particularly important besides the nation, but rather another modern social institution, the church. The religious authority constitutes a more serious challenge to the nation than the family, the descent group or the village community. None of these compete seriously with the national community for the loyalties of the people. At the same time, however, one could have expected an even higher emphasis on the religious identity, considering its importance in local events as late as 1964. It may be suggested, therefore, that the religious quarrels, which took place in Buhaya around independence, must have been confined to certain localities.

Among the respondents who believed that it is more important to teach a child to work for his religious group rather than the national community, Catholics and Muslims are slightly overrepresented. Of the four Protestant respondents three were actively engaged in church activities, and their answer can at least partly be explained in that light. If this is considered the pattern becomes more conspicuous. It is difficult to draw too much inference from the attitudes of the relatively small number—in all 40—who claim the religious institutions are more important than the nation, but it is not a coincidence that Catholics and Muslims rather than Protestants lean in that direction. To the former, religion is mainly a social institution, to the latter a way of life. The Catholic Church, ever since its establishment in Buhaya, has constituted an important sub-community. Its influence has extended far beyond the purely religious sphere of activities, as shown in previous chapters.[4] The demand for subordination to the church authorities have been strong. This to a large extent also applies to the Muslim sects, in which political and social questions often are viewed in the light of religion.[5]

[4] See e.g., Ch 7, pp. 138—39.
[5] For an account of Islam in East Africa, see Trimingham, *op.cit.*

The implication of what has been said, however, is not that a considerable number of Bahaya experience a constant crisis of identity, not knowing whether to convert completely to religion or to secular political beliefs. First of all, it should be emphasized that the information presented is rather superficial, and it would have been extremely difficult to obtain such information without a well-designed psycho-analytic survey, a task which lies far beyond the purpose of this study.

Whether religious identity goes deeper than national identity is impossible to establish on basis of the material presented here. One can assume however, like Welbourn,[6] that religion and politics to many Bahaya are "different modes of expression of the same fundamental personality". Most often people can keep religion and politics separated; religious loyalties are not viewed as contrary to loyalties towards modern secular institutions. Sometimes however, particularly in areas where religion has contributed to social cleavages, political tensions may at times occur as has been the case in Buhaya. The minutes of the Bugombe Village Development Committee, for instance, give an indication that religious differences at a number of occasions during 1963—65 have hampered the cooperation for development of the local community.[7] The references to speeches by political leaders about the lack of cooperation between political leaders and between various sectors of the local population are more frequent in Bugombe. One should not exclude the possibility that this is so simply because the secretary of the Bugombe VDC has been more thorough and perhaps sincere than the other secretaries. Local interviews made by the present author, however, have also confirmed that religious differences have influenced politics in Bugombe.

It should be emphasized that if one compares the distribution of the total population in each parish, by religion, there is no indication that one religious community or another is discriminated in the VDCs.[8]

Table 8. Number of VDC members in the five parishes; by religion.

	Bugom-be	Kiten-dagulo	Bwatan-gabo	Kaba-gunda	Kiru-ruma	Total
Roman Catholic	10	15	15	6	13	59
Protestant	5	12	—	6	5	28
Muslim	3	—	8	2	—	13
Animist	1	1	1	—	—	3
No infor	—	—	—	1	—	1
Total	19	28	24	15	18	104

[6] Welbourn, op.cit., p. 54.
[7] Minutes of the Village Development Committee, Bugombe 1963—65.
[8] Cf., Appendix II.

There is no information which confirms that the election of members to the VDC should directly be influenced by the religious factor. Certainly it is not the only factor, age, "progressive attitude", education, and personal popularity being others.[9] It is true, however that indirectly, religion plays a part. The local village community may not elect a Christian only because he is a Christian, but because he is generally more educated than a Muslim or an Animist. Therefore, there may be a tendency in some places to favor educated Christian candidates.[10]

The strong orientation towards the Tanzanian nation, recorded in Table 7, also came out in the answers to the question of how proud they are to be citizens of Tanzania. The pattern of answer was very uniform: 90 percent replied "very proud", the remaining 10 percent "a bit proud"; nobody felt he was "not proud at all". These answers as well as those presented in Table 7 were given to closed-choice questions, and it is obvious that far-reaching conclusions cannot be drawn from that material only. Attempts were therefore made to find out more specifically what determines their high "system affect".[11] Their motives were to a large extent reflected in the answers to the question about what they think is the most outstanding quality of their nation:

Table 9. Opinions about which is the most outstanding quality of the new nation of Tanzania; by parish. Absolute number in brackets.

(in %)	Bugombe		Kiten-dagulo		Bwatan-gabo		Kaba-gunda		Kiru-ruma	
peace, peaceful independence	48	(28)	50	(28)	58	(57)	31	(22)	32	(14)
diligent leaders	5	(3)	5	(3)	10	(10)	7	(5)	4	(2)
obedience to leaders	13	(7)	7	(4)	3	(3)	—	(0)	—	(0)
unity and cooperation	8	(5)	8	(5)	3	(3)	3	(2)	—	(0)
richness	2	(1)	4	(2)	1	(1)	3	(2)	—	(0)
poverty	4	(2)	5	(3)	—	(0)	—	(0)	—	(0)
good agriculture	—	(0)	7	(4)	10	(10)	15	(11)	27	(12)
others	8	(5)	5	(3)	1	(1)	14	(10)	22	(10)
don't know	13	(7)	9	(5)	13	(12)	27	(19)	14	(8)
total	100	(58)	100	(56)	100	(98)	100	(72)	100	(44)

[9] Cf., Welbourn, op.cit., particularly his account of Buganda in Ch XI.
[10] Educational attainment seems to have influenced the voters in the general election in Tanzania 1965. Cf., Cliffe (ed), op.cit., p. 263.
[11] This concept is used by Almond and Verba in their account of the political culture in five different countries, op.cit., pp. 64—68.

This table reveals several things, first of all, the extent to which people mention political qualities. There are no words about the grand national parks or the beautiful mountains, and, not unexpectedly in these rural communities, the non-political quality most often mentioned is the agriculture of the country.

The second thing is that so many—in average 45 percent of the total sample—name "peace" or "peaceful achievement of independence" as the most outstanding qualities of the country. Much of the pride in the nation is therefore likely to be based on their evaluation of the way the new system was established, not by violence but by peaceful means. It is, of course, impossible to trace the national pride only to such a factor as "the peaceful achievement of independence", but it is an important finding that independence does have an important impact on the ongoing process of politics. This is a parallel case to that reported by Almond and Verba about the impact of the Mexican revolution on political attitudes in Mexico today.[12] It is true that the Mexican revolution lies much further back in history, and therefore the Mexican case is more startling than that reported here. Still, in the African context it is significant. Other political scientists, who have studied other African countries, have reported about the waning importance of independence,[13] and there is empirical evidence to support their opinion, the disintegration of Nigeria, and the decline of the nationalist movements in several states being the clearest cases in point.

The high Haya affection for the Tanzanian nation is also likely to have grown out of events in the immediate international environment, notably Uganda, Rwanda and the Congo. Reference to the political disturbances in these countries were often made when the respondents mentioned "peace" as the most outstanding quality of Tanzania. The geographical position of Buhaya on the border to Rwanda and Uganda and the proximity to the Congo has been a relevant factor in the development among the Bahaya of a pride in their own system. It is worth remembering that Tshombe's name and that of the tribal Kabaka Yekka party in Uganda were used to describe those in Buhaya who obstructed TANU immediately after independence.[14]

The frequency with which people are mentioning political qualities as opposed to others or none at all is higher in the three eastern parishes, Bugombe, Kitendagulo and Bwatangabo than it is in the southern, Kabagunda, and the western, Kiruruma, parishes. In the latter two some mention agricultural production, while another large group is unable to state

---

[12] *Ibid.*, pp. 66—67.
[13] See, e.g., Coleman and Rosberg, *op.cit.*, pp. 655—91, and Zolberg, *op.cit.*, particularly Ch. 5.
[14] Cf., p. 134.

any quality at all. Since the number of educated people and those who regularly follow any mass media is smaller in Kiruruma and Kabagunda one may assume that the "don't knows" belong to these categories. This is also confirmed by the findings in the following table.

Table 10. Respondents who mention "peace" or "peaceful independence" as special qualities of the Tanzanian nation and those who cannot mention any quality at all; by education, media exposure and party membership. Absolute number in brackets.

	Education			Media exposure			Party membership		
Mention:	none	some	much	very often	often	not so often	never	yes	no
(in %)	(143)	(119)	(66)	(34)	(67)	(95)	(116)	(225)	(55)
"peace" or "peaceful independence"	41	50,5	47	55,5	47,5	51	40	27,5	22,5
no quality at all	18	16	10,5	12,5	9	18,5	22	18,5	21,5

It appears therefore, that education and frequent media exposure make the respondent more predisposed to feel affection for the system because it has attained independence peacefully or events in Tanzania after independence have remained peaceful. Party membership does have the same effect, although not so clearly. The most parochial respondents—those who cannot mention any quality at all—are found most frequently among the non-educated and those who never or only rarely listen to radio or read newspapers.

The dominant position that the "nation" seems to occupy in the minds of the rural Bahaya was also revealed in the supplementary interviews that were carried out with a cross-section of the original sample. Five out of six respondents mentioned specifically "I am a Tanzanian" or "I am a good citizen" when asked the question: "If a man asks you who you are, what will you answer?" The others said they were "good villagers" or "ordinary citizens". One should not exclude the possibility, when asking this type of questions, that the respondents give an answer which they believe that the interviewer expects, and not an answer reflecting their sincere opinion. When asked to explain why they feel a strong identity with the Tanzanian nation, however, the answers suggested that their opinion is not false or based simply on a superficial pride. Here are some of the explanations given.

A 35 year old Muslim woman in Kabagunda, who does not know Kiswahili said:

I identify with the nation because I know I belong to one big family of Tanzanians with one leader, Mr Nyerere.

A Rwanda-born, 30 year old Muslim bar owner in the same parish, with only two years of formal education maintained that:

... I am a man with a national mind. If, for instance, war breaks out in Tanzania I am going to fight.

Another woman, 42 years old, staying alone with her children in a small house in Kitendagulo, having no education and with hardly no cash income had very much the same to say:

I feel I am a Tanzanian, because if something happens elsewhere in Tanzania, for instance a war, I will also be affected.

The list of statements confirming the same orientation could be continued, but more interesting to note is perhaps the fact that even those who would feel the loyalty to the family or the tribe to be most important had a consciousness of the nation. They do not conceive of identification with the tribe as something contrary to national identity, but simply as complementary. A 70 year old farmer, who claimed that he went to one of the first unregistered bush schools started by the Roman Catholic missionaries, now living in Bugombe, put it this way:

I feel the tribe is most important. We have many different tribes. Our nation is made up of tribes, so in fact, if I belong to a tribe, in a certain sense I belong to the nation as well.

A 24 year old farmer in Bwatangabo, with four years of formal education who had never travelled outside Bukoba District, and identified himself with the extended family—*ujamaa*—thought:

Since the nation starts with the family, or rather the nation is composed of several families, I feel I am primarily a member of my family.

All these opinions and attitudes are rather different shades of the same phenomenon—the affect for and identity with the nation—than a reflection of a divided political culture. But we are now turning to the second dimension of the assimilation process.

TANU and the process of assimilation

The significance of membership in TANU is twofold. It implies a positive inclination towards national unity; a member is more likely than a non-member to identify with the new system. Secondly, a member will be more exposed, and perhaps also more amenable, to the dissemination of national symbols. It is probably true that there are many persons who have joined the party for reasons of expediency, and that membership itself therefore is not a sufficient indicator of political involvement in the process of national assimilation. The distinction between a member and a non-member might in some situations, as this study will indicate, be difficult to draw.

Still membership can be used as an indicator of national assimilation, particularly if consideration is taken to when people joined the party. Those who joined TANU at an early stage, while independence still was considered distant, must have taken this step aware of the fact that both government and religious authorities would try to make life more complicated for them. There is very little information about the rank and file members in any African political party and comparisons are difficult to make. The figures in Table 11 show that at least in Buhaya, which, it is true has had a long tradition of African participation in political associations, a large number of people in the rural areas joined TANU in its first years of existence. This may not be surprising if one knows the political history of Buhaya, but it confirms one important thing, that TANU ever since its formation has had a strong backing in the rural areas. This has of course been of utmost importance for the efforts to create a national identity by political means. The struggle for independence in Tanzania has not simply been a matter of a new African elite replacing the colonial wielders of power.

Table 11. Distribution of respondents according to when they first became members of TANU; by parish. Absolute numbers in brackets.

(in %)	Bugombe	Kiten-dagulo	Bwatan-gabo	Kabagunda	Kiruruma
1956—59	48 (28)	23 (13)	39 (38)	21 (15)	21 (9)
1960—61	10 (6)	11 (6)	15 (15)	11 (8)	21 (9)
1962—65	14 (8)	21 (12)	13 (13)	22 (18)	34 (15)
Total number of respondents	(58)	(56)	(98)	(72)	(44)

An average of 30 percent joined in its first years when the date for independence was still unknown. This figure is quite high considering the short span of time, three years, and the fact that no election was held in these years. The influx of members in these early years was particularly remarkable in the densely populated eastern part, although Kitendagulo is somewhat of an exception.

The low figures in Kitendagulo could be explained with reference to its higher degree of differentiation. Unlike Bugombe and Bwatangabo, this parish is not socially homogeneous, and evidence from other countries suggests that people, who live under similar conditions, develop similar needs and interest and therefore tend to view the world through the same eyes, are more inclined to act in a similar fashion than members of a highly differentiated community.[15]

The figures for Kiruruma, the Karagwe parish, does not support the assumption made by TANU leaders in the early years that it was easier to muster support in Karagwe;[16] most of the respondents in Kiruruma have joined only after independence or immediately before it was achieved. On the other hand, Kiruruma is not likely to have been one of the first destinations of the party organizers, since it is located so far off the main roads.

Another important finding is that membership in a particular religious community or educational attainment did not predestinate people to join TANU, at least in the villages. Christians, Muslims and Animists, educated and illiterate people alike, joined the ranks of TANU in its formative years in roughly the same proportions, as is shown in Table 12.

Table 12. Respondents joining TANU in 1956—59; by religion and education. Absolute number in brackets.

	Religion				Education		
joined:	R. C.	Prot.	Muslim	Anim.	none	some	much
(in %)	(196)	(50)	(37)	(42)	(143)	(119)	(66)
1956—59	30,5	34	43	33	31	33	32

The only notable exception is that the proportion of Muslims is slightly higher. Since the absolute number of respondents analyzed is rather low any farreaching conclusions should not be drawn. The figure suggests, however, that it is true what was said about the Muslims in Ch. 7, that they, perhaps more than others, found in TANU an appropriate platform for their demands on the society.

Table 11 also shows that the influx of members to TANU did not come to an end with independence. A substantial number of people have joined the party after 1961. We do not know the reasons why these people have become members but the figures certainly suggest, that the party leadership has not ceased its efforts to make TANU a true mass party. The aim

[15] Lazarsfeld P. F., Berelson B. and Gaudet, H., *The People's Choice,* (New York 1948), pp. 148—49; also K. W. J. Post, *The Nigerian Federal Election of 1959,* (Oxford 1963), p. 376 ff.
[16] Cf. p. 127.

has been to make TANU identical with the national community. Our data indicates that TANU has remained a genuine mass party also after independence. It is true that party organizers have difficulty in collecting membership fees, but, as will be shown further in the next chapter, people do accept TANU as the legitimate instrument to run community affairs.

TANU's own capacity to maintain a functioning political organization in the countryside and thereby providing a new network of communication channels has given the political leaders of Tanzania great opportunities to really create a sense of national identity by political means. Today TANU symbols penetrate all walks of life. The respected village elder, when walking to church on Sundays, always ties his TANU Elders' badge on his coat before leaving. VDC meetings are generally opened by a prayer and by everyone singing "Tanzania, Tanzania", a kind of "second" national anthem. Saba saba Day, the birthday of TANU, is at least as important a national holiday as Uhuru Day, and so on. People are constantly reminded of their common experience and identity, and the important role of TANU as the "patron" of the new nation.

Haya attitudes towards the domestic society

The political community is only one example of division of labor invented by human beings to serve a particular purpose and it is not always the most important, although in some countries—in Africa as well as elsewhere— political leaders want it to be that way. One main purpose of this study has been to find out to what extent actions taken by the political community can be used to control the impact of the social, or the economic, system on politics. It would be wrong, however, not to examine more closely how the social system, or rather the social community, as Easton prefers to call it,[17] affects the political community.

This may be particularly relevant in a country which pursues a policy of political mobilization—the deliberate creation of a new political consciousness to serve the interest of the country—, the reason being that mobilizing political systems often trigger off forces in society, over which it is difficult to achieve control. People, leaving a traditional way of life, move into new positions in society, in which they often feel insecure and lack ways of communicating with other people. This is a particularly dangerous phenomenon in less developed countries, where material resources do not suffice to meet

[17] Easton, "A Systems Analysis . . ." *op.cit.*, p. 183.

the demands of the people. Local sub-communities formed in the new urban areas find themselves unable to communicate with each other; ethnic, or other parochial sentiments tend to grow strong in such situations.[18]

Karl Deutsch has most convincingly argued for the necessity of a certain degree of social communication as a prerequisite for the emergence of a sense of identity within a community.[19] Mobilization of men without a capacity to communicate with each other along similar lines of thought is likely to lead to tensions in society. Other political scientists have argued in the same vein. Quincy Wright writes that the danger of great tension arises when groups within a society with inconsistent value systems come in close contact.[20] Easton argues that a stable, integrated political system is in most cases not achieved through homogenization but rather by developing a deeper sense of mutual awareness and responsiveness among incapsulated cultural units.[21]

There is therefore, in the culturally fragmented new African states, a strong case for making the community grow faster than the society. Political mobilization as an instrument for national assimilation is most likely to be successful in countries where people will have developed a capacity for communicating with each other and feeling a responsibility towards their national community before they are mobilized into new positions in society.

Tanzania has pursued a policy along these lines. As shown in Ch 2[22], the government has taken deliberate steps to move unemployed people away from the urban centers and offer them opportunities to work in their home area. At the same time, it has pressed on the use of Kiswahili in all walks of life and maintained a network of communication channels between the center and the periphery of the political system.

Our aim has been to find out whether the Bahaya are satisfied with their social environment; if they are prepared to stay where they are, or if they have strong desires to break up from their home society in order to find new avenues for social and economic advancement elsewhere. One could assume that if there is a high degree of dissatisfaction and social restlessness, the assimilation of these people into a viable national community would be endangered, considering the limited opportunities for social mobility that exist in a country like Tanzania. One of the questions they were asked therefore was: "If you could move anywhere you want in Tanzania, where would you move?" The answers were distributed in the following way:

---

[18] Cf., Young's account of politics of ethnicity in Congolese towns, op.cit., Ch XI.
[19] Deutsch, op.cit., Ch 7. Cf., also p. 23.
[20] Q. Wright, "The Nature of Conflict", Western Political Quarterly, (Vol 4, June 1951), p. 196.
[21] Easton, "A Systems Analysis . . .", op.cit., p. 250.
[22] Cf., p. 47.

Table 13. Places to which people would like to move; by parish. Absolute number in brackets.

(in %)	Bugombe	Kiten-dagulo	Bwatan-gabo	Kaba-gunda	Kiru-ruma
other place in Buhaya	40 (23)	54 (31)	44,5 (44)	40 (29)	20 (9)
outside Buhaya	— (0)	9 (5)	2 (2)	13 (9)	— (0)
nowhere	52 (31)	26 (14)	51,5 (50)	42 (31)	80 (35)
don't know	4 (2)	— (0)	— (0)	5 (3)	— (0)
no information	4 (2)	11 (6)	2 (2)	— (0)	— (0)
total	100 (58)	100 (56)	100 (98)	100 (72)	100 (44)

The two most notable things in this table is that so many absolutely reject the idea of moving elsewhere, and the fact that almost all those who can think of going to another place mention another part of Buhaya. The pattern is striking in all five parishes, although most conspicuous in Kiruruma. Karagwe where there is still available land for cultivation is the most popular choice of those who can think of moving. Only 5 % of *all* respondents had any inclination to migrate to town, whether Bukoba, Dar es Salaam or Mwanza.

The young, educated farmers and those with a non-agricultural occupation can most easily conceive of moving somewhere else. This pattern is even more accentuated in the answers to the probing question whether the respondent had ever seriously considered making a move to the place he had mentioned. Only 8,5 % of the total sample claimed that they had done so. This is shown in Table 14, in which the answers have been analyzed according to some basic socio-economic variables.

le 14. Respondents who can think of moving elsewhere and who have seriously considered doing y age, education, size of farm and occupation. Absolute number in brackets.

%)	Age			Education			Size of farm			Occupation	
	young	middle-aged	old	none	some	much	small	middle-size	big	agr.	non-agr.
	(132)	(130)	(63)	(143)	(119)	(66)	(108)	(126)	(63)	(270)	(58)
think moving	49	48,5	38	43	45,5	54,5	44,5	43,5	49,5	41,5	70
seriously sidered it	15	5,5	1,5	1,5	13	16,5	5,5	9,5	8	6	19

The attachment to the home land, whether voluntary or not, is most clearly determined by age, education and occupation, but also size of farm does determine to some extent the willingness to move. The middle-size and the large farmers are slightly more inclined to move than the small farmers, whom one would expect should be most interested in moving elsewhere for economic, if for no other, reasons. The wealthy farmers are therefore the more mobile. They have enough money to afford the risk that is implied in moving from one place to another. They are probably also more removed from traditional beliefs about land tenure and methods of cultivation, and consequently more inclined to view their situation in a "business-like" manner. This question will however, be dealt with more specifically in Ch. 10.

If one accepts the thesis that the division of labor caused by material factors should not be allowed to grow faster than the creation of common channels of communication and mutual responsibility between local subcommunities—if the process of national assimilation is to be successful—the stable rural orientation of the majority of the population is a precondition for the maintenance of a viable national community in a country like Tanzania. To that extent the attitudes of the rural Bahaya are not likely to be contrary to the objective of creating and maintaining a national identity. One reservation which should be made is that the interview population uniformly comprises people with a permanent income and property of land. Those who do not belong to this category have not been considered here; in fact, they are hardly at all represented in the parishes studied.

One may ask why the Bahaya have such a strong attachment to their home land. There is, first of all, the fact that they have always been dependent on the cultivation of bananas and coffee; much of their culture has been based on this material condition. The primitive methods of cultivation have reinforced this pattern. In this respect, the Bahaya do not differ from other people living under similar conditions. A second factor of importance is that Buhaya has remained a single-tribe area. There has been no pressures by neighboring tribes to the south to move to Buhaya in search for land. People have come to Buhaya from other, less rich areas, but they have come to work for the Bahaya. They have accepted the position of a rural proletariat, rather than competing with the indigeneous Haya population for already scarce land resources.[23] This pattern has been particularly conspicuous in eastern Buhaya.

What is important to note therefore is that the immigrants to Buhaya, the majority being temporary laborers, have not disturbed the existing social structure; they have, by and large, accepted a subordinate role. This has probably reduced the threat of social or political conflicts in Buhaya.

---

[23] These people who come to work in Buhaya, mainly Banyarwanda, Barundi, Basubi and Bahangaza, are somewhat derogatorily referred to by the Bahaya as *bashuti*.

The strong rural orientation of the Bahaya when it comes to selection of places to work and live is not a complicating factor in the process of national assimilation. This fact is apparent from the figures in Table 13 and 14. The relatively stable character of the social relations in rural Buhaya and the fact that the impact of many traditional elements, social and political, was reduced already before independence, are likely to be two important explanations of this situation.

Conclusions

The family in the present Haya context is not simply a traditionally oriented institution. The answers of the family heads reveal both pride in the new nation of Tanzania and an awareness of a political community wider than that of the village or the tribe. This does not exclude the possibility that local conditions still determine to a large extent the way people think and act in politics; there is still a distinct political sub-culture, that is likely to be the framework within which the Bahaya carry out most of their political actions. This will be discu..sed further in the following chapters. The most important finding is, however, that the Bahaya are not only "inward-looking"; their self-consciousness does not lead to hostility towards other tribes, at least in the present social and political context. Instead they show a great capacity to absorb the values of the new Tanzanian leadership. They feel that they find a meaningful guidance from the present Tanzanian leaders. The Haya respondents certainly do not resemble the Italian peasants portrayed by Banfield,[24] when he says that one of the main characteristics of these peasants is that they cannot conceive of political action to solve problems of a common interest to the whole community.

The distinction between the family and other modern socializing agencies such as the school, is not likely to be as clear-cut and simple as suggested by Le Vine and Coleman.[25] The adult population on the whole have a strong sense of pride and identity with the new nation, and in fact, a comparison with school children in St VIII in the same rural areas shows that the adults are more aware of their obligations to the nation than the younger generations.[26]

[24] Banfield, *op.cit.*, p. 98 ff.

[25] Cf., p. 144.

[26] A full account of this study appears in an unpublished paper by the present author, "Attitudes among School Children and Adults in a Rural area in Tanzania", The Political Science Research Programme, Makerere University College, (Kampala 1966).

Edward Shils a few years ago wrote that the sense of membership in the new nation is still rudimentary and frail in Asian and African countries.[27] Our data, however, despite its limitations, indicates that, at least in a rural area of Tanzania like Buhaya, people are not merely revealing a high system affect, but several respondents also show an awareness of their duties to the new national community. It is also important to note with reference to Buhaya, that those primordial sentiments which were expressed immediately after independence, for instance, in the 1963 district council election, have not been permanently integrated in the local political culture of the area. Religious and other similar social identities, which were so important before and around independence, are not likely to be principal determinants of political behavior, at least not in the type of local communities studied here.[28]

[27] Edward Shils, *op.cit.*, p. 283.
[28] Geertz, *op.cit.*, in one chapter called "The Integrative Revolution" maintains the point that political instability in some new countries is due to the prevalence of primordial sentiments in the political culture.

Chapter 9.   # The problem of legitimacy

In the last chapter, focus was on the political community. In this chapter we will be concerned with the regime, the problem of creating—and maintaining—new structures, values and norms. We will see the problem from the viewpoint of the rural population in the periphery of the Tanzanian political system. How do they react to the institutionalization of the prerequisites for the running of a modern government? This question is particularly pertinent since one of the attributes of modern government with reference to local politics is "increased central supervision, intervention and control."[1] This means that an increasing part of the daily life in the villages will be affected by politics; the regulation of social and political behavior will be extended.

The process of building new structures, values and norms has, however, in most African countries been complicated. Many African political systems are likely to remain even today, what Zolberg calls, "syncretic".[2] The societies remain unintegrated; modern and traditional elements survive side by side. Members of the political system are influenced by at least two sets of structures, values and norms.

A viable political organization is not only an important instrument in keeping together a newly born political community, but it is also an essential means of internalizing with the population the belief that the new regime is legitimate. Even in those states, however, in which a strong central party has existed problems have arisen as a result of insufficient expansion of political control by the central authority. Buhaya 1963 is a case in point. Although Buhaya is not necessarily typical for Tanzania as a whole, because of its special political history, it is symptomatic for the situation after independence in almost all African states. In 1963 the political sub-system of Buhaya was still divided, partly as a result of old cleavages in the social system. Certain groups were not prepared to yield to pressures for centralization and subordination to a central authority controlled by TANU.

The crisis in Buhaya at this time has similar features to the events in Buganda in 1966, when the Uganda government decided to put an end to the semi-autonomy of Buganda and its king, Kabaka Mutesa II. Both

[1] Robert E. Ward, "Introduction to Village Government in Eastern and Southern Asia: A Symposium", *Far Eastern Quarterly*, (Vol. XV, February 1956), p. 178.
[2] Zolberg uses the concept in a paper for the 7th World Congress of the International Political Science Association in Brussels, September 18—23, 1967, entitled "The Structure of Political Conflict in the New States of Tropical Africa" p. 4.

Buhaya and Buganda have been better advanced than neighboring areas in their respective countries. Both had, in the colonial period, grown accustomed to a high degree of autonomy. When moves were taken after independence to reduce the local autonomy, there were forces strong enough to threaten the success of these efforts.

The Baganda were, however, able to offer a much stronger resistance to the central government by virtue of their strategic position in Uganda, geographically, socially and politically. While the Bahaya were split, the Baganda by and large acted in an identical manner the critical days of May 1966.[3] Finally, the central government of Uganda at that time did not enjoy the same strong authority as its Tanzanian counterpart; it lacked, moreover, the advantage of a well organized political party like TANU. The Uganda experience underlines the importance of a strong party organization, if used properly, in the process of building up a new regime.

An attempt will be made in this chapter to analyze the general predispositions of the rural Bahaya towards the new regime. Three aspects have been selected: (1) the Haya reaction to the new value of "equality", put in practice in Buhaya for the first time with the new independent regime; (2) their attitude towards the political norm, that a government should act quickly; and (3) their opinion about the structural arrangement of the one-party system. The last section of the chapter will be devoted to an analysis of the relation between the national set on the one hand, and the traditional set of values, norms and structures, on the other.

No analysis will be made in this chapter of government performance on specific issues, although it is likely to affect the legitimacy of the regime. This type of government output, however, will be dealt with in Chapter 10 and 11. The focus here is on political dispositions towards the regime and the capacity of the system to control political conflicts growing out of the general process of change.

Attitudes towards the regime

We have already noted that one of the principal features of the relation of the centre of the political system to the periphery in the colonial period was that of exploitation, while after independence the prescription has been that of reciprocity.[4] The new political leaders have made a case of identifying themselves with the peasants. It is true that the most important single example of this is the Arusha Declaration,[5] which was not adopted until

---

[3] For background information on Buganda, see e.g., Apter, "The Politics ..." *op.cit.*, his book on Buganda, *op.cit.*, and Fallers, "The King's Men", *op.cit.*
[4] See pp. 105 and 139.
[5] See Ch 2.

January 1967. The efforts of adapting the political goals more closely to the aspirations of the majority of the people have, however, been a permanent feature of Tanzanian policies since independence. Some of our questions therefore related to the value of "equality". Do the rural inhabitants have expectations of equal treatment? We are not concerned here with their feelings towards governmental authorities as much as we are with their opinion about what type of regime they prefer. When the following statement "The government should give fair and equal treatment to all" was read to them almost all respondents tended to agree. This could perhaps have been expected, and the question was therefore superfluous. On the other hand, it should be remembered that the principle of equality was by no means commonly accepted in the pre-colonial and colonial society. In fact, in the traditional society people accepted an unegalitarian society, and much of the same thinking prevailed in the colonial period. As late as the 1950s members of the Hinda clan believed that they had the right to enjoy privileges, which other people should not. It was only under pressures from the new political elite that the old ruling dynasties in Buhaya changed their attitudes and accepted a wider social intercourse with other members of the society.

In order to substantiate the information on this point the respondents were asked a question with direct relevance to Buhaya: "Do you agree or disagree with the following statement: 'The abolition of the *nyarubanja* system was a step in the right direction' ". The reason for asking this question was to find out who would agree with a political decision that was likely to affect human relationships in Buhaya in the direction of a higher degree of social and economic equality. The answers were distributed in the following way:

Table 15. Opinions about the abolition of the *nyarubanja* system; by parish. Absolute number in brackets.

(in %)	Bugombe	Kitendagulo	Bwatangabo	Kabagunda	Kiruruma
agree	89,5 (52)	94 (53)	94 (92)	95,5 (69)	90,5 (40)
disagree	10,5 (6)	6 (3)	6 (6)	4,5 (3)	9,5 (4)
Total	100 (58)	100 (56)	100 (98)	100 (72)	100 (44)

The origin of the *nyarubanja* system was connected with the way by which rewards and patronage were distributed in the old Haya society. A holder of *nyarubanja* land was a member of the "upper class". He combined political office with high status and economic privileges. Tenants on his land were by and large dependent on the holder, and had to pay an annual tribute to him. The burden increased in the colonial period, when tenants besides tribute to their master had to pay local tax.[6] Although probably no more than every fifth or sixth person was a *nyarubanja* tenant in the colonial period,[7] the system had in the final phase of that period become a "hot" political issue; TANU took a strong stand against its perpetuation.[8]

The pattern of answers in the five parishes is very uniform. Nine out of ten respondents think the abolition of the feudal land tenure system was correct. A combination of personal experiences and the exposure to new values, disseminated by educational institutions and the new political organization, TANU, is a likely explanation for the consolidation of an egalitarian orientation in various walks of life. In the TANU message at the time of independence was a promise of a better life ahead; of people becoming their own masters. The nationalist movement prescribed an alternative way of life, aimed at all men regardless of religious, ethnic or other social differences. The question in which we were particularly interested was to what extent independence still was regarded as a turning-point on which human predispositions depended. The villagers were therefore asked the following, open-ended question: "Can you think of any event in the life of this country, not just something that has happened in the village or district, but some event that has affected the whole nation, which has also made a difference in your life?" The answers are recorded in the following table.

Table 16. Opinions about what has made a difference to the nation and to the respondent's life; by parish. Absolute number in brackets.

(in %)	Bugombe		Kitenda-gulo		Bwatan-gabo		Kaba-gunda		Kiru-ruma	
independence	22,5	(13)	9	(5)	32	(31)	30,5	(22)	20,5	(9)
abolition of traditional authorities	5	(3)	—	(0)	4	(4)	4	(3)	7	(3)
a better govt.	7	(4)	5,5	(3)	4	(4)	1,5	(1)	9	(4)
a worse govt.	4	(2)	11	(6)	9	(9)	1,5	(1)	—	(0)
other non-political events	10	(6)	—	(0)	9	(9)	5,5	(4)	9	(4)
none or don't know	51,5	(30)	74,5	(42)	42	(41)	57	(41)	54,5	(24)
total	100	(58)	100	(56)	100	(98)	100	(72)	100	(44)

[6] Cf., p. 101.

[7] Reining in her paper on Haya land tenure, *op.cit.*, claims that 16,5 % of the landholders in Buhaya are only tenants, not owners of their land. In this figure, however, she also includes a more recent system of tenancy, which developed in the colonial period and was based on somewhat different principles than the original *nyarubanja* system.

[8] See p. 130.

The figures indicate that independence is still regarded as the most important event by a considerable number of people. The change of regime has brought about something different, supposedly something better, although there are a few who maintain that the present government is worse than the colonial government. This number is, however, small. One might have expected that a larger number of respondents would have mentioned the abolition of power of the traditional authorities. After all, that was in a sense a much more concrete political move. The inference that could be drawn from this is that a considerable number of respondents do think in terms of the total political system, and not just in terms of what goes on at the local level.

The other important finding, however, is that a large percentage cannot mention any event at all. One possible explanation would of course be, lack of interest in the affairs outside the local community; the persistence of parochial attitudes. But it is not likely to be the only explanation. A very large percentage of this category of respondents come from Kitendagulo, the most developed, at least the most socially differentiated, parish of all. They probably have other motives such as the fact that materially the condition may not have improved significantly in the last decade, due among other things to a low coffee price. The inhabitants of Kitendagulo have the greatest reason to consider material conditions, as they, more than the others, due to their proximity to town, are likely to have developed the strongest material needs.

The Bahaya appreciate concrete steps in the direction of equality, such as the abolition of the *nyarubanja* system; and a substantial number of people do consider independence as an important event, and are therefore likely, although not necessarily, to identify with the present regime. In short, the Bahaya have high expectations of the new regime. What implications this will have on their opinion of the performance of the government authorities will be the subject of the two following chapters.

Tanzania is a nation in hurry.[9] It is one of the poorest countries in the world. It has been a deliberate policy of independent Tanzania to make a case of trying to "catch up" with other nations. In the first years the strategy had been to rely mainly on foreign aid. After the Arusha Declaration the emphasis has shifted in the direction of a higher degree of reliance on domestic resources—the principle of "self-reliance". The way the Haya villagers thought of the pace of change in 1965 is reflected in the following table:

[9] This is the title of a recent book on Tanzania: A. MacDonald, *Tanzania—Young Nation in Hurry*, (New York 1966).

Table 17. Opinions about whether "a government should get things done quickly"; by parish. Absolute number in brackets.

(in %)	Bugombe	Kitenda-gulo	Bwatan-gabo	Kaba-gunda	Kiru-ruma
agree	77,5 (45)	87,5 (49)	95 (93)	83 (60)	80 (36)
disagree	22,5 (13)	12,5 (7)	5 (5)	17 (12)	20 (8)
total	100 (58)	100 (56)	100 (98)	100 (72)	100 (44)

There is a uniform pattern in each of the parishes. At least four out of five respondents are interested in quick government action. The answers therefore indicate a strong predisposition in favor of rapid social and economic development. Other material also suggest that the Bahaya by and large are "development-conscious" rather than "power-conscious"; they are more interested in obtaining positions whereby they directly can make a concrete contribution to development. This may be through positions such as doctor, teacher or engineer, rather than in positions which primarily carry power in society—politician or police officer.[10]

Rapid development, however, also implies a large contribution by the people itself, particularly in a less developed country, where resources are scarce. One of our questions therefore aimed at illuminating to what extent people in the villages really feel that the government is pressing them too much under present circumstances: "Do you think the government expects too much of the people?"

Table 18. Beliefs about whether the government is expecting too much of the people; by parish. Absolute number in brackets.

(in %)	Bugombe	Kitendagulo	Bwatangabo	Kabagunda	Kiruruma
yes	30 (17)	40 (22)	36 (35)	51,5 (37)	81 (35)
no	63 (37)	51 (29)	57 (56)	37,5 (27)	17 (8)
don't know	7 (4)	9 (5)	5 (5)	11 (7)	2 (1)
no infor	— (0)	— (0)	2 (2)	— (0)	— (0)
total	100 (58)	100 (56)	100 (98)	100 (72)	100 (44)

There is a clear difference here between the answers obtained in the three eastern parishes, on the one hand, and Kabagunda and Kiruruma on the other. The feeling that the government expects too much of the people

[10] Hyden, "Attitudes among School Children . . .", op.cit.

is particularly widespread in the Karagwe parish. This suggests, as Kiruruma and Karagwe are generally poorer in terms of per capita income, that this opinion is closely related to economic status. We will return to discuss that assumption later in this chapter. With reference to the material in Table 17 and 18 one may establish the fact that by and large people do not mind a high pace of change, but it is more difficult for them to agree that they themselves should have to make a contribution to development, or that the government can ask them to make sacrifices in the name of development. This suggests that a large portion of the population have a subject orientation towards the political system; they expect primarily rewards of the political system.[11]

The third set of questions refer to the legitimacy of the one-party structures. The complete domination by one political party is a relatively recent phenomenon in Buhaya. Other parties existed in Buhaya until 1963. Not until then did TANU become the single recognized political authority in the area. In the pre-colonial times, however, the Bahaya were accustomed to one political authority. Much of this thinking is likely to have survived also in the modern context. Therefore, one important thing to know is whether the villagers were prepared to give any credit to a system based on the principle of competition for power or they preferred a system in which only one authority was allowed to wield power. The following statement "A good government cannot exist without a one-party system" was read to them, and the answers were distributed in the following manner in the five parishes:

Table 19. Opinions about the one-party system; by parish. Absolute number in brackets.

(in %)	Bugombe		Kitendagulo		Bwatangabo		Kabagunda		Kiruruma	
agree	89,5	(52)	78,5	(44)	89	(87)	80	(58)	84	(37)
disagree	10,5	(6)	21,5	(12)	10	(10)	17	(12)	16	(7)
no infor	—	(0)	—	(0)	1	(1)	3	(2)	—	(0)
total	100	(58)	100	(56)	100	(98)	100	(72)	100	(44)

This reveals a strong preference for a system in which competition for loyalties to the regime is minimal. The conclusions to be drawn from this table are limited because, inter alia, of the way such a question had to be asked in order not to frighten the interviewee. In order to obtain supplementary information on this matter, the villagers were requested to give

[11] Cf., Almond and Verba, op.cit., pp. 17—18.

their view on another statement: "Any person who opposes TANU policy or TANU leaders should be detained." These are the answers:

Table 20. Opinions about the detention of those who oppose TANU; by parish. Absolute number in brackets.

(in %)	Bugombe		Kitendagulo		Bwatangabo		Kabagunda		Kiruruma	
agree strongly	41	(24)	21,5	(12)	41	(40)	50	(36)	52	(23)
agree	41	(24)	34	(19)	27,5	(27)	43	(43)	37	(16)
indifferent	1,5	(1)	9	(6)	1	(1)	—	(0)	2	(1)
disagree	5,5	(3)	3,5	(2)	4	(4)	6	(4)	7	(3)
disagree strongly	1,5	(1)	3,5	(2)	4	(4)	1	(1)	—	(0)
no infor	9,5	(5)	28,5	(15)	22,5	(22)	—	(0)	2	(1)
total	100	(58)	100	(56)	100	(98)	100	(72)	100	(44)

The figures in this table confirm those of the previous table. The Bahaya have a clear preference for a system with an undisputed political authority. Those who oppose the authority in power are regarded as being opposed to the whole system. A very large number of the respondents consequently believe that these people should be detained.

So far the presentation in this chapter has been made solely by parish, and we have seen that there exists on most of the matters a high degree of consensus in each parish. Nor are there any significant differences between the parishes; the pattern of answers to most of the questions is rather uniform. There are, however, persons who deviate from the majority opinion; those who believe that the *nyarubanja* system was good; those who disagree with a rapid pace of change; and those who disagree with the idea of a one-party system being the best form of government. We are now therefore turning to the question: "Who are these people?" Can differences in opinion be referred back to social or economic characteristics? The answers are found in Table 21.

Only a very small group—in fact less than 10 per cent of the total sample —found that the abolition of *nyarubanja* holdings was a bad move. It is obvious therefore, that any farreaching conclusions cannot be drawn from an analysis of the respondents who objected to the policy. All the same, it may be worth while pointing out—as the trend is quite clear—that those who are disagreeing with the general opinion on this matter are, by and large, people with such characteristics as old age, no education, farm occupation and low exposure to mass media. The figures also suggest that people with large coffee farms are more inclined to disagree than those with

Table 21. Comparison between selected answers to questions on the legitimacy of the regime; by age, education, size of farm, occupation, media exposure and party membership. Absolute number in brackets.

percentage who answer:	Age			Education			Size of farm			Occupation		Media exposure				Party membership	
	young (132)	middle-aged (130)	old (63)	none (144)	some (118)	much (66)	small (108)	middle-size (126)	big (63)	agr. (270)	non-agr. (58)	very often (34)	often (67)	not so often (95)	never (116)	Yes (225)	No (55)
disagree with the abolition of *nyarubanja* holdings	3,5	4,5	17,5	9,5	4	4,5	5,5	7	11	8	—	3	4,5	7	9,5	8	7
mention independence as most important event	30	21,5	25,5	22	23,5	35,5	20	22	30	25	26	26,5	25	27	25	30,5	25,5
do not like government to get things done quickly	13,5	13	17,5	12,5	13,5	18	22	14	6	13	19	11,5	10,5	16,5	16,5	16,5	16,5
government demands too much	57,5	38	33	44,5	52,5	30	56,5	40,5	37,5	46	36	35	33	42	49,5	44	56
one-party system not necessary for good government	13,5	18	9,5	12,5	13,5	19,5	15,5	14	12	13	20	20,5	18	14,5	12	17,5	12,5
TANU opponents should not be detained	14,5	4,5	12,5	6	10,5	15	7,5	12,5	6,5	9,5	12	12	18	9,5	8,5	12	10,5

middle-size and small farms. Party membership, however, does not seem to influence the opinion of the respondent on this issue.

The most significant finding with regard to the opinion of the respondents on the *nyarubanja* question is the general satisfaction with its abolition. Those who feel the other way, however, are most likely to be people, whose minds still are extensively guided by traditional values, because they are old, have not been exposed to modern education or modern mass media, et cetera. The finding is not surprising.

The people who answered that political independence in 1961 was an important event to them as well as to the nation is the next category worth further examination. Their answers indicate to what extent people view the new regime as legitimate, or at least to what extent people tend to view the new regime as basically different from the previous one. We are interested to know to which category of people independence has meant much. As the figures in Table 21 show, young people more often than middle-aged and old people tend to mention "independence". Similarly, those with high education do it more often than less educated, and large farmers more often than other farmers. There is also a tendency for party members to mention it more often than those who are not members. Interestingly enough, degree of media exposure does not seem to determine a person's inclination to mention independence as the single most important event with effect both on the nation and on the respondent himself.

There were some people who could not mention a national event, but who did mention, in answer to a supplementary question, local events, such as the fall of the coffee price. By and large, people who could mention an event with impact on themselves as well as the wider community referred to events with a positive connotation, such as "independence", "better government leaders" and so forth. That young and educated members of the society should feel the impact of independence most strongly could be expected. After all, they have potentially greater chances to reap the benefit of *uhuru* than, in particular, the old people.

One probable effect of independence is that people's expectations have risen. The promises of a better future, of an egalitarian society with more education and better health facilities have, as shown above, not been forgotten. Moreover, as the figures in Table 17 suggest, the villagers want their government to accomplish these reforms immediately. Some however, do not feel that rapid government action in exclusively desirable. A large portion of this category are small farmers, but another considerable group are the educated persons in non-agricultural professions. It is hard to decide whether their answers reflect a genuinely "conservative" attitude. One could assume that small farmers have the greatest problem of accomodating to extensive reforms; at least they believe themselves that this is the case. Even if there are advantages to be drawn from rapid government execution of policies, they think that the disadvantages are more acute. The reluctance of the educated members of society may be based on more sophisticated reasons, and be partly connected with the general performance of the government authorities. They believe that money could be allocated more effectively; that the policies should rest on firmer basis of facts. This conclusion is at least supported by the answers to another question, about the ideals of good government and good statesmen, which reads as follows: "Which do you think is more important: that the political leaders have good ideas that they can carry out, or that they do not waste money?" Members of the more highly educated sector of the population tend to prefer the latter alternative in a larger proportion than those without or with only a few years of schooling. Since the pattern is relatively similar in all five parishes the analysis has been made only by education.

Table 22. Preference for leaders with good ideas or for leaders who do not waste money; by education. Absolute number in brackets.

	Education		
prefer: (in %)	none (143)	some (119)	much (66)
leaders with good ideas	33 (47)	32,5 (39)	24 (16)
leaders who do not waste money	65 (93)	65,5 (78)	74 (49)

One gets additional information on the attitudes towards change by further analyzing the answers to the question if the government expects too much of the people. As the figures in Table 21 suggest, young small farmers with none or only little education constitute a large portion of those who believe that the government has too high expectations of the people. As they are young, and supposedly, therefore, have quite high expectations themselves about what to achieve in life, they may feel the implications of the low coffee price and the increasing tax rates even more than other categories of respondents. They are conscious about the need for development but incapable of materializing any improvements for themselves. They feel that it is the duty of the government to do more for them rather than they for the government. This group of people as suggested on p. 165, is the one which finds life hard under the present regime, although it is true of course, that the fault of their hardship is not necessarily that of the present regime and its incumbents. As is shown in the following table, the dissatisfaction is much more widespread among the young uneducated small farmers than it is among uneducated elders with a comparable size of the farm:

Table 23. Proportion of young and old small farmers with no formal education of the total number of respondents answering that the government expects too much of the people; by parish. Absolute number in brackets.

(in %)	Bugombe (17)	Kiten-dagulo (22)	Bwatan-gabo (35)	Kaba-gunda (37)	Kiru-ruma (35)
young, uneducated small farmers	23,5	36	31	20,5	40
old, uneducated small farmers	11,5	13,5	8,5	13	8,5

The pattern is relatively uniform in each parish. Somewhat exceptional is the situation in Kabagunda, where the proportion of young farmers is lower than elsewhere. The reason that the pattern is different in Kabagunda can at least partly be explained by the fact that several of the young farmers also engage in trading and fishing and hence have a second source of income. Their economic hardship due to the small size of the farm is therefore eased.

The idea that the government expects too much also came out in the course of the supplementary interviews which were held with a selected group of the original sample. One of the young small farmers in Bugombe said:

... Nowadays people are poorer, because taxes have increased, and so have the prices of many things; moreover, food is scanty...

Another respondent belonging to the same category, also from Bugombe, maintained that:

People are getting discouraged because they believe that the government is sucking up all their money...

In the supplementary interviews there were also mentioned as reasons for the poverty the fact that the government was no longer relying on outside foreign help like the British colonial government used to do. Reliance on foreign aid is sometimes said to be the easiest way out of the economic problems that Tanzania is facing. This opinion runs, however, contrary to the policy of the present government, particularly of course after the adoption of the Arusha Declaration. The people who are holding this opinion are likely to get little sympathy from a government, which rather wants to pursue a policy of self-reliance.[12]

There is another interesting factor implied in the answers of the small farmers. This is the idea that the government, rather than the people

[12] Cf., pp. 48—50.

themselves, should bear the responsibility for the well-being and development of society. The prevalence of this idea suggests that traditional values persist in the modern context. In a society like Buhaya, where communal labor for the benefit of the whole community was unknown, it was believed that the chief, and only the chief, was responsible for the well-being of his chiefdom.[13] The same opinion was reinforced by the colonial regime although a change in opinion took place in certain sectors of the population, particularly those who had withdrawn their support for the traditional authorities. Still, however, a very large part of the population is likely to believe that the primary aim of the political system is to offer its members rewards.

The small farmers who believe that government expects too much of the people are seldom or never exposed to radio or newspapers; this is particularly true of the old, uneducated farmers. There is, finally, an indication that party members are less likely to express agreement with the view that the government is "pushing the people" too far. Party allegiance may therefore make them more prepared to accept sacrifices in the interest of the whole community.

There is wide consensus in the rural communities in Buhaya that a one-party system is a precondition for a good government. A larger part of the respondents also find it correct that people opposing the regime—and also the incumbent authorities—should be detained. The young educated people who occupy non-agricultural positions constitute, however, an important group opposed to this idea. These people are more inclined to accept that authority in society can be diffuse—that it can be shared by two or more institutions or groups. The figures in Table 21 tend to confirm, what has sometimes been maintained in Tanzania, that it is the more highly educated sector of the population who have found it most difficult to subordinate themselves to the authority of one political party.[14] The reasons are probably many. It is likely to be related to their exposure to new values at school, their own position in society, and so forth.[15]

That such a large a number of people prefer a one-party system is not simply expressed in fear of intimidation or out of sheer compliance. After all, the idea of unlimited power in the hands of one single authority is the only one which people traditionally know. In the old Haya society opposition to this authority, the chief, was regarded as illegitimate; it was a way of destroying social peace and harmony in society.[16] The Bahaya have al-

[13] Cf., p. 83.
[14] Cf., pp. 133—34.
[15] See President Nyerere's speech on "Education and Self-reliance", *The Nationalist,* February 10, 1967; reprinted in *Africa Report,* (Vol. XII, June 1967).
[16] The Haya conception of life can be compared with the information on other African tribes in D. Forde's *African Worlds,* (Oxford 1954).

ways aspired to live in peace, *emilembe.* One implication of this way of looking at life is that it must be bad to create dissension within the community. According to the Haya conception such a man associates himself with the destructive forces in the world.[17] He departs from the ideal, which is to be a *muntu murungi,* or in Kiswahili, a *mtu wa amani.* Many people in Buhaya even today profess the same ideal, when asked about for which quality they want to be admired:

Table 24. Opinions about personal qualities for which the respondent want to be admired; by parish.[18] Absolute number in brackets.

(in %)	Bugombe	Kitendagulo	Bwatangabo	Kabagunda	Kiruruma
peaceful, love others	65 (37)	73 (41)	78 (76)	28 (20)	32 (14)
hard-working	12 (7)	7 (4)	5 (5)	5,5 (4)	7 (3)
rich	— (0)	2 (1)	1 (1)	5,5 (4)	2 (1)
others	18 (11)	13 (7)	10 (10)	18 (12)	22 (10)
don't know	5 (3)	5 (3)	6 (6)	43 (32)	37 (16)
total	100 (58)	100 (56)	100 (98)	100 (72)	100 (44)

To "love others" or to be "peaceful" are the most desirable qualities of which people can think. The pattern is particularly conspicuous in eastern Buhaya. In Kabagunda and Kiruruma several respondents felt it hard to answer the question or simply did not, for various reasons, want to mention any quality at all. Even in these parishes, however, no other single quality was so frequently mentioned as "peaceful" and "love others". This suggests that the Bahaya pay very much attention to how a man behaves; they appreciate him according to his contribution to a peaceful community.

The point is, however, that it is becoming increasingly more difficult to uphold this ideal in a society which becomes more and more differentiated; in which people move into new roles, and where traditional patterns of relations are destroyed. This brings us to the question of whether the modern regime has replaced the traditional one, or whether the latter still survives; whether the character of the political sub-culture in Buhaya is such that it supports Zolberg's point about the African societies being "syncretic".[19]

[17] An interesting analysis of the Haya conception of life is found in Bennetsson, *op.cit.*

[18] It is worth noting that when asked how they would describe themselves an almost identical pattern of answers was obtained.

[19] Cf., p. 159, footnote 2.

"The cultural gap"

The question of how modern and traditional sets of values, norms and structures relate to each other has only very recently been the subject of research in the new African states.[20] The question is very pertinent and the answers that will be provided from research on this matter are likely to increase our understanding of along which lines the political culture in the African states may grow.

In order to substantiate our material from the interviews, a closer look has been made at the minutes of the Village Development Committees in the five parishes. This way we will get material not only about how people think but also about how they *act*. This exercise may be particularly relevant since the VDCs have replaced traditional institutions at the local level and been prescribed to perform primarily different functions from those of the old structures. The VDCs are first of all meant to be tools in the development process, while the former village councils and the mukungu as their main responsibility had to maintain law and order. One interesting question is what functions the VDCs *really* perform. Have they taken over some of those performed by the old structures?

So many new potential areas of conflict at the local level have emerged as a result of the modernization of the society itself and the decline of the social and political autonomy of each village or parish community. One can expect that in an area like Buhaya which has always been so concerned with order and peace in society,[21] alternative practices are going to grow up if it is proved that the original objectives of the new institutions, the VDCs, do not include control of all major aspects of social life.

One objective of this study has therefore been to read through the VDC minutes in the five parishes in order to find out more specifically with what types of matters they are dealing. As the minutes are not very exhaustive, it is impossible to grade the matters according to their importance to the local community at a particular time. It should also be noted that some VDC secretaries are more careful and ambitious than others; consequently there is necessarily a variation in quality of the minutes. All the same they give a rough indication of what does concern the local community and can be used as an additional way of showing how modern and traditional structures, values and norms interact.

All matters brought up before the VDCs in a two year period, 1963—65, have been read and classified according to which developmental problem

[20] The question is dealt with by, for instance, Violaine Junod, "Community Development and National Planning: The Tanganyika Case", *International Review of Community Development*, (Rome 1966).

[21] The concern with peace and order is typical of all peasant societies; cf. Banfield, *op.cit.,* p. 93.

they refer. Hence, calls for unity or the use of Kiswahili at public occasions are listed under the problem of identity; matters concerning the rights and duties of the VDCs or criticism of the political leaders under the problem of legitimacy, and so forth.

From the figures in Table 25 one can conclude that problems relating to the regulative and extractive capability of the system are most frequently discussed. It is very common that the VDC meetings are characterized by the leaders exhorting the people to contribute to the building of a school or a new health clinic, but also by the leaders informing the villagers about new rules regarding the sale of beer or the paying of fees and licences, and so forth. The new Tanzanian government is not satisfied with leaving the local communities with a high degree of autonomy. It operates according to universal principles. The whole society has to be imbued with the same values. The material from the VDCs suggests, however, that the transmission of new values and new regulations is complicated; the expansion from the centre is a gradual process. It takes long time for the many rural inhabitants to realize the need for a higher degree of centralization. When the customary law becomes less and less valid for guiding the relationship between men, they have to be constantly reminded of the new rules and regulations. Our material indicates that the VDC leaders are prepared to assume this burden, and help improve the expansion of the modern set of structures, values and norms.

Table 25. Matters brought up before the Village Developmei. Committees between March 1963 and March 1965.

Problem type:	Bugombe	Kiten-dagulo	Bwatan-gabo	Kaba-gunda	Kiru-ruma	Total
Identity:						
call for unity and cooperation	5	2	1	1	1	10
call for cooperation between leaders	5	1	2	—	—	8
organization of national celebrations	2	—	1	1	—	4
call for use of Kiswahili	—	1	—	—	—	1
Legitimacy:						
rights and duties of the VDC	6	10	6	4	3	29
critique of political leaders	3	1	—	3	2	9
local rules read	37	14	14	18	3	86

	Bugombe	Kiten-dagulo	Bwatan-gabo	Kaba-gunda	Kiru-ruma	Total
Legitimacy:						
cases where rules have been broken	33	22	18	21	15	109
people criticized for abuse of political leaders	2	3	5	2	1	13
others	25	11	7	6	—	49
Penetration:						
general information from district or national level	6	3	1	4	—	14
general call for self-help work	4	5	9	5	1	24
call to:						
build schools	17	6	7	8	6	48
cultivate	26	14	18	14	5	77
health clinic	10	2	13	9	5	39
build roads, and other projects	7	4	12	13	—	36
Allocation:						
tax remittance and other tax issues	20	3	20	5	5	**53**
request for govt assistance in:						
agricultural projects	2	2	2	—	—	**6**
other projects	5	2	2	1	—	10
gratitude expressed to the people	3	2	4	2	—	11
Participation:						
matters related to local participation in politics	24	16	6	7	3	56
others	3	4	2	3	1	13
Total	245	128	151	128	51	703
Number of meetings held	47	32	23	27	17	146

One may therefore say that the modern government structures are visible in the local communities, and the fact that the village or parish leaders accept to be agencies of the central government is likely to affect also the local political culture. Some VDCs meet more frequently than others; one may, for instance, compare Bugombe to Kiruruma in order to realize the differences, in terms of visibility and effectiveness of the VDCs, that exist at the local level. One finding, when reading through the VDC minutes is, however, that the local committees take on rather too many than too few functions. In the pre-independent society, when local autonomy was still considerable, there were special institutions to deal with local matters, such as sorcery and witchcraft, land disputes, and so forth. Nowadays these are not allowed to exist, or they are no longer trusted by the people. They therefore turn to the VDC, which also tends to operate as an adjudicative authority. This indicates that people have confidence in their leaders and the new institutions. But often the VDCs go beyond their original powers. In a dispute between two villagers the VDC may sentence one of them to pay fines. The committee has no right to do this; the case should have been brought to the local court. Still this type of cases occur, and explains why the minutes contain paragraphs which say that a government leader from Bukoba has told the committee members what powers they have, and not have. There might be some confusion as to the powers of the VDC also among higher government officials, but as one local government officer explained, the VDCs cannot deal with land cases or coffee smuggling, in which the law of the country clearly is involved. It can, however, punish people who, for instance, refuse to participate in self-help projects. In these cases the political leaders are allowed to pass judgment. Whether or not the VDC can decide to ostracize a person from the local community who has not committed a legal crime is, however, a more sensitive matter. It has happened on a number of occasions in Buhaya during 1963—65, that the VDC has decided to ostracize a person who has been accused by others of bewitching certain people. According to customary law, the parish chief had the right to ostracize a person, if he found this man was threatening the order of his community. Nobody can say with any certainty whether the VDCs have the same right.[22] This is a clear case therefore, of where traditional values have remained important, because there is no specific reference to this type of cases in the modern regulations. There is a cultural gap or a vacuum, in which the VDC acts as the bridge between the national and local community and between modern and traditional values.

The strong concern in the VDCs with upholding rules and regulations can also be explained in the face of a widespread feeling that crimes have

[22] This information was obtained in conversations with local government officers in the Bukoba District Council at various occasions in 1965—66.

increased and that the central government does not do enough to break the trend. The dissolution of traditional codes of behavior and the increasing rate of crimes are also considered as main problems by a selected sample of Village Executive Officers in Bukoba and Karagwe Districts.[23] This category of local leaders maintains that it does not get enough help from the superior government agencies to solve the problems that the local population considers most urgent. There is, therefore, in the village communities, a feeling that the government is not doing enough to regulate the behavior of people. Despite attempts by the VDC leaders to make government presence at the local level meaningful, some people, including the VEOs, do not see the benefits of the new regulations, since they relate to problems which are not regarded as equally important by the local population.

It is against this background one has to view the relatively common opinion in the rural communities of Buhaya that the abolition of chiefly power has created a vacuum in their home areas. This question was asked with the specific aim of finding out whether the traditional authorities still meant anything to the villagers.

Table 26. Opinions about whether the abolition of chiefly power has left a vacuum in society; by parish. Absolute number in brackets.

(in %)	Bugombe	Kiten- dagulo	Bwatan- gabo	Kaba- gunda	Kiru- ruma
agree	43 (25)	28,5 (16)	30 (29)	50 (36)	58,5 (26)
disagree	57 (33)	71,5 (40)	69 (68)	48,5 (35)	41,5 (18)
no infor	— (0)	— (0)	1 (1)	1,5 (1)	— (0)
total	100 (58)	100 (56)	100 (98)	100 (72)	100 (44)

It is very difficult to know exactly how these figures should be interpreted. It is most unlikely, however, that it should be taken as a proof that the villagers wish to restore the old order. It is probably rather connected with the idea that the reduced importance of the traditional authorities so far has not been compensated by a corresponding increase in the capacity of the present government to regulate the behavior of the citizens so that criminal and other mischievious activities are reduced. Age, education, religion, occupation, and so forth, are on this matter less important variables than the geographical location of the parish. Government presence is less visible in Kabagunda and Kiruruma. There are fewer VDC meetings and

[23] G. Hyden, "Problems of Village Administration in Tanzania" paper prepared for the Political Science Research Programme, Makerere University College, (Kampala 1966).

the two parishes are less accessible for government officials from Bukoba. Kabagunda and Kiruruma have visits by superior government officials much more seldom than places like Bugombe, Kitendagulo and Bwatangabo. The widespread agreement, in places like Kabagunda and Kiruruma, with the statement that—chiefly power has left a vacuum in society—is, therefore, likely to depend on the reasons just stated.

A final comment about the figures in Table 25 is that problems relating to the creation of cooperation and a national identity have been brought up rarely compared to other problems. This tends to confirm, therefore, that the Bahaya in their present socio-economic and political position in the country-side are not opposing the attempts to create a national political community, in which the local sub-communities will have to accept a wider framework of cooperation and mutual responsibility. Another interesting feature in the minutes is that, there are few references to actual requests for government assistance in various local development projects. There is less traffic of demands "upwards" than "downwards". This suggests the following conclusions: (a) A large number of matters are solved at the local level without the need for government assistance. There is also some evidence to support this. A number of local self-help projects in these parishes have been completed without outside help. The consequence is that the demands on the system itself are reduced; central government authorities are being less "overloaded" by local demands. (b) The local leaders may also be aware that it does not pay to ask for government help, either because the government is not able, or it is not willing, to satisfy local demands. (c) The third conclusion is that the local leaders may not know how to use the political structures to their advantage. They lack what Almond and Verba call "civic competence";[24] they do not think they can affect governmental decisions by using their influence. More about this will be discussed in Chapter 12.

In many countries in the world, the legitimacy of the regime depends on who are the incumbents in government roles. Members of such political systems judge the validity of the regime on basis of such questions as, "Which group do the incumbent authorities represent?" "What qualifications do they have?" and so forth. One might say that a political system has passed a critical stage of development when its members are able and willing to distinguish between the legitimacy of the regime and the legitimacy of the incumbent government authorities. The costs of system maintenance is likely to be reduced if the members can afford to make a distinction between change of political incumbents and change of regime; that one must not lead to the other, or be achieved simultaneously. Most African states, like several states elsewhere in the world, including Western

[24] Almond and Verba, *op.cit.*, Ch. VI.

Europe, have not reached this stage yet. The regime depends on the authority of one or a few persons. It is possible, however, that the Tanzanian political system is less exclusively depending on the authority of a few persons than many other countries in Africa, although much of the legitimacy of the present regime can be attributed to the authority of President Nyerere himself.

The high turn-out at the polls in the 1965 general election in Tanzania is an indication that the regime itself enjoys a high degree of legitimacy. In Buhaya, for instance, two thirds of all registered voters—which is approximately two thirds of the estimated adult population—voted. As was found in both Dar es Salaam and Buhaya, the reasons why people did not vote were almost exclusively connected with private incapacities.[25] While the electorate showed a high degree of confidence in the regime by going to the polls, they rejected a large number of incumbent political leaders, at the national as well as the regional and district level. In Buhaya, for instance, Edward Barongo, was defeated.

The problem of the legitimacy of the government leaders is very severe, particularly in countries where resources are scarce and where there is little sign of general development in society. Persons who very rapidly have reached the apex of the political system are likely to be viewed by others as "self-seeking", if their way of life or general behavior is also altered as a result of their quick promotion. Some of this opinion came out in the supplementary interviews that were made. One young educated man said:

... The situation has become worse in recent years because President Nyerere chose leaders who only know how to talk, but are not at all educated.

Another man had the following opinion about the behavior of certain political leaders:

... There is at lack of competent and sincere leaders. Each and every one wants to feel a boss in his area.

Political leaders are always blamed for lack of development in society, although in many cases the reasons for this lie beyond the influence and control of these leaders. Many political problems in African countries, for instance, are due to the low prices offered on the world market for certain primary products. All the same, in Tanzania the low price on coffee and cotton is often blamed on the government, which is said to take all the money away from the farmer by a system of fees and taxes.[26]

People in a rural area like Buhaya, certainly, do not lack articulate opinions about their political leaders. They believe, for instance, that a success-

[25] K. Prewitt and G. Hyden, "Voters Look at the Election", in L. Cliffe (ed), *op.cit.*, pp. 275—76. See also p. 229.
[26] In 1966 the Tanzanian Government sent out a brief circular to all cotton farmers in Sukumaland explaining the reasons for the low income of the individual farmers.

ful politician should be equipped with such qualities as "being social with the people", "honest" or "frank",[27] which indicates that they have high expectations of their leaders. The President himself is also aware of these opinions among the people. He realizes that the legitimacy of the regime is not enough. The leaders must also be legitimate. The people must have confidence not only in their government but also in their government leaders.[28] This awareness on part of the principal leader of government is likely to serve as a moral check also on other leaders, and should therefore help upholding a popular confidence in the incumbent authorities.

Conclusions

The last two chapters have shown that the impact by an increased measure of contact with the national political life has been among the villagers, not alienation or resistance, but rather an identification with the new nation and the new regime. The strong support for the prescribed values, norms and structures also implies, however, very high expectations of actual government performance. One of the problems that may arise from this situation is, that the government leaders always fail to live up to the prescriptions of the regime. This is not, of course, a problem unique to Tanzania. It exists in every country in the world, but it is likely to become particularly grave in the less developed countries, where the freedom of action of the government is constrained by lack of material resources. There are, for instance, as shown above, some indications that the Bahaya would blame actual problems in the country on the political leaders. The relation between the legitimacy of the regime and the incumbent political leaders will be subject to further discussion in the next chapters.

Another conclusion is that lack of confidence in the government is little related to such questions as the existence of a one-party system. The majority supports the idea that political authority should be undivided, as they agree with the principle of equality and rapid political change. When it comes to questions about regulation of human behavior, people in the villages would like to see a stronger and more visible government authority. There is a substantial group of people who feel that the government does not pay enough attention to this aspect of political development.

[27] Prewitt and Hyden, op.cit., pp. 283—84.
[28] This is an idea, which is most clearly expressed in the "Leadership resolution" of the Arusha Declaration.

Chapter 10.   The problem of penetration

In the previous two chapters, references were made to the general pre-dispositions of the Haya population towards the national political community and the political regime. If, like in Buhaya, the members of the system have favorable attitudes towards the regime and the community, the costs of running the political system are likely to be lower than in a system where the community and the regime are seriously questioned. This does not mean, however, that the members necessarily have a high opinion of the performance by the government authorities. If something goes wrong it is often the political incumbents who are blamed. This is, as indicated before the case particularly in less developed countries where scarce material resources put very severe restrictions as to what government leaders can do to placate the people.

In fact, one of the chief problems in less developed countries is that the leaders instead of satisfying the needs of the people have been forced to ask them for larger contributions to the development of the society. To the individual citizen this means that taxes and fees to the public have increased; that his work is increasingly viewed in terms of its contribution, not only to the needs of a family but the needs of the society and its development. Government authorities have, in order to extract more energies from the individual for the system, begun to penetrate an increasing number of aspects of the daily life of the individual citizen. Of particular interest, in the case of Buhaya, has been the government call for improvement of the coffee cultivation as a way of enlarging the material resources of the country. Haya attitudes to the calls for agricultural improvement have to a large extent been determined by existing land resources and the limited opportunities to extend these without considerable capital investments. Important has also been certain aspects of the local culture, which, as indicated in Ch 4,[1] has been based on the cultivation of coffee. Like peasants in other parts of the world, the rural Bahaya have been used to a social rather than an economic way of reasoning.[2] They created their own rationale for a life in relative seclusion in the village communities based on the ideas of peace, security and self-sufficiency. Much of the traditional thinking has now been abandoned, but some of it still prevails. This has been exempli-

[1] See pp. 82—83.
[2] Cf., e.g., W. I. Thomas and F. Znaniecki, *The Polish Peasant*, (New York 1958), p. 173, and R. Redfield, *Peasant Society and Culture*, (Chicago 1956).

fied in the Haya reaction to the policy of coffee rejuvenation. This policy was originally pursued by the colonial authorities, but the Haya reaction then was very negative.[3] The British had not paid enough attention to the peculiarities of Haya society and since the policy ran contrary to the traditional Haya beliefs, the peasants were reinforced in their resistance to the project. The situation after independence has improved; many Bahaya have accepted the idea of uprooting old coffee trees. Still, government authorities are not totally satisfied. Despite increased efforts by both the agricultural extension service, the Bukoba Cooperative Union and some voluntary agencies to demonstrate and teach methods of cultivation, production figures have not increased significantly.[4] In recent years production of coffee, both Arabica and Robusta, has remained around 10.000 tons a year.[5] In other coffee-producing areas of the country a steady increase has been recorded. The value of the coffee crop in Tanzania rose from £ 6 m. 1963 to £ 11 m. 1964, but according to Mr. Barongo, the Junior Minister for Agriculture, this was mainly due to improvement in quality of the coffee grown in other areas than Buhaya.[6]

Improvements in methods of cultivation have been easier to achieve in some parts of Buhaya than in others. According to BCU, the best response to rejuvenation of coffee has been obtained among farmers in the southern and western parts of Buhaya, including areas around Kamachumu and Lake Ikimba in Kianja. This is where the coffee tradition is least strongly rooted, where land is least scarce, the size of the farms large[7] and where Arabica, which commands a higher price on the world market, rather than Robusta coffee is grown.[8]

Another problem which is as prevalent in Buhaya, as elsewhere in less developed countries, is that individual farmers are reluctant to reinvest capital resources in agricultural development. Some observers of developmental problems in Asia and Africa[9] maintain that economic development

[3] Cf., pp. 115—16.

[4] A report by the West Lake Regional Agricultural Officer, quoted in *The Standard*, (April 1, 1966), says the overall effect of demonstrations to the farmers had been encouraging in that the farmers were applying better husbandry practices. This comment also referred to the methods of growing bananas.

[5] Compare this figure with the diagram on p. 99.

[6] Edward Barongo, "Bukoba coffee suffers from years of neglect", *The Standard*, August 9, 1965.

[7] This information was obtained in interviews with Mr Martin Wamala, Publicity and Education Officer of the BCU; cf., also Appendix II.

[8] A sharp drop in the Robusta price took place in 1965; see *Uganda Argus*, July 24, 1965.

[9] See, e.g., René Dumont, *L'Afrique noire est mal partie*, (Paris 1962), and J. H. Boeke, "Capitalist Development in Indonesia and Uganda: A Contrast" in UNESCO, *Social Change and Economic Development*, (Leiden 1963), pp. 95—96.

will only take place when the male is replacing the female as principal agriculturist; when production for subsistence is ousted from the first place by production for the market and for profit; when occupation becomes business and the family provider becomes an entrepreneur. To some extent these changes have already, it is true, been achieved in Buhaya but still, however, a great number of people in the villages adhere to the traditional beliefs about agricultural production. Men are, for instance, only reluctantly inclined to take the place of women in agriculture. The President, on one of his recent visits to Buhaya, made a specific reference to this fact. "Discard old habits", he said, and continued: "Since men and women are equal it is imperative that they all participate fully in productive labour."[10]

We are in this chapter particularly concerned with how agricultural production, as a means of increasing the income of the country, can be improved, how government can extract new resources from the country. From what has been said above, this problem, in an area like Buhaya, is likely to be conditioned by the following factors: (a) the neglect of the farms; (b) the scarce land resources; (c) the low price of coffee, particularly Robusta, on the world market; and (d) the prevalence of old habits.

It is worth keeping in mind that the resistance to improvement of the coffee cultivation was "legitimized" by the political events in the colonial period.[11] The fact that the leaders of TAA and chiefs alike publicly opposed the improvement schemes reinforced the belief of the individual farmer that resistance was correct.

Land resources have only marginally changed in Buhaya, as people have showed no interest in opening up new farming areas on the poor grassland. Furthermore, only a very limited number of farmers in the eastern part, where land is particularly scarce, have opened up farms elsewhere, e.g., Karagwe. Although some Bahaya have been able to increase the productivity of their farms, the economic situation for the majority of the farmers has not improved in recent years. The low price of coffee on the world market is of course the major reason that so many farmers feel that their economic situation has not improved after independence.[12] This also helps explain why traditional beliefs have survived. Economic incentives to alter methods of cultivation have been lacking. There is a vicious circle: A constantly low income from coffee production reinforces old beliefs, which, in turn makes the farmers regard any change in agricultural production as an enterprise beyond their means.

[10] *The Nationalist,* January 11, 1967.
[11] See pp. 115—16.
[12] Cf., also Ch 11.

Attitudes towards land and cultivation

Because of the importance of agricultural improvement to both the villagers and the government, the respondents were asked a number of questions relating to land and cultivation. The distribution of the answers to some of the most important questions are shown in Table 27.

The first thing we were interested in was the opinion of the coffee rejuvenation policy among the Haya farmers. The respondents were asked if they agreed or disagreed with the following statement: "The current policy of uprooting the old coffee trees is a bad policy." The second question referred to how the respondents think they would use their economic resources if they received a capital increase, such as a credit or an additional income. Would they use it for reinvestment in agriculture or would they simply increase their ordinary consumption. The question reads: "Suppose you have got an average income of 1000/— a year, but this year you get an increase of 200/—, what would you do with the additional money you earned?" The interviewees were requested to list three things that they most urgently would do. If this question was intended to throw some light on how they were going to spend their money, it was not likely to indicate whether they preferred to invest capital in production for subsistence or for the market. They were, therefore, asked another, more specific question: "What do you consider most important to grow on your farm?"

The answers to the first question confirm that the resistance to the policy of coffee rejuvenation has been strongest in eastern Buhaya, where land is most scarce, the tradition of coffee growing particularly long and Robusta is the prevailing type of coffee. Those who believe that the current policy of uprooting the old trees is bad are particularly many in Bugombe and Kitendagulo. The low percentage of people opposing the policy in Kiruruma can be explained by the fact that most of the farms have been created recently. People arrived in the area only a few years ago and bought the farms. Cultivation is therefore not tied up with certain traditional beliefs in the same way as it is in eastern Buhaya. In Kiruruma and Bwatangabo people grow almost exclusively Arabica coffee, and the farms are on the whole larger than in parishes like Bugombe and Kitendagulo. Out of the five parishes studied here coffee cultivation is most advanced in Bwatangabo. Interviews with the staff of BCU have confirmed this fact.[13]

The Bahaya reveal a strong orientation towards land and agriculture in their answers to the question what they would do with an additional income. Around 40 % would like to use it for increasing their land resources or improving already existing farm land. This pattern is again most conspicuous in eastern Buhaya. In places like Kabagunda and Kiruruma the

[13] Personal communication with Mr Wamala, February 23, 1966.

emphasis is rather on buying cows and building better houses. Both are natural preferences in areas where cows rather than land are most highly evaluated and where houses by and large are of poor quality. In Kiruruma, for instance, it happens, according to information obtained from the local population, that wild animals visit the parish in the night and sometimes cause severe damage to the property of the inhabitants.

Table 27. Attitudes towards various aspects of agricultural improvement by parish. Absolute number in brackets.

(in %)	Bugombe		Kiten-dagulo		Bwatangabo		Kabagunda		Kiruruma	
Uprooting of old coffee trees not a bad policy?										
Agree	40	(23)	37,5	(21)	22	(21)	29	(21)	18	(8)
Disagree	60	(35)	50	(28)	74	(73)	68	(49)	82	(36)
No infor	—	(0)	12,5	(7)	5	(4)	3	(2)	—	(0)
If more money, how use it?										
Buy land	22,5	(13)	27	(15)	25	(24)	16,5	(12)	11,5	(5)
Improve culti-vation	29,5	(17)	16	(9)	23	(22)	16,5	(12)	11,5	(5)
Build a house	16	(9)	9	(5)	15	(15)	14	(10)	22,5	(10)
Pay tax or school fee	8,5	(5)	9	(5)	11	(11)	14	(10)	9,5	(4)
Invest in business	—	(0)	5	(3)	2	(2)	5,5	(4)	4	(2)
Buy cows	8,5	(5)	7,5	(4)	8	(8)	4	(3)	18	(8)
Buy clothes, food	10	(6)	16	(9)	8	(8)	8,5	(6)	11,5	(5)
Others	5	(3)	10,5	(6)	8	(8)	21	(15)	11,5	(5)
Most important to grow on the farm?										
Bananas	83	(48)	82	(46)	80	(78)	77,5	(56)	84	(37)
Coffee	7,5	(4)	11	(6)	11	(11)	8,5	(6)	—	(0)
Beans	5	(3)	5	(3)	4	(4)	10	(7)	14	(6)
Cassawa, maize	3	(2)	2	(1)	2	(2)	1,5	(1)	—	(0)
No information	1,5	(1)	—	(0)	3	(3)	2,5	(2)	2	(1)
Total	100	(58)	100	(56)	100	(98)	100	(72)	100	(44)

Only a few respondents would consider buying such things as clothes, food, or a bicycle. Nor is any larger number interested in investing their money in a business enterprise, such as a small *duka*.[14] On the whole, therefore, the Bahaya still have a very strong orientation towards land. This would look like a good sign for a government that is keen to engage people more actively in modern agriculture. It is hard to say, however, whether the attitude of the Bahaya is determined by traditional ties to the land or by the modern idea of agriculture as a business enterprise. There are certain indications that it is the first rather than the second factor that determines their attitude. Although several respondents mentioned that they would spend their money on improving their cultivation nobody specifically said that he would buy modern farming equipment.

The Haya farmers can be compared with farmers in other parts of East Africa. Their system of preference resembles that of the farmers in Buganda, although the latter are more inclined to invest money in building houses.[15] The Ganda and Haya patterns, however, stand in contrast to that of the Embu farmers in Kenya, as reported by Jon Moris. Many more farmers in Embu District think in terms of reinvesting money in, not just land and cattle, but also modern farming equipment.[16] This suggests that the latter have a more modern approach to agricultural production than the Bahaya. They look upon it more as a business enterprise. They are also more mobile. While only 8,5 % of the Haya respondents[17] had considered moving elsewhere, the information given by Moris is that two-thirds of the Embu farmers had worked elsewhere as wage-earners for some time.[18] This can be explained by the fact that a major urban area, Nairobi, is located not far from Embu. It is possible, therefore, that Haya farmers would have had a different outlook on economic activities, had there been a major town in the immediate neighborhood. Bukoba cannot offer any great number of employment opportunities and does not encourage a high degree of social and geographical mobility as a place like Nairobi does.

The rather traditional approach to agricultural production comes out also in the Haya opinion about what is most important to grow on the farm. Over 80 % of the respondents mention bananas whereas only 8 % mention coffee. This suggests that the Bahaya by and large prefer producing for subsistence rather than for the market. Land scarcity and low productivity, as well as lack of economic incentives, are likely to explain this preference. Bananas, being the staple food, will remain most important to the

[14] Kiswahili for 'shop'.
[15] Personal communication with Mr Archibald Mafeje, Department of Sociology, Makerere University College, November 12, 1966.
[16] J. Moris, "Education and Training of the Farmer", paper presented ti the Conference on Education, Employment and Development, at Kericho, Kenya, September 25—October 1, 1966, p. B 14.
[17] Cf., p. 155.
[18] Moris, *op.cit.*, p. B 14.

farmer as long as his income does not allow him to buy food on a larger scale.

In this connection it is worth while pointing out that the Haya farmers, when encouraged in 1962—63 to prepare their own local development plans, later to be integrated in the regional and national development plans, they expressed crop targets for maize, beans and groundnuts, but ignored the major cash crop, coffee. The targets were set by the VDCs, but little notice of these was taken in the West Lake regional plan.[19] Our data suggests that the strong preference for food production rather than cash production still prevails in Buhaya.

Although the trend in the answers presented in Table 27 is clear it is by no means uniform. The next task therefore will be to find out more specifically who are the people: who dislike coffee rejuvenation, who prefer investing in land and improved cultivation, and, lastly, who believe growing coffee is more important than growing bananas. Furthermore, attempts will be made to analyze the connections between individual responses to these questions. The answers are shown in Table 28.

Not unexpectedly, the resistance to the policy of uprooting old coffee trees and planting new ones, is particularly strong among the elders. Yet, the opposition among young people is also considerable. Reluctance to accept the policy is prevalent among people without education or only a few years of schooling, and among people in possession of small or middle-size coffee farms. It is important to note that high media exposure does not necessarily make people more favorable to the policy of uprooting coffee trees. This suggests, therefore, that media participation does not necessarily have such a decisive modernizing impact, as Lerner maintains is the case in the Middle East, and that there are other factors, which are equally important in determining the attitudes of the farmers towards agricultural improvement.[20] This point will, however, be discussed, more specifically, later in this chapter.

It would seem as if many of the respondents who *dislike* the policy of coffee rejuvenation favor investment in land and improved cultivation. The percentage who are interested to invest extra money in agriculture, is particularly high among respondents of young age, good education and relatively high cash income. The frequency of answers in favor of growing coffee rather than bananas is also higher among younger, educated people with a sizeable coffee farm.

The relationship between the answers to these three questions is, however, not as simple as that. Although one could assume that those who

19 "Mipango ya uchumi na kazi za kujenga taifa" (Plans for the task of nation-building), worked out by VDCs in Buhaya 1962—63. Also personal communication with the Regional Agricultural Officer, Bukoba, December 1964.
20 D. Lerner, *The Passing of Traditional Society*, (New York 1958), pp. 34—75.

Table 28. Differences in attitudes towards agricultural production; by age, education, size of farm and media exposure. Absolute number in brackets.

(in %)	Age			Education			Size of farm			Media exposure			
	young (132)	middle-aged (130)	old (63)	none (143)	some (119)	much (66)	small (108)	middle-size (126)	large (63)	very often (34)	often (67)	not so often (95)	never (116)
Do not like uprooting of old coffee trees	20,5	30,5	42,5	33,5	32,5	10,5	31,5	32,5	19	26	26,5	26	26
Want to invest in land or improved cultivation	43	44	31,5	36	39,5	53	35	42	55,5	50	49	41	39
Believe coffee is more important to grow than bananas	9	10,5	1,5	3,5	11,5	12	6	9,5	12,5	9	10,5	9,5	7,5

are opposed to the rejuvenation policy would have only a limited interest, if any, in improving cultivation or extending their land-holding, this assumption does not hold true with reference to all categories of respondents. It does hold true, for instance, with the old, uneducated small farmers, among whom the resistance to the rejuvenation policy, as indicated in Table 28, is widespread. Their attitude, however, is in great contrast to that of other categories of respondents. Old, uneducated persons with large farms, for instance, are much more favorable to the uprooting of old coffee trees. Quite a few of them are also inclined to spend their extra money on buying land or improving cultivation. This category of respondents is also represented among those who would prefer growing cash crops before food crops as is shown in Figure 12.

Table 29. Attitudes of certain categories of respondents towards coffee rejuvenation and farm cultivation. Absolute number in brackets.

(in %)	old, un-educated small farmers (25)	old un-educated big farmers (17)	young, educated small farmers (25)	young, educated big farmers (13)	young, uneducated small farmers (51)
Dislike coffee rejuvenation (total 94)	72	29	16	7,5	35
Prefer investing in land and cultivation (total 134)	8	64	24	23	52,5

The latter group includes both educated and uneducated respondents. Interestingly enough, it is the young people with the small farms who show the greatest inclination towards growing cash crops instead of food crops. For those who have education this is understandable, as most of them already have another occupation and therefore are more economically independent. More unexpected, however, is the fact that quite a number of the uneducated young small farmers, who dislike the rejuvenation policy, have a favorable attitude toward investment in agriculture and growing cash crops. This in perhaps the most important finding about the attitudes of the Bahaya towards agriculture. It is obvious, since the number of each category of respondents is relatively small, that no farreaching conclusions can be drawn. Still, however, it is worth noting that the trends are quite clear. As the figures in Table 29 indicate very few old uneducated small farmers who oppose the coffee rejuvenation policy are interested in investment in land and cultivation. In case of the young, uneducated small farmers, however, despite the fact that several of them object to uprooting old coffee trees, as a whole, they favor investment in land and cultivation. The implication of this finding is that the resistance to coffee rejuvenation in Buhaya does not simply grow out of the traditional belief system and lack of exposure to new ideas.

Figure 12. Total number of respondents preferring to grow coffee rather than bananas, divided into major categories.

(6)	young, educated small farmers
(2)	young, educated large farmers
(7)	young, uneducated small farmers
(2)	old, large farmers
(3)	middle-aged, large farmers
(5)	others

This was also confirmed in the supplementary interviews, where two separate types of opinions crystallized: one traditional, a second indicating that lack of economic resources is the principal reason for opposition to the rejuvenation schemes.

Many of the elders feel it is very difficult to uproot the old trees and their main reason is deference to traditional beliefs. Six of the respondents, who were approached for supplementary interviewing—five of them old small farmers—mentioned that they cannot uproot trees planted by their fore-fathers. This would bring them misfortune. One person went as far as claiming that it was an insult to do such a thing.

The other attitude which is more prevalent among young and middle-aged people is connected with the fear of taking economic risks. The far-mers are afraid of uprooting the old trees, which despite their low yields, give the owner a regular amount of money every year. They believe that before the newly planted trees will give a sizeable yield, at least two years will pass, und during this period they will have to live on a lower income than at present. Some also object because they find the new husbandry too complicated and costly, and this becomes an additional reason for not abandoning the old methods of cultivation.

One young female farmer in Kitendagulo said:

We do not like to uproot the old coffee trees, because it will cost too much money to plant new ones—and it will take long time before the new trees can produce any coffee.

A young, uneducated small farmer in Bwatangabo felt very much the same way:

... Uprooting the old trees means that we are going to lose the coffee which we already have at hand.

One can say, therefore, that resistance to the coffee rejuvenation policy, among the old uneducated small farmers, is principally based on traditional values, while in the case of the young small farmers, resistance is mainly due to economic considerations. The latter feel too poor to dare take such a step. This suggests, therefore, that unlike the old people, who cannot be expected so easily to discount future benefits for present ones, the young have a desire to change, but need to be helped over the economic barriers they are facing. Improved credit facilities, for instance, would be one way of helping these poor farmers, who do not lack the positive attitude towards investment in agriculture. Existing circumstances meant, however, at least before the Arusha Declaration, that these farmers were excluded from loans, since their opportunities to pay back were limited.[21]

There is a great deal of evidence to suggest that this category of farmers would become more favorable towards coffee rejuvenation, if more generous credit facilities were offered. Such a step would also be in line with the spirit of the Arusha Declaration, which aims at minimizing the social and economic differences between various sectors of the population. It would probably also have the effect of making the male sector of the population more committed to agricultural production, an important step towards modernization, as stated in the introduction of this chapter.[22]

Another way of improving the situation in the rural communities of Buhaya would be to make more effective the flow of information into these communities. Several farmers tend, as indicated above, to overdramatize the difficulties involved in the transition from the old to the modern way of cultivation. The rest of this chapter will therefore be devoted to the question of how the rural inhabitants get their information about politics in general and agricultural policies in particular.

From where does the information come?

A precondition for overcoming the problem of penetration is a well-functioning network of communication. People living in isolated rural communities must be exposed to the outside world; they must be convinced that they have to change their customary way of life. We have seen so far that

[21] Personal communication with Mr Wamala, February 23, 1966.
[22] Cf., pp. 182—83.

their general predispositions are in favor of allegiance to a national community and deference to existing values, norms and structures. The material in this chapter has, however, indicated another thing—that people, because of adherence to traditional beliefs or due to economic restrictions, find it difficult to comply with government calls for specific projects of agricultural development.

We were interested to find out how the information is transmitted to the villagers. One can assume that the largest amount of information reaches them by face-to-face communication, since the number of radios in these communities is small and the spread of newspapers limited. Only 8,5 % of the total sample reported that they owned their own radio.[23] The greatest number of radio sets were found in Bugombe and Kitendagulo, while in Kiruruma nobody had a radio. Approximately one third of all respondents—approximately 50 % in Kabagunda and Kiruruma—never listened to radio. 57,5 % of the total sample never read newspapers; furthermore, the percentage is particularly high in Kabagunda and Kiruruma, where the distribution of newspapers is very poorly organized. The Catholic Church is the main distributor, and consequently the most widely read papers are also owned and published by that Church. One quarter of the respondents read the *Kiongozi;*[24] the second most popular is the *Rumuli,* the local Catholic paper in Buhaya. Hardly any government-owned paper, whether Swahili or English, reaches the villagers in Buhaya, while a few mention that they read the *Bukoba Cooperative News,* published by the BCU.

Table 30. Answers from where the respondents get their information about politics; by parish. Absolute number in brackets.

(in %)	Bugombe		Kiten-dagulo		Bwatan-gabo		Kaba-gunda		Kiru-ruma	
Family, friends	43	(25)	59	(33)	74	(72)	63	(46)	80	(35)
Radio, newspapers	29,5	(17)	32	(18)	10	(10)	23	(18)	4	(2)
Govt circulars	24	(14)	9	(5)	13	(13)	14	(10)	14	(6)
No information	3,5	(2)	—	(0)	3	(3)	—	(0)	2	(1)
Total	100	(58)	100	(56)	100	(98)	100	(72)	100	(44)

[23] This figure can also be compared to Uganda, where according to one survey 36 % of the respondents (in total 416 all over the country) reported that they owned their own radio set. See Anthony Obershall, "Media Exposure, Information Level and Aspirations in Rural Uganda", paper prepared in the Department of Sociology, Yale University, August, 1967.

[24] Published bi-monthly by the Catholic Church Office in Tabora.

Although listening to the radio may be a popular pastime for some respondents, and newspapers are carefully read by some people, most people could be expected to depend primarily on other sources of information than mass media. This was also confirmed when the respondents were asked from where they get their information about politics.

The greatest number obtain their political information mainly from other family members, fellow-workers or friends. Government circulars read at public meetings in the parishes serve only to a limited extent as primary sources of information. The highest proportion of respondents relying on government circulars is found in Bugombe. One possible explanation for this could be that the VDC there meets more frequently than the others. The inhabitants of that parish are in fact exposed to government information at public meetings more often than they get the newspapers to their homes—twice a month.

Four out of five respondents feel satisfied with the information they get. The villagers were also asked to whom they would turn in case they wished to know more about a certain political matter. Would they go to a friend, who is usually well-informed, would they tune to Dar es Salaam for political news, or would they turn to the official documents which are distributed to the parish? By and large it is the same pattern as in the previous table that emerges. Those who regularly obtain information from a friend will turn to him if they want to know more, those relying on mass media would turn to radio or newspapers, and so forth.

Table 31. Distribution of answers how the respondents obtain additional information about politics; by parish. Absolute number in brackets.

(in %)	Bugombe		Kiten-dagulo		Bwatan-gabo		Kaba-gunda		Kiru-ruma	
Family, friends	31	(18)	57,5	(32)	64	(62)	65,5	(47)	84	(37)
Radio, newspapers	27,5	(16)	25,5	(14)	15	(15)	19,5	(14)	—	(0)
Govt circulars	40	(23)	17	(10)	19	(19)	14	(10)	16	(7)
No infor	1,5	(1)	—	(0)	2	(2)	1,5	(1)	—	(0)
Total	100	(58)	100	(56)	100	(98)	100	(72)	100	(44)

The only important change is recorded in Bugombe, where a substantially higher number would turn to government documents rather than to their friends. This suggests a situation which is unusual in small communities—that people tend to have greater trust in "external" that in "internal" sources of information. The most important conclusion to be drawn from this table is, however, that by and large people are more prepared to turn to friends or to government sources than to mass media for additional political information.

Media exposure or participation is a basic indication of modernization, according to Lerner.[25] On basis of material from the Middle East he suggests that urbanization, literacy, media participation and political participation are four consecutive phases of modernization. The way by which these variables will affect the modernization process in sub-Saharan Africa is, however, likely to be different from that of the Middle East. Certainly in East Africa, urbanization is a process which has gained momentum only very recently, and in fact in Tanzania it has deliberately been retarded.[26] In Tanzania media participation has moreover been considered only a secondary matter. Instead, emphasis has been placed on teaching people how to handle new situations by extending formal education and by involving people in a political organization, through which they can become part of a wider political and social community.

Lerner writes in a different context[27] that the mass media are the primary resource for developing societies-in-a-hurry. They reach the most people fastest and cheapest with their message. The question to which Lerner does not address himself, however, is whether mass media is also the most effective way of transmitting messages. The Tanzanian government has not considered investment in mass media as important as investment in a strong political organization as a channel of communication, downward as well as upward. The correctness of such a policy seems to be confirmed by the material presented here. The majority of the persons interviewed prefer a system in which the message is "legitimized" by a person or an authority before it is accepted. This is not an unusual situation in areas where an oral tradition has been prevalent for a long time, and where the degree of personal trust may not be very high.[28] This is, of course, of great significance to the whole process of penetration. A message may lose its meaning and effect before it reaches the local communities, to which it is addressed, because it is transmitted by an authority whose legitimacy is in question.

There is, however, a natural barrier against a wide spread of such a tendency in the Haya parishes due to the strong loyalty to the system by the majority of the population. This is likely to serve as a guarantee that infor-

[25] Lerner, op.cit., pp. 52—65.

[26] Cf., p. 47.

[27] D. Lerner, "Communication and the Prospects of Innovative Development" in Lerner and Schramm (eds), Communication and Change in the Developing Countries, (Honolulu 1967), p. 316.

[28] For a summary of the literature on this subject and for stimulating hypotheses, see Ithiel de Sola Pool, "Mass Media and Politics in the Modernization Process" in Pye (ed), "Communication . . .", op.cit., pp. 234—53.

mation transmitted from one person to another is not going to get seriously distorted. The mass party in Tanzania, however, also makes reliance on mass media less necessary. A party that really functions as a channel of communication can more easily be used to overcome the problem of "the revolution of the rising expectations". Mass media may encourage consumer tendencies without a correspondingly appreciation of the means by which increased benefits can be obtained. A political organization, however, can more easily be adapted to a communications strategy which also aims at teaching people how to achieve these things on their own.

This has not been said to underestimate the importance of mass media, but simply to point out the essential role of the political organization. People often tend to rely on political leaders for guidance. This was verified when the respondents were asked questions about how they obtained information and in particular about agricultural activities. There are three main categories of leaders, from which the farmers can obtain information, the Village Executive Officer or the VDC leaders, both primarily involved in transmitting a general type of information about agriculture; the representatives of the local cooperative society; and the Agricultural Extension Officer, the chief representative of the Ministry for Agriculture at the local level.

Table 32. Answers from whom the farmers get agricultural information; by parish. Absolute number in brackets.

(in %)	Bugombe	Kiten-dagulo	Bwatan-gabo	Kaba-gunda	Kiru-ruma
VEO or VDC	31 (18)	37,5 (21)	49 (48)	71 (51)	82 (36)
Coop leaders	31 (18)	34 (19)	19 (19)	12,5 (9)	12 (5)
Extension officer	28 (16)	21 (12)	28 (27)	10 (7)	4 (2)
No information	10 (6)	7,5 (4)	4 (4)	6,5 (5)	2 (1)
Total	100 (58)	100 (56)	100 (98)	100 (72)	100 (44)

As the figures in Table 32 indicate the VEO and the VDC leaders are by and large the most important. The impact of the extension officer and the coop leaders decreases the further away one gets from Bukoba; at the same time the role of the VDC and the VEO increases in importance. The reasons are probably many. One could be that the organization of the coops and the extension service is poorer in the less densely populated areas of southern and western Buhaya. Another is probably that in Kabagunda and Kiruruma, where people on the whole are less educated, adherents to the traditional religion, and poorer—if exception is made for the trading community in Kabagunda—they may be more inclined to rely on the old established authorities,[29] that is, in particular the VEO, who is viewed by many as the "new version" of the old parish chief.[30]

The figures in Table 32 also suggest that the party and government organization really functions as an important channel of communications. They also indicate that the people have a favorable orientation towards the political system, which is of great importance to the functioning of the system itself.

One problem that arises out of this situation is, however, that the VEO has very limited opportunities to be an agricultural "innovator", since his main contribution to the operation of the system lies in his role as chief tax collector. This is the principal preoccupation of the VEOs, and they claim themselves that in present circumstances they have no, or little, time to such activities as agricultural improvement.[31]

The VDC is an important body of disseminating information, but the effective contribution to agricultural development by individual members of the VDC varies from place to place. In at least some of the areas, the VDCs are dominated by elders, who, although favorable to the regime and the government in general, are unlikely to take steps to improve agricultural production. They simply do not have the knowledge and motivation needed. One difficulty with the present system therefore, is that the local leaders, in whom the villagers place such great confidence, have neither time nor enough interest and skill, in serving as agricultural instructors. The situation could of course be improved by either facilitating for these leaders to engage more actively in agricultural improvement, or strengthening the role of the extension service or the coop agricultural advisers.

Table 33. Opinions about which type of leaders has the greatest impact on the local population; by parish. Absolute number in brackets.

(in %)	Bugombe		Kiten-dagulo		Bwatan-gabo		Kaba-gunda		Kiru-ruma	
National leaders	16	(9)	7,5	(4)	13	(13)	8	(6)	9,5	(4)
Regional and district	3	(2)	16	(9)	5	(5)	4	(3)	4	(2)
Parish and village	81	(47)	76,5	(44)	81	(79)	88	(63)	86,5	(38)
No information	—	(0)	—	(0)	1	(1)	—	(0)	—	(0)
Total	100	(58)	100	(56)	100	(98)	100	(72)	100	(44)

[29] That situation is, for instance, prevalent among traditional farmers in Thailand; cf. N. Luykx, "The Role of Rural Development in Agriculture in Thailand", Comparative Administration Group: Occasional Papers, (Bloomington 1964), p. 43.
[30] For a more detailed account of the role of the Village Executive Officers, see Hyden, "Problems of Village . . .", op.cit.
[31] Ibid.

Whatever means employed, however, it is clear that the local political leaders play a key role in the penetration process. In comparison to leaders at higher levels in the political hierarchy, the village, or parish, leaders, are most important to the local population. This the respondents themselves strongly emphasized.

One should not assume that the official leaders at the local level necessarily are the most influential, or at least, not the only influential people in the villages. A study from the coastal region of Tanzania suggests that a number of "hidden" leaders, such as the leader of the Muslim sect, have a greater impact on the members of the village community than the politically appointed leaders.[32] It is also reasonable to assume that in Buhaya, for instance, religious leaders have a considerable influence. Material in previous chapters have indicated this.[33] All the same, the material in this chapter has clearly indicated that the political leaders are viewed by the common man as both important and influential. What they say and what they do, therefore, is likely to mean more to the ordinary person than what other members of the local community are doing, and even more than what the superior political leaders are doing. The rural inhabitants prefer to follow the advice and orders of an "in-leader", a permanent member of the village or parish community. Even if they have a favorable attitude towards membership in the national community and approve of the regime, the villagers need to have their new code of behavior constantly reinforced by words and deeds of the official leaders in their immediate environment.

Conclusions

We have devoted much space in this chapter to the question of agricultural improvement, and rightly so, as it is regarded by the Tanzanian government as an important condition for economic development in the country. It renders the individual farmer a higher cash income; it may help increasing government revenue from a larger export, and so forth. In Chapter 9 we showed that a general feeling among the Bahaya is that the government expects too much of them. This point has been further underlined in this chapter by the information on the question of agricultural improvement. Many respondents are interested in adopting new methods of cultivation but fear to take the step since their economic means are very limited.

A great deal of the problem of how to improve the extractive capability of the political system is related to the communication strategy employed.

[32] See N. Miller, *op.cit.*
[33] Cf., pp. 133 and 145—46.

Mass media is often used simply to raise the expectations—to make people believe in things that cannot happen—rather than to teach the public how to achieve the things that are promised. The opportunities to avoid the negative consequences of such a false strategy, however, are great in an area like Buhaya. People are not highly dependent on mass media for information about government and politics, and they show on the whole greater trust in direct face-to-face communication with friends, or in official government documents. This emphasizes the crucial role that the political organization plays in the developmental process in the country-side. TANU has perhaps in the first years of independence not taken advantage of these opportunities in the rural areas, but the new emphasis on rural developmental problems, which is one consequence of the Arusha Declaration, may well lead to an enhanced role of TANU in concrete developmental tasks in the villages.[34]

[34] The blueprint for the transformation of Tanzania's rural life in the direction of so-called *Ujamaa* (brotherhood) villages is found in a pamphlet by President Julius Nyerere, *Socialism and Rural Development* (Dar es Salaam 1967).

Chapter 11. ## The problem of allocation

One of the implications of the Tanzanian policy of equality has been attempts to level out the differences in economic and social development between various regions or parts of the country. This political strategy has affected Buhaya, one of the most advanced parts of the country before independence. Some people have, quite naturally, felt that the rate of development has not been satisfactorily in recent years. Not all of them are blaming the government; in fact, some of the critics express a high degree of self-criticism, pointing to "the lack of interest" in development among the local Haya population. The following quotation is from a letter to the Editor of *Rumuli,* the local Catholic paper, and is rather typical of a number of such letters in the local press:[1]

Some time ago Buhaya was more highly developed than other places in Tanzania with regard to education, agriculture and local government. It is terrifying to see now our Buhaya decline and die. Poverty is our first problem. Secondly, there is hunger ... The number of people in Buhaya is increasing, while food is decreasing. We also lack schools ... We have no money to make our children continue schooling. Coffee price is also very low ...[2]

The letter contains a number of things with which the writer, and one can assume a large part of the population, is dissatisfied. It refers to lack of money, to the low production of agriculture, and to inadequacies in the educational sector. We believed that the attitudes of the respondents to these aspects of life would give an indication of their degree of satisfaction —or dissatisfaction—with the present life. We were also interested to find out their hopes for the future and how these related to their opinion about the present life.

This would, however, not give us any idea of their opinion about the way government allocated the resources of the society. It is possible, for instance, that the local population believed that the reasons why their situation had not improved after independence were *not* connected with an unsatisfactory performance by the government authorities. We therefore asked the respondents a series of questions relating to the process of distribution. On which groups or sectors of the population is government spending most of its resources? The relevance of this type of questions is underlined by the

[1] *Rumuli* is published by the local Catholic Church in Bukoba Diocese. It appears once a month.
[2] *Rumuli,* "Buhaya kuhemuka kiki?", June 15, 1966.

fact that in most societies, in which "subject"[3] attitudes prevail, people have a strong orientation towards the "output side" of the system. People have high expectations of the system. They think in terms of rewards which they can get out of it rather than in terms of what contribution that they can make to its successful operation.

In short, what we are concerned with, in this chapter, is the material aspirations of the individual citizens and how government authorities are trying to meet them.

Satisfaction with life and hope for the future

Much has been written on the "revolution of rising expectations" in the less developed countries, and the deep imbalance between achievement and aspiration that exists among wide sectors of the population in these countries.[4] Desires are created more rapidly than can be satisfied. This hypothesis has, however, only recently been empirically tested in tropical Africa.

The degree to which people feel satisfied or dissatisfied with important aspects of their life is likely to affect their general appreciation of the society in which they live. The Haya respondents were therefore asked a number of questions about what they thought of their income, house, job, education, village and nation. The answers to the last two items need not to be presented in detail here. They revealed a very strong satisfaction among almost all respondents, and the answers simply confirm the pattern presented in Chapter 8.[5] With regard to the more material aspects of life, the situation was different.

The majority of the respondents do not feel very satisfied with the material conditions under which they live. Their complaints are particularly strong of the financial and educational situation. Almost two thirds of the total sample express some degree of dissatisfaction with the amount of education that they have. Nearly half the number wish they had a higher income. This is a clear indication that they feel restrained by economic factors in their attempts to achieve more and better things. It is worth noting that the grievances are as a widespread in the western and southern parishes as they are in the eastern ones. This suggests then that even in the most remote parts of the country people have a very strong desire for education. This is a desire which is not only limited to urban areas or to already well advanced rural areas.

[3] Cf., Ch. 9. p. 165.
[4] See e.g., Lerner, *op.cit.*, Pye, "Communications . . .", *op.cit.*, E. M. Rogers, "Mass Media Exposure and Modernization among Colombian Peasants", *Public Opinion Quarterly*, (Vol 29, No 4), pp. 614—25.
[5] See pp. 149—50 and 154—57.

Table 34. Degree of satisfaction felt among the respondents with regard to their income, housing situation, job and education; by parish. Absolute number in brackets.

(in %)	Bugombe		Kiten-dagulo		Bwatan-gabo		Kaba-gunda		Kiru-ruma	
present income:										
very satisfied	14	(8)	9	(5)	8	(8)	7	(5)	20	(9)
satisfied	22,5	(13)	7	(4)	31	(30)	15	(11)	20	(9)
neither-nor	27,5	(16)	27	(15)	17	(17)	30	(21)	4	(2)
dissatisfied	29	(17)	35,5	(20)	38	(37)	43	(31)	56	(24)
very dissatisfied	7	(7)	21,5	(12)	5	(5)	5	(4)	—	(0)
house one lives in:										
very satisfied	21	(12)	10,5	(6)	8	(8)	12,5	(9)	28	(12)
satisfied	22,5	(13)	10,5	(6)	22	(22)	19,5	(14)	22	(10)
neither-nor	26	(15)	32	(18)	31	(30)	23,5	(17)	11,5	(5)
dissatisfied	24	(14)	32	(18)	34	(33)	40	(29)	36,5	(16)
very dissatisfied	6,5	(4)	15	(9)	5	(5)	4,5	(3)	2	(1)
job one has:										
very satisfied	44	(26)	14	(8)	23,5	(23)	16	(12)	25	(11)
satisfied	24	(14)	28,5	(16)	36	(35)	22,5	(16)	8,5	(4)
neither-nor	19	(11)	28,5	(16)	20,5	(20)	29	(21)	20	(9)
dissatisfied	9	(5)	25	(14)	18	(18)	25,5	(18)	44	(19)
very dissatisfied	4	(2)	4	(2)	2	(2)	7	(5)	2,5	(1)
amount of educational one has:										
very satisfied	27,5	(16)	7	(4)	13	(13)	9	(6)	13	(6)
satisfied	21	(12)	19,5	(11)	13	(13)	12	(9)	2	(1)
neither-nor	15,9	(9)	19,5	(11)	8	(8)	9	(6)	4,5	(2)
dissatisfied	19	(11)	36	(20)	56	(54)	38	(28)	44	(19)
very dissatisfied	17	(10)	18	(10)	10	(10)	32	(23)	36,5	(16)
total	100	(58)	100	(56)	100	(98)	100	(72)	100	(44)

Dissatisfaction with income is very widespread in Kitendagulo, and one can assume that this is due to the proximity of the parish to Bukoba. They are exposed to material attractions, such as good houses, new types of consumer goods, and so forth, and this is likely to have its effect on the evaluation of their own situation. The case of Kitendagulo will be discussed further below.

Table 35. Proportion of respondents who express some degree of dissatisfaction with education, income and job; by age, education, size of farm and occupation. Absolute number in brackets.

| (in %) | Education | | | Age | | | Size of farm | | | Occupation | |
	none	some	much	young	midd-le-aged	old	small	midd-le-size	large	agr.	non-agr.
	(143)	(119)	(66)	(132)	(130)	(63)	(108)	(126)	(63)	(270)	(58)
dissatisfied with:											
education	74	57	42	68	56	57	70	62	53	64	62
income	63	44	51	52	40	49	66	47	36	53	47
job	21	25	31	30,5	24	19	31	18	25	17	36

On the whole, people are least dissatisfied with their jobs, and as is shown in Table 35, this is largely due to the fact that so many respondents are farmers. They take a pride in their occupation and are less likely to express dissatisfaction than representatives of other occupations. This feeling is particularly strong in eastern Buhaya—as shown in Table 34—where the agricultural tradition is most deeply rooted.

The figures in Table 35 reveal several things. As could be expected, people without education feel most discontented with their own educational attainment. Emphasis in public speeches and discussions, before independence as well as after, has been on the importance of formal education, and it is understandable, therefore, that so many people would feel this way. The percentage of persons with primary education or above is, however, also high. Several of these probably wish they could obtain a higher degree or certificate. Education gives both status and a greater capacity to improve one's economic position. Surprising is the fact that age does not determine the opinion of their educational attainment. Old and young people express the same opinions to about the same extent.

The small farmers are most frequently reporting dissatisfaction with their income, while age and occupational status are no significantly determining variables. Education, to some extent, is an important variable. Those who lack formal education are most inclined to reveal dissatisfaction also with their income. As illustrated in Table 36, it is the category of respondents who feel most dissatisfied with their income, which reports that the government expects too much of the people.[6]

As regards the attitudes towards their occupational status, it is worth noting, in addition to the fact that farmers are less dissatisfied than non-farmers, that the degree of dissatisfaction with the present job situation is

[6] See pp. 168—71.

higher among younger than among older people. This may be a reflection of a not uncommon notion among the younger generation in the rural areas of the less developed countries that farming is an occupation that belongs to the past, that the future lies in other walks of life. This illusion was, at least, not recognized in the Haya villages at the time this research was conducted.

This should of course not be taken as an indication that there is a strong desire to move away from the rural areas of Buhaya. As shown in Chapter 8, the vast majority of the respondents are not inclined to move outside Buhaya.[7] Quite a large number of people wish that there was a higher degree of social mobility in the rural areas, that is, that one could move up the social ladder without having to leave the home area. This comes out in the answers to the question about what hopes they have for their children. For instance, 84,5 % (278) of all respondents want their sons to get at least a secondary school or university education; 76 % (251) hope their daughters can reach the same educational attainment. At the same time, however, 49 % of all respondents want their children to work in the rural areas. This could, of course, be interpreted in many different ways. One may say that the respondents simply view education, and particularly higher education, as a status symbol. People may therefore express this opinion without considering the dilemma, that people with high education are predestinated to work in urban rather than rural areas. It could also, however, be interpreted as a genuine feeling of dissatisfaction with the present situation; that the rural areas benefit very little from the social and economic improvement that have taken place in Tanzania after independence. We will return below to the question how much truth there is in such an interpretation.

Table 36. Proportion of some selected categories of farmers reporting dissatisfaction with income. Absolute number in brackets.

(in %)	young, small uneducated (51)	old, small uneducated (25)	old, big uneducated (17)	young, big educated (13)	young, small educated (25)
expressing dissatisfaction	77	38	17	15	24

As seen from the data presented here, much of the dissatisfaction is connected with an insufficient degree of education, or complete lack of it, as well as lack of money to realize some of their material aspirations. The

[7] See p. 155.

Haya respondents do not differ in this respect from the attitudes of rural Ugandans.[8] The spread of dissatisfaction with education, income and other central, material factors is about the same as in Uganda.

The fact that the overwhelming majority of the respondents have a firm root in the land and in agriculture, is likely to make the situation in Buhaya better than in certain other parts of Tanzania, where people have got more extensively used to regular incomes from non-agricultural occupations. Among the Nyakyusa people in south-western Tanzania, for instance, several male inhabitants used to work in the copper mines of Northern Rhodesia, before that country became Zambia in 1964. After independence, however, the Zambian government has given priority to employment of its own subjects. Workers from other countries have in large number been compelled to leave the mines. As a result, several Nyakyusa have returned to their home districts in Tanzania. Some have not found land at all; others have simply not been interested to take up cultivation again. This, according to information by some local people, have caused restlessness and some tension between governmental authorities and the local people.[9]

Rural Bahaya maintain by a 3:1 ratio that their life has improved in the last ten years. This figure compares favorably to Uganda, where Obershall found that those who reported life in the villages was better now than before were twice as many as those who said life had become worse.[10]

Daniel Lerner suggests that the spread of dissatisfaction in the less developed countries can be attributed to the central role that mass media plays as a creator of new aspirations.[11] Radio, television and newspaper are given the responsibility for creating new aspirations in a society undergoing rapid change; where old norms and values are on their way to languish. His assessment of the role of mass media assumes that the change is complete or abrupt. Criticism has, however, been raised against Lerner's thesis, which is principally based on Middle East material.[12] Social scientists are more prepared to accept that there is a certain degree of continuity in the process of social change. People have a greater capacity to relate their aspirations more extensively to concrete conditions than so far assumed. It is not surprising that the conditions, described above, should apply to the situation in tropical Africa. When compared, for instance,

[8] Cf., Obershall, *op.cit.*

[9] Cf., "Letters to the Editor", *The Standard,* January 18, 1966.

[10] Obershall, *op.cit.,* p. 35.

[11] Lerner, "Towards a Communication Theory of Modernization" in Pye, "Communications . . .", *op.cit.,* p. 333.

[12] For a recent contribution, see Joseph Gusfield, "Tradition and Modernity: Misplaced Polarities in the Study of Social Change", *American Journal of Sociology,* (Vol 72, January 1967).

with the Middle East, it is clearly apparent that factors, which affect the modernization process, operate in a different fashion in this region.[13]

As the figures in Table 37 indicate degree of media exposure does not, as Lerner's hypothesis proposes, determine the evaluation of one's own life situation in such a plain way. The same can be said about geographical mobility. It is true, however, that people who have travelled more extensively do reveal dissatisfaction in slightly higher percentages. As to the third variable, party membership, people who are members are somewhat more inclined to express dissatisfaction than non-members. The most important finding, however, is that no systematic differences emerge when media exposure, geographical mobility and party membership are introduced as variables in the analysis of those who express some degree of dissatisfaction with their educational attainment, income and occupation.

Table 37. Proportion of respondents who express some degree of dissatisfaction with education, income and job; by media exposure, geographical mobility and party membership. Absolute number in brackets.

(in %)	Media exposure			geographical mobility travelled outside:				party membership	
	very often	often	not so often	never	village	district	nation	member	non-member
	(34)	(67)	(95)	(116)	(84)	(100)	(131)	(225)	(55)
Dissatisfied with:									
education	58	53	60	49	48	63	58	54	48
income	41	52	58	53	57	49	51	51	45
job	19	29	27,5	23	16	29	22	30	26

The reasons why there are no marked differences in satisfaction level expressed by groups differing on media exposure, geographical mobility and party membership are likely to be many. One important reason is that media exposure does not play a key role in transmitting information to the rural communities. As illustrated in the previous chapter, people have other channels of communication, on which they rely more heavily.[14] Radio and newspapers do not "monopolize" the process of transforming the minds of the local inhabitants. People become aware of the world through other channels as well, and these as in the case of the party organization, may impart to the villagers a more realistic level of expectation.

[13] See Ch. 10, p. 194.
[14] See Ch. 10, pp. 192—93.

These factors also help to explain why people who have only travelled outside the village, but not the district, express roughly the same degree of dissatisfaction as those who have travelled more extensively, that is, beyond the home district or to other countries. Levels of expectation are similar regardless of what category of people is asked, or regardless of where they live, with the only exception that those living in Kitendagulo, near Bukoba, are slightly more dissatisfied, as shown in Table 34.

It seems therefore that constant exposure to the urban way of life may affect the level of satisfaction of the respondent. Simple geographical mobility does not create marked differences in the way people evaluate their own situation. A considerable number of respondents have travelled to Uganda or Kenya. Many have lived for some time in major urban areas; some have even worked there temporarily. The experience gained in these cities, however, is not likely to make them unhappy of their own situation. Certainly in some cases, people in the urban areas make money, but this is not a universal experience. A constantly increasing number of people in the major towns of Africa is becoming dependent on means other than a regular income from work or trade. Even among those who get money regularly, urban life is not like life in paradise. Food is expensive. Housing conditions often poor.[15]

It is this world to which the urban visitor is exposed, as much as to the world of cinemas, white-washed and shining houses and well-dressed people. No wonder such a person feels satisfied with his own position in the countryside. Conditions in the urban areas of East Africa do not necessarily compare favorably to the rural areas. We have seen in Ch. 8, only a very small percentage of the respondents had any desire to move, if it were possible, to an urban area. The Bahaya have a very high opinion about being a landowner, and they feel that they enjoy a higher degree of economic security on the land than in the towns. Furthermore, the material aspects of life are not likely to be better in town than in the village, unless one gets an extremely well-paid position. These facts are often overlooked when talking about urban experience as a factor contributing to a steep rise in the level of expectations of people.

In order to understand the exceptional case of Kitendagulo, it should be pointed out that the inhabitants there have come to look upon urban life as

[15] There are a number of good studies on the question of urban migration in Africa. These include Ph. Mayer, "Migrancy and the Study of Africans in Towns", *The American Anthropologist,* (Vol 64, 1962), pp. 576—92; J. C. Mitchell, "Africans in Industrial Towns in Northern Rhodesia", *Report of the Duke of Edinburgh's Study Conference* (Vol II, Oxford 1957); P. H. Gulliver, "Incentives in Labour Migration", *Human Organization,* (Vol 19, No 3, 1960); A. W. Southall and P. C. Gutkind, *Townsmen in the Making,* (Kampala 1957); and A. W. Southall (ed), *Social Change in Modern Africa,* (Chicago 1961).

a permanent experience. They, unlike inhabitants in the other parishes, have lost their status as primarily rural peasants, an identity which is more easily kept by the visitor or the urban immigrant, who comes to work only temporarily. It is likely therefore, that urban experience is only going to increase the level of dissatisfaction in those rural areas, where the economic —and social—conditions are very poor.[16]

Because the political organization of TANU pervades the local communities extensively, chances are that very few people can avoid getting affected by its presence, whether they are members or not. Party membership does not, however, reduce the feeling of dissatisfaction with certain important material aspects of life. Ordinary party members do not seem to be so committed to the goals of the party that they are prepared to sacrifice material improvements of their own life for the symbolic gratification of membership in the party.

le 38. Distribution of opinion about their income, housing situation, job and education among local tical leaders, members of TANU and non-members. Absolute number in brackets.

%)	Income			Housing			Job			Education		
	l (36)	m (196)	n-m (48)	l (36)	m (196)	n-m (48)	l (36)	m (196)	n-m (48)	l (36)	m (196)	n-m (48)
ress:												
faction	44,5	29	35	25	35	35	55,5	51	40	11	30	31
ner-nor	8	23	35	36	24	29	16,5	23	31	14	10	14,5
tisfaction	47,5	48	40	39	41	36	28	26	29	75	60	44,5
	100	100	100	100	100	100	100	100	100	100	100	100

aders;   m = members only;   n-m = non-members.

The same can be said about the office-holders. By and large, they are as dissatisfied as any other group. In fact, with regard to education, the highest percentage of dissatisfied people are recorded among the leaders; three out of four respondents. The inference that can be drawn from the figures in Table 38, therefore, is that leaders are likely to become aware of the need for education while holding office. As leaders they are continually exposed to situations, where they have to explain matters to the public. Often in such situations, education would be a great benefit. This assumption is supported by the data obtained in the general election 1965, where

[16] This is an argument that has been presented by some writers on urban migration in Africa. Cf., Ali A Mazrui, "Political Superannuation and the Trans-class Man", paper prepared for 7th World Congress of IPSA, Brussels, September 18—23, 1967.

educational attainment influenced the voters' choice; in most cases, the more highly educated candidates defeated the less educated ones.[17]

The figures also suggest, however, that in the rural areas the process of recruitment to office in the local political institutions is open. The financial and educational position of a person does not exclude him from being elected, although the office-holders perhaps more than other categories of people become aware of the need for education. To that extent political involvement contributes to a rise in the expectations of these people.

The findings from Buhaya can readily be compared with those that Obershall presents in his rural survey in Uganda, particularly as cultural and economic conditions of the two areas are rather similar. He also concludes that the talk about the "revolution of rising expectations" is exaggerated. Certainly media exposure does not in itself produce awareness about objects and desire to obtain these things.[18] The same holds true for urban experience in Uganda. Like media exposure it does not increase the level of dissatisfaction, a pessimistic evaluation of progress or heigthened desires and expectations. One difference between the Haya and the Uganda surveys should be noted: influentials, which include political and other leaders in the local communities, are, in Uganda, by and large more satisfied than the rank and file. Obershall attributes this phenomenon to the fact that they are more prosperous. The distinction made in this study is only between political office-holders and others; but we have seen that the leaders reflect opinions similar to those of the members and the non-members of TANU. Certainly it would be wrong to talk, therefore, about an elite-mass gap in the local communities.

This, however, should not lead us to conclude that the villagers are not interested to improve their conditions, or that they do not conceive of the economic differences that exist between people in different social and economic environments. This fact came out in the answers we obtained when the interviewees were asked what was the principal difference between various people living in their communities. 45 % referred to economic inequalities; another 9 % mentioned that some people are employed, others are not. Another major distinction that the villagers made was between "honest" and "dishonest", "peaceful" and "quarrelsome" peoples; 31 % thought this was the main difference between the inhabitants in their area.

The awareness of economic differences are, as expected, particularly wide-spread among the small farmers. As many as 72 % of them mentioned economic differences, as compared to 42 % of the respondents with middle-size farms, and 40 % with large farms. Among the small farmers, the largest proportion was young and middle-aged persons.

[17] Cliffe (ed), op.cit., pp. 262—64.
[18] Obershall, op.cit., p. 38.

It is hard to know what solution that the villagers would like to see to the problem of economic inequalities. When the respondents were asked an open-ended question, what they thought that the government should not change, 27 % answered land tenure. This was the singlemost important item mentioned. Instead of government take-over of their most valuable resource, the land, they are likely to prefer a situation in which the rich people would be more generous and share their wealth. This is a rather "traditional" solution to the problem, but not an uncommon opinion among the farmers. A middle-aged Muhaya once told the author:

The majority of the people are poorer nowadays. Only a few are rich. It is a trouble in the villages. People complain of difficulties to send their children to school. Maybe it is God's decision... People care too much about themselves nowadays. Many leave the villages, and they forget us who stay behind...

The implication of this statement, which was not obtained in the actual survey, but supplements the answers in it, is that those who have left the rural areas to work in the towns should make greater contributions to the improvement of life also in the rural areas.

Opinions about government allocation

The feeling among the rural inhabitants that they are neglected by the people who have come from their own communities, but now live and work in the towns, is not surprising. It is likely to develop in all societies which undergo a rapid change from traditional agricultural activities to modern industrial activities. The farmers have difficulties to see that living in towns is quite different; to understand, for instance, that the economic conditions for life are not the same as in the villages. It is often very hard for the individual urban resident to meet the many economic demands that are put on him by the relatives in the rural areas.

Almost every little village in Tanzania has some person who has taken the step from the village to the town. Certainly this is true in Buhaya. When talking to the villagers one gets convinced that they are proud of "their sons" who have climbed the social ladder. The village elders can usually name all the youngsters who have got employed somewhere else, privately or by the state. These elders, however, also reveal certain expectations of the young people; expectations, which are very similar to those referred to above. The young people should help their parents. The latter look upon them as a "life insurance". They should build their parents a decent house, or they should pay the education of their younger brothers and sisters, and so forth. This type of expectations are very common.

The feeling that the younger generations, which have moved to the urban areas, do not pay enough attention to the problems of the villages is also likely to have influenced views about how the government is allocating its resources. The rural inhabitants by and large believe that the government prefers spending its money in the towns rather than in the country-side, on industries rather than on assistance to small farmers. Even more serious is the fact that they believe government is spending more on salaries to the MPs than on actual development projects.

Table 39. Beliefs about government allocation of money; by parish. Absolute number in brackets.

(in %)	Bugombe	Kiten-dagulo	Bwatan-gabo	Kaba-gunda	Kiru-ruma
Government spends more on:					
industries or	80 (46)	90 (50)	81 (79)	82 (59)	66 (29)
small farmers*	20 (12)	10 (6)	19 (19)	18 (13)	34 (15)
villages or	20 (12)	9 (5)	20 (20)	15 (11)	34 (15)
towns	80 (46)	91 (51)	80 (78)	85 (61)	66 (29)
development projects or	50 (29)	23 (13)	32 (31)	28 (19)	50 (22)
salaries for MPs	47 (27)	77 (43)	65 (64)	71 (51)	48 (21)
no information	3 (2)	— (0)	3 (2)	1 (1)	2 (1)
total	100 (58)	100 (56)	100 (98)	100 (72)	100 (44)

* as opposed to estate owners

The trend in the answers to the first two parts of the question is clear. It is the urban areas and the industrial sector, the farmers believe, that are favored. As will be seen in Table 40, there are no marked differences between young and old people, educated and uneducated or TANU members and non-members. Opinions are equally distributed among all categories. The answers, which are given, are not factually wrong. According to the Five Year Development Plan, the amount reserved for agricultural development is only 14,5 % of the total capital expenditure for the period 1964 —69, while the share for industrial expansion is 24 %.[19]

[19] The Republic of Tanganyika, *The Tanganyika Five-Year Plan for Economic and Social Development*, (Dar es Salaam 1964), p. 3.

One can assume, however, that factors other than factual knowledge have influenced the answers of the villagers, particularly when comparison is made with the third part of the question. An average of 63,3 % believe that the government allocates more money on salaries to incumbent leaders than on development projects. One may assume that some people expressing this opinion are highly critical of the government. They believe it consists of "self-seekers". This assumption is supported by the fact that the percentage of more educated people is rather high among those who believe that government is allocating more money on salaries to MPs than development projects. We do not know for sure, of course, whether the educated respondents are critical and not just simply ignorant. We found in Ch 9, however, that this category is critical of certain aspects of the political system.[20] In the supplementary interviews critical opinions of the political incumbents were also expressed. One, more educated, man, asked to explain why he thought things had become worse in the last ten years, maintained: It is because Nyerere chose other leaders, who are not educated, and who only know how to talk.

An even harder judgment was passed by an *mzee* (elder) in Bwatangabo:

Our situation has deteriorated, because there is a lack of good leaders. The present leaders are not educated and they do things as they like.

The discontent, which is explicit or implicit in the answers we have obtained may well have another reason, which is connected with the type of political culture that persists in the rural areas. We saw, in Ch 9[21], that the respondents have very high expectations of government performance, and they expect the government to be the principal agent responsible for development. With such values prevailing, it is not surprising if the villagers choose to blame primarily the government for lack of social and economic advancement.

Some people may also seriously believe that the situation has not changed after independence; still political leaders, as in the old times, do get very high rewards for their work; in other words, is it not surprising to the people if more money is spent on remunerating the leaders than on development of the society. In addition to this, it should be pointed out that very few people have been exposed to visible signs of government assistance in the development of the rural areas. Most of the local development projects have been organized and carried out on a self-help basis.[22]

[20] See pp. 167—69.

[21] See pp. 169 and 180.

[22] See p. 50.

Table 40. Beliefs about how government allocates its resources; by age, education and party membership. Absolute number in brackets.

(in %)	Age			Education			Membership	
	young	middle-aged	old	none	some	much	member	non-member
	(132)	(130)	(63)	(143)	(119)	(66)	(225)	(55)
Spends most on:								
small farmers	28	17,5	18	32	16	18	22	18
villages	26	15	20	30	17	18	25	15
MPs	75	61	58	60	58	79	61	68

The rural Bahaya, regardless of age, educational attainment and party membership, feel government is spending too little on the development of the villages. At a general level, however, there exists a congruence between the Haya view of how the government *should* allocate its money and the way government actually spends it. Among the items in the national budget that the Haya respondents consider to be of critical importance are: education, health, agriculture and communications. This fact comes out clearly in the answers recorded in Table 41.

Table 41. Preferences about how government should allocate its resources; by parish. Absolute number in brackets.

(in %)	Bugombe	Kiten-dagulo	Bwatan-gabo	Kaba-gunda	Kiru-ruma
education	60 (35)	67 (38)	64 (62)	43 (31)	50 (22)
health	14 (8)	23 (13)	7 (7)	23,5 (17)	28 (12)
agriculture	17 (10)	3,5 (2)	14 (14)	4,5 (3)	2 (1)
roads, communications	— (0)	— (0)	6 (6)	10 (7)	7 (3)
others	9 (5)	— (0)	1 (1)	6,5 (5)	— (0)
don't know	— (0)	6,5 (4)	8 (8)	12,5 (9)	13 (6)
total	100 (58)	100 (56)	100 (98)	100 (72)	100 (44)

What is striking in this table is not only the relatively high consistency in the answers from one parish to another, but also the fact that so many respondents express a clear opinion on this matter. They all seem to have a very definite desire about what government should do; very few are indifferent.

The Haya concern with education is once again documented. People, regardless of social and economic background, consider it the most important object for government expenditure. The central government, as well as the local District Council, have spent considerable portions of their budgets on education. Still this has not satisfied the expectations of the villagers. Local discontent with educational expansion in the country has continued to grow in many areas. Often the reason is that the government investments in education have been aimed at a target, which is not identical with that preferred by the local inhabitants. A disparity has evolved between the choice made at the national level and the choice made at the local level. For instance, government has shown little interest in building secondary schools in the countryside, but has rather concentrated this type of schools to the urban areas. People in the rural areas, however, have requested that even they should get secondary schools in their immediate vicinity. The local inhabitants cannot always be expected to have understanding for the arguments that government presents in favor of its alternative choice of allocation.

An important aspect of the process of distribution is what determines the opportunities for people to advance in society. We have seen how lineage descent was a major determinant of social mobility in the traditional society, and how religious affiliation largely determined the achievement of new status in the colonial society. "Particularistic"[23] elements played a very predominant role in the process of recruitment to office in these two types of society. The new Tanzanian government has made deliberate efforts to reduce the influence of particularism in social relations. Such things, as religious affiliation or tribal and racial descent, should not be allowed to affect social or political advancement of people.

The government has been equally keen to make it clear that promotion should primarily depend on election or merit. Personal contacts or membership in a special social group should not be allowed to affect recruitment to office. What is said in a public connection, however, may not always be followed in practice. Our way of finding out to what extent the principle of universalism, as opposed to particularism, is followed in Tanzania was to ask the respondents what they think make people succeed in life: good education or good personal contacts, hard work or good family background? We also included the question what is most important: intelligence or sheer luck, in order to find out to what extent they feel they themselves have control of their life, or depend on forces beyond their control. The answers are recorded in Table 42.

---

[23] For a more lengthy explanation of the use of this concept in the study of political cultures, see Almond and Coleman, *op.cit.*, p. 22 ff.

Table 42. Opinions about what is most important in order to succeed in life; by parish. Absolute number in brackets.

(in %)	Bugombe		Kiten-dagulo		Bwatan-gabo		Kaba-gunda		Kiru-ruma	
good education	82,5	(48)	98	(55)	87	(85)	91,5	(66)	93	(41)
or										
good personal contacts	17,5	(10)	2	(1)	13	(13)	8,5	(6)	7	(3)
family background	14	(8)	2	(1)	13	(13)	21	(15)	11,5	(6)
or										
hard work	86	(50)	98	(55)	87	(85)	79	(57)	88,5	(38)
intelligence	19	(11)	6,5	(4)	8	(8)	18	(13)	11,5	(6)
or										
providence (luck)	81	(47)	93,5	(52)	92	(90)	82	(59)	88,5	(38)
total	100	(58)	100	(56)	100	(98)	100	(72)	100	(44)

It is obvious from the figures in this table that the vast majority of the respondents in the rural communities believe that the public authorities will not act arbitrarily, pushing such factors as merit and hard work aside. The high conformity of the answers also indicates that new values have reached even the most distant parts of Buhaya. The percentage of people who believe that the road to success in life lies in good education and hard work are as many in Kiruruma as they are in Bugombe or Kitendagulo.

As Table 43 indicates, the opinions are not markedly determined by such factors as age and education. If any inference at all should be drawn from the figures in this table, it is that educated more than uneducated believe good contacts to be more important in society than good education. This reinforces the impression of the more educated sector of the population as having rather a low evaluation of government performance.[24] That the more highly educated persons should be critical is not surprising. They, perhaps more than any other group in society, have had to make a considerable adjustment to the government policy of equality. The problem of this sector of the population in Buhaya was dramatized by the crisis that followed the 1963 district council election.[25]

People in Buhaya by and large believe that certain rational principles guide the promotion of individuals in society. This is a great asset to the political system as the prevalence of these opinions is likely to reduce the influence of such factors as tribalism or other parochial loyalties.

[24] See pp. 169 and 171.
[25] See p. 134.

Table 43. Proportion of those who believe "good personal contacts", "good family background" and "intelligence" determine success in life; by age and education.

| (in %) | Education | | | | Age | |
| | none | some | much | young | middle-aged | old |
	(143)	(119)	(66)	(132)	(130)	(63)
good contacts	7,5	8	18	12	8,5	9,5
good family background	14,5	11,5	12	15,5	12	9,5
intelligence	12	12,5	15	12	4	17,5

Traditional values, however, still influence the respondents in their opinion of what matters most for success in life: luck or intelligence. Almost nine out of ten respondents feel that their fate is in the hands of God. The local word that is expressing their opinion on this question is *omugisha*—blessing. It has always been a common belief in Buhaya that a human being needs *omugisha*—blessing by the supernatural powers—in order to succeed. The prevalence of this belief also today was clearly reflected in the answers we obtained. Success therefore, although it is promoted by such factors as education and hard work, is, in the opinion of the villagers, ultimately due to an "invisible hand" rather than to the capacity of one's own mind.

Conclusions

In this chapter we have found that a large percentage of the rural population feel dissatisfied with the conditions under which they live; they express discontent with education, income, job and housing situation. The hypothesis, raised by Lerner on basis of his Middle East experience, that level of aspiration and expectation is correlated to media exposure, is not supported by the data obtained in this study. Our survey, as well as one made in rural Uganda, suggests that the situation in East Africa may be different.

Party members are as dissatisfied as people who are not members. Nor do political leaders feel more satisfied than others. On the contrary, there is some evidence that holding a political office may make a person become more dissatisfied, unless he already has those attributes that are held in high respect by the local community, notably education but to some extent also, a good house and a decent income.

The knowledge of the actual process of allocation in the country that the respondents have, suggests that they by and large are familiar with the fact that the government spends more money on industries and urban development than on agriculture and rural development. Quite a large number of the respondents also believe that more money is spent on the MPs than is allocated to development projects. People may have answered this way simply out of sheer ignorance, and/or may seriously believe that this is the case. It is interesting that in this latter category quite a number are highly educated. This group, the more highly educated ones, reveals the most critical appraisal of government performance also when asked what determines success in life. More than any other category of respondents, they believe good personal contacts rather than good education is the guide to success.

This opinion is, however, exceptional. The majority seriously believe that certain objective principles guide promotion in society and they seem to expect treatment by public authorities accordingly. This is no doubt a great strength to the young Tanzanian nation. People may be dissatisfied with their life, and also blame the government for this, but they do not express opinions which indicate political alientation or cynicism.

Chapter 12.   The problem of participation

The previous chapters in this part of the book have dealt exclusively with the opinions and attitudes of the Haya villagers towards the "output side" of the system; their outlook on symbolic outputs, on government regulations, extractions and allocations. This chapter will deal with the input side; how members are involved in the political system.

For the political system increased political participation may imply two things: increased supports and/or increased demands. At one stage members may participate to increase the energies of the system; this often happens, for instance, in a case of national crisis. At another time, however, popular participation at a high degree may simply devastate the energy of the system. People get involved solely to "take out" as much as possible from the system.

The prevailing pattern is determined by situational context and political culture. People may be highly politically conscious, but still constitute a burden to the system, since they rely primarily on the system for problem-solving, and they view themselves as unable to change their own situation. People are lacking civic competence.[1] Such is the situation in most countries in the world, particularly in those countries where people by and large have a low socio-economic status, and a political tradition characterized by a high degree of authoritarianism.

The strong inclination towards the output side that the Bahaya have manifested means that they regard the government as responsible for the welfare of the people. There are also indications that certain sectors of the population believe that the government expects too much of the people. This is a situation likely to be common in all countries where the government leaders, in attempts to reduce the burden of demands on the system, have increased the extractive efforts by raising taxes and requiring a growing number of services from the people. The situation is often made even more complicated, for instance, by the fact that most people do not have full information about the limits of the government.

The discussion about political participation at the parish level in Buhaya will centre around the following four questions: (1) How are the people involved? (2) Do they discuss politics, and how often? (3) What

[1] Almond and Verba, *op.cit.*, Ch. VI. Cf., also p. 178.

is their knowledge of politics? (4) How do they behave at election time? Some of the material presented here has been obtained in a special election survey, and presented at full detail elsewhere.[2]

Political involvement

The degree to which people are involved in the fate of their political system varies in all societies. Some people are not involved at all. They are apathetic and do not mind about politics. Others act as spectators. They regard, and evaluate, political activities with a varying degree of interest. A third category are the politically active people, who regularly attend meetings, being candidates for office or already holding a public office. One may talk, therefore, about a hierarchy of political involvement, ranging from political "gladiators" to political spectators with the apathetics constituting a special category withdrawing from all kinds of political stimuli.[3]

Voting, initiating a political discussion and wearing a party badge are generally considered as spectator activities, contacting a public official or attending a political meeting as transitional activities, and holding office or publicly campaigning for a political organization as gladiatorial activities. The question is how one should regard membership in a political organization. In most Western countries membership in a political party is considered as a rather high degree of political involvement. Becoming a member is a deliberate step in the direction towards a stronger involvement. We have seen, in previous chapters,[4] that membership in TANU is not a crucial variable in determining political behavior in the country-side. Members are not, for instance, more inclined to give prominence to special political qualities of the Tanzanian nation than non-members; they do not regard the regime as more legitimate, and they are as dissatisfied with material conditions as non-members. When a distinction was made between "spectators" —ordinary members—and "gladiators"—office-holders—there were only minor differences expressed in the level of satisfaction.[5]

It is, therefore, rather difficult to draw farreaching conclusions from the fact that 69 % of the sample are members of TANU. We need to know more about their political involvement. The village meetings organized by the VDC—the local TANU body—are usually well attended. In some parishes there is a compulsion to attend. Those who are absent from the public

[2] Cliffe (ed), *op.cit.* See also Appendix I.
[3] These concepts have been borrowed from L. W. Milbraith, *Political Participation,* (Chicago 1965), p. 16 ff.
[4] See e.g., pp. 167 and 205.
[5] See p. 207.

village meetings organized by the VDC leaders may expect some public rebuke at the next meeting. Most people, therefore, prefer to comply rather than to be rebuked in front of all other villagers. This remark should, however, not lead to the conclusion that the villagers are forced to the meetings. A very large number do attend voluntarily. The traditional belief in the area is that once a meeting is called for, everyone should attend. High attendance is therefore expected.

A special opportunity to measure political involvement in this area was offered by the general election, which was held in September 1965. We were, for instance, interested to find out how many would go to the campaign meetings. Such meetings were held at least once in each parish.

Table 44. Attendance at campaign meetings in the 1965 general election; by parish.[6] Absolute number in brackets.

(in %)	Bugombe	Kiten-dagulo		Bwatan-gabo	Kaba-gunda	Kiru-ruma
attended	55 (29)	20	(8)	53 (40)	22 (16)	44 (19)
did not attend	43 (23)	72,5	(29)	46 (35)	77 (55)	52 (23)
no information	2 (1)	7,5	(3)	1 (1)	1 (1)	4 (2)
total	100 (53)	100	(40)	100 (76)	100 (72)	100 (44)

There is a striking difference between Kitendagulo and Kabagunda on the one hand, and the rest of the parishes, on the other. Only about one out of five attended campaign meetings in Kitendagulo and Kabagunda, while in the others the average was close to every second person in the sample. The main reason, however, is not political. By far the majority of the respondents who did not attend in Kitendagulo and Kabagunda claimed that they could not be present because they were "busy with other things"; in most cases they were working. In Kitendagulo a large number have employment in Bukoba township; in Kabagunda a large number are engaged in fishing. Other people who did not attend maintained that the meeting was held too far away; still another group had not been informed about the meeting. Hardly any, however, said he "did not care".

Among those who attended, one finds that political leaders attended more frequently than ordinary members and non-members; 76 % of the leaders, 41 % of the members and 36 % of the non-members. The diffe-

[6] The interview population in the electoral survey was originally supposed to be the same as in the general survey, but a number of respondents could not be traced for post-electoral interviews. The total number of the sample was consequently reduced to 285. In Table 44, percentages are worked out on basis of this figure. Cf., Appendix I.

rence between members and non-members is minimal, and the latter seemed, by and large, to be as keen as the former group to attend the campaign meeting. That such a high percentage of leaders were present can partly be explained by the fact that they were involved in the organization of the meeting and in the mobilization of people to attend.

Campaign meetings in the Tanzanian election 1965 were principally a spectator activity for those who attended. Only the candidates talked and no questioning was arranged after the speeches. The attendance figures for Buhaya were by no means low, particularly considering the predominantly rural character of the parishes. Personal contacts are likely to have facilitated the attendance in these rural communities, where there is a widespread inclination towards conformity in behavior. In places like Bugombe and Bwatangabo the high degree of social homogeneity may also have facilitated a high attendance.

There are few organized activities besides those of the VDC in the rural communities. As many as 61 % of the respondents claim that they are members of the Bukoba Cooperative Union, or its primary society in the area. The percentage is lower in Kabagunda and Kiruruma than in the other parishes. 11 % are enrolled in NUTA—the national trade union movement. 8 % are members of voluntary religious societies. Except for the latter societies which organize domestic training courses, or similar activities, group work and meetings are rare.

Attendance at other meetings than those organized by the VDC is therefore relatively low, although it is true, that attendance even in a society with a highly developed set of interest groups would probably not be much higher.

Table 45. Attendance at meetings other than those organized by the VDC; average for all five parishes. Absolute number in brackets.

(in %)		
once or twice a week	3	(11)
once or twice a month	10,5	(35)
once or twice a year	50,5	(167)
never	36	(115)

Only 2,5 % have ever been office-holders in the cooperative society or any other voluntary group besides TANU. If one looks closer at those who have attended once a month or more often, it turns out that a very high proportion—67 %—are people with at least upper primary education. Although the number of respondents, who are considered in this analysis, is small, only 46, it is worth pointing out that our data corroborates findings made in Western countries that education or higher socio-economic status, in general, stimulates participation in both political and non-political activities.[7]

One very interesting observation is that very few respondents, only 11 % of those who are members of cooperative societies, NUTA or other voluntary associations, considered these organizations as "political". The vast majority looked upon them as non-political. The respondents by and large would not consider using them for political purposes. There are probably several explanations why the respondents should be "turning down" the importance of these associations in the political sphere of action. One would be that they are not inclined to use an institution like the BCU for political objectives, because it can be interpreted as a threat to the hegemony of TANU. Another reason would be that there is a strong inclination to regard politics as the monopoly of a single institution in society.[8] A third reason, and perhaps the most important one, is that they do not consider working through NUTA or BCU as very effective ways of reaching political goals. This opinion was revealed when we asked which they thought were the most effective techniques of influencing the government.

Table 46. Opinions about the most effective technique to influence government; by parish. Absolute number in brackets.

(in %)	Bugombe		Kiten-dagulo		Bwatan-gabo		Kaba-gunda		Kiru-ruma	
voting	46,5	(27)	75	(41)	55	(53)	45,5	(33)	61,5	(27)
writing a letter to MP or member of district council	18,5	(11)	12	(7)	17	(17)	22	(16)	18	(8)
using personal contacts	16	(9)	7,5	(4)	12	(12)	23,5	(17)	16	(7)
working through BCU or NUTA	17	(10)	7,5	(4)	15	(15)	7,5	(5)	4,5	(2)
no information	2	(1)	—	(0)	1	(1)	1,5	(1)	—	(0)
total	100	(58)	100	(56)	100	(98)	100	(72)	100	(44)

The figures illustrate clearly that working through BCU or NUTA is considered least effective of the four choices given to the interviewees,[9] even

---

[7] Cf., Almond and Verba, op.cit., pp. 380—81, S. M. Lipset, *Political Man*, (New York 1960), and R. E. Lane, *Political Life: Why People Get Involved in Politics*, (New York 1959).

[8] See pp. 165—66.

[9] This question was constructed as a closed-choice question after pre-testing, that gave some indication of which techniques people were conscious.

less effective than using personal connections, a method particularly associated with the pre-independent period. Voting is, by 57 % of the sample, considered to be most effective, while a considerable number believe writing to the MP or the local representative in the District Council will have greatest influence.

The conclusion is that the importance of voting is widely recognized, and people consider the individual political representative a more effective political instrument than an interest group such as the cooperative union or the trade union. Our data suggests that there is little activity in the parishes, which would make people feel that BCU or NUTA are capable of influencing the government in the interest of their members. The organizations do not primarily work as a platform for individual consumer interests, and the villagers themselves regard them as non-political.

Political matters can, however, preoccupy the minds of people even in situations where there are limited organized activities of such a character. Certain issues may be taken up in informal discussions among people. This leads us to the second question: How often do the villagers discuss politics?

Milbraith writes that of all stimuli about politics that an individual may encounter, those which come through personal discussions are probably the most influential.[10] Studies from several countries also show that persons participating in informal political discussions are more likely than non-discussants to vote and participate in other ways in the political process.[11] Our survey shows that the percentage of non-discussants is very small; that the vast majority at least sometimes get involved in a political discussion. A large number discuss as often as once or twice a week.

Table 47. Frequency with which respondents discuss political matters; by parish. Absolute number in brackets.

(in %)	Bugombe		Kiten-dagulo		Bwatan-gabo		Kaba-gunda		Kiru-ruma	
every day	10	(6)	16	(9)	3	(3)	8,5	(6)	7	(3)
once/twice a week	32,5	(19)	19,5	(11)	27	(27)	40,5	(29)	48	(21)
less than once a week	40	(23)	48,5	(27)	65	(63)	33	(24)	36	(16)
never	17,5	(10)	16	(9)	4	(4)	15,5	(11)	2	(1)
no information	—	(0)	—	(0)	1	(1)	2,5	(2)	7	(3)
total	100	(58)	100	(56)	100	(98)	100	(72)	100	(44)

[10] Milbraith, op.cit., pp. 39—47.
[11] Cf., e.g., G. Karlsson, "Voting Participation among Male Swedish Youth", Acta Sociologica, (Vol III, fasc. 2—3), pp. 98—111; also S. Rokkan and A. Campbell, "Norway and the United States of America", International Social Science Journal, (Vol XII, No 1), pp. 69—99.

We have seen already[12] that direct face-to-face communication is the most common channel for obtaining information about political matters. Most of the transformation of political information is likely to be in the form of discussion. Surely, one part may be more of a recipient part than the other, but on the whole the transformation of political facts and values takes place under informal discussions. In Buhaya, most of these discussions are held at public places. 77 % claim that they discuss politics at public places like bars. It is a common preoccupation for the male inhabitants in these communities to meet in the bars at least a few times every week.

One particular question of interest is the following: "Who are the people discussing most frequently?" Do they belong to any particular category of people? The answers are presented in the following table.

Table 48. Proportion of people who discuss politics at least once a week; by education, media exposure and political involvement. Absolute number in brackets.

(In %)	education			media exposure				political involvement		
	none	some	much	very often	often	not so often	never	office holder	member	non-member
	(143)	(119)	(66)	(34)	(67)	(95)	(116)	(36)	(189)	(55)
discuss at least once a week	38	33	58	57	45	30	37	75	37	35

Certain trends are discernable. People with much education are discussing more often than others, although there is little difference between those with some education and those without any formal education. This finding is not extraordinary. Several studies, as already indicated, confirm the same pattern.[13]

The affect of media exposure on willingness to discuss politics is perhaps less clear. Those who are exposed most often also tend to be most inclined to discuss. This suggests that frequent exposure to newspapers and radio serves as a political stimulus.[14] On the hand, however, equally interesting is that people who are *never* exposed to this kind of stimulus tend to discuss even more often than those are exposed occasionally (not so often).

Political office-holders are quite naturally much more often engaged in political discussions than ordinary members. Their gladiatorial activities necessarily make them discuss often. From this rule, local Haya political leaders are no exception. Hardly any distinction, however, exists between members and non-members with regard to frequency with which they discuss politics.

[12] See pp. 192—93.
[13] See p. 221, footnote 7.
[14] Cf., B. R. Berelson, P. F. Lazarsfeld and W. N. McPhee, *Voting*, (Chicago 1954).

Next question that we are addressing ourselves to is: What knowledge do the villagers have about politics? We asked a series of questions with the purpose of finding out both how well-informed they are about their leaders and some national events with great symbolic significance, and how knowledgable they are about ways to resolve political problems in their community. How would they go about if a problem arises which has a bearing on the whole community?

Knowledge about who is who in the political hierarchy of the country may not increase the political competence of a person, but it will indicate to what extent people are aware of the political hierarchy outside their own little community; to what extent they pay attention to individual leaders, events and institutions of national significance. We asked a series of information questions, the answers to which are recorded in the following table.

Table 49. Knowledge of the name of certain key political leaders and dates of selected national events; by parish. Absolute number in brackets.

(in %)	Bugombe		Kiten-dagulo		Bwatan-gabo		Kaba-gunda		Kiru-ruma	
Knows name of:										
President (Nyerere)	98	(57)	98	(55)	98	(96)	97	(70)	95,5	(42)
First Vice-President (Karume)	27,5	(16)	33,5	(19)	16	(16)	15	(11)	2	(1)
Second Vice-President (Kawawa)	38	(22)	32	(18)	22	(22)	12,5	(9)	4,5	(2)
Secretary-General of TANU (Kambona)[15]	5	(3)	12,5	(7)	10	(10)	4	(3)	—	(0)
Regional Commissioner (Marwa)	48	(28)	53,5	(30)	42	(41)	15	(11)	4,5	(2)
Area Commissioner (Tosiri/Kafanabo)[16]	10,5	(6)	30	(17)	15	(15)	2,5	(2)	47,5	(21)
Knows date and meaning of:[17]										
Uhuru Day	60	(35)	40	(22)	55	(54)	30,5	(22)	25	(11)
Saba saba Day	46,5	(27)	32	(18)	41	(40)	15	(11)	2	(1)
Union Day	7	(4)	16	(9)	8	(8)	1,5	(1)	—	(0)

[15] Mr Kambona resigned as Secretary-General in June 1967, and the post was abolished at the National bi-annual Conference of TANU at Mwanza in October the same year. See The Nationalist, October 19, 1967. Cf., p. 45, footnote 36.
[16] Tosiri is Area Commissioner in Bukoba District, Kafanabo was Area Commissioner in Karagwe District until 1966.
[17] Uhuru Day is celebrated 9th of December, Saba saba Day—the birthday of TANU—7th of July, and Union Day on 26th of April.

The rather low score on First and Second Vice-President can partly be explained by the fact that the introduction of two vice-presidencies was only made in 1964, when the union between Tanganyika and Zanzibar was first established. Before that time Kawawa had been the only Vice-President. Hence in the answers several mentioned Kawawa as First Vice-President. This recent change in the political leadership had not permeated the local communities. It was further confirmed by the fact that only 6 % knew when the Union Day is celebrated. Surprisingly few could mention the name of the Secretary-General of TANU, an indication that to the local people this role was not regarded as very important.

The Regional Commissioner was more well-known to the people than the Area Commissioner, although they had been in Bukoba about the same length of time. The reason may well be that the former had travelled more extensively in the various parts of Buhaya. A striking exception from this trend, however, is found in Kiruruma, where hardly anybody knows the Regional Commissioner, but almost every second person the Area Commissioner. This has a special explanation. In Karagwe District, the Area Commissioner was in 1965 a man of the area, a person with a name that was familiar to most people, because it was indigeneous and because this person had been involved in local politics since before independence.

The most essential implication of the figures in Table 49 is, however, not how many people know who is who, but the distribution of this knowledge. The geographical location of the parish and its social characteristics seem to determine level of information about these matters. Except for the case of the President himself, people in Kabagunda and Kiruruma are much less informed than those in Bwatangabo, Kitendagulo and Bugombe. People living in the latter three parishes are likely to have seen and heard most of these leaders at least once, as they are located in areas, to which political leaders often have paid visits. In these areas local celebrations of the national holidays have also been organized. Political knowledge in this sense is also determined by education and degree of participation in political discussions, as is shown in Table 50.

Again, our data confirms two findings made in Western countries; that education and interest in politics—e.g., participation in political discussions —are correlated to knowledge about politics. There is no distinct correlation, however, between political knowledge and media exposure. This corroborates, therefore, our earlier finding that mass media are not so important as stimuli for political and non-political aspirations and activities.[18] Other factors, such as face-to-face communication and the elaborate political organization in the country-side, are likely to be more important.

[18] See pp. 204—05. Note, however, that people often exposed to mass media are more inclined than others to discuss political matters. Cf., p. 223.

Table 50. Proportion of those who can name at least three key political leaders and two nation[al] events; by education, frequency of political discussion, and media exposure.[19] Absolute number [in] brackets.

(in %)	Education			Political discussion				Media exposure			
	none	some	much	every day	once/ twice a week	less than once a week	never	very often	often	not so often	neve[r]
	(143)	(119)	(66)	(27)	(107)	(153)	(35)	(34)	(67)	(95)	(116)
people who know at least three key political leaders and two national events (92)	19	25	56	40,5	31,5	27	17.	29,5	28	29,5	26,[ ]

A person who believes he can influence a government decision or in any other way be politically influential is called, by Almond and Verba, "subjectively competent".[20] This competence must be widespread if the citizenry is to have any influence on government policies. The perception of the ability to exert influence, that an individual has, may be unrealistic. Still it is important since a person who feels he has such an ability is more likely to exert influence, than those who lack such a perception. Banfield in his study of a backward rural area in southern Italy illustrates the situation where people lack interest and ability to participate in public affairs.[21]

Our interviewees were asked a question whether there was anything they thought they could do to make it likely that the government would provide a service, such as a better road or a new school, if there was a need for this in their home area. More than four out of five respondents believe that they can do something.

Table 51. Beliefs about whether people can do anything or not to make government provide a service for their home area; by parish. Absolute number in brackets.

(in %)	Bugombe		Kiten-dagulo		Bwatan-gabo		Kaba-gunda		Kiru-ruma	
believe they can do	79,5	(46)	76,5	(43)	86	(84)	88,5	(64)	86	(38)
believe they cannot	18,5	(11)	23,5	(13)	12	(12)	7	(5)	14	(6)
no information	2	(1)	—	(0)	2	(2)	4,5	(3)	—	(0)
total	100	(58)	100	(56)	100	(98)	100	(72)	100	(44)

[19] From our point-of-view, knowledge of at least three persons in the hierarchy, e.g., the President, the Regional Commissioner and the Area Commissioner, plus the two most important national events, Uhuru Day and Saba saba Day was considered an indication of "political knowledge" in this case.

[20] Almond and Verba, op.cit., p. 137 ff.

[21] Banfield, op.cit., p. 85.

It is remarkable that the distribution of subjective competence is roughly the same in each parish, despite their distinct social and economic characteristics. This should probably be credited to TANU, as TANU itself and its activities is likely to have contributed most to the growth of political consciousness in an area like Kiruruma, geographically isolated and with few educated people. Unlike the situation in most of the countries studied by Almond and Verba, subjective competence is not highly correlated in our study to educational attainment.[22] The competent persons were 79 % among those with no education, 85 % among those with some, and 84 % among those with at least upper primary school education.

We were also interested to know what strategy that the competent people would try to use in order to influence the government. In replying to the question what they could do to influence the government to provide a new school or a better road, there was a certain vagueness; several respondents simply replied "ask for government help". Others, however, were more specific.

Table 52. What "competent" villagers report they would do to make the government provide a service to their community; by parish. Absolute number in brackets.

(in %)	Bugombe		Kiten-dagulo		Bwatan-gabo		Kaba-gunda		Kiru-ruma	
voluntary work	17,5	(8)	51	(22)	52,5	(44)	94	(60)	98	(37)
ask for government help	50	(23)	30	(13)	46	(39)	3	(2)	—	(0)
contact VEO	6,5	(3)	—	(0)	1,5	(1)	—	(0)	—	(0)
contact VDC	13	(6)	14	(6)	—	(0)	—	(0)	—	(0)
contact private agency, like mission	—	(0)	2,5	(1)	—	(0)	3	(2)	—	(0)
other ways	13	(6)	2,5	(1)	—	(0)	—	(0)	2	(1)
total	100	(46)	100	(43)	100	(84)	100	(64)	100	(38)

It is highly probable that in the minds of those who answer "ask for government help" is an intention to do this through the local government representatives, the VEO or the VDC. We have seen earlier that quite a large number of matters are brought before the VDC.[23] One reservation should, however, be made. The matters discussed by the VDCs are almost exclusively local parish problems or brought to the notice of the VDC by a superior political authority. Very few matters are forwarded to the district or national level, as has been illustrated in Table 24. Requests for govern-

[22] Cf., Almond and Verba, op.cit., pp. 159—67.
[23] See pp. 174—75, Table 25.

ment assistance are very few compared to other items discussed in the VDCs. For this reason one should be careful to draw the conclusion that what the respondents say, they will necessarily also do.

The most interesting finding, however, is that such a large percentage mention "voluntary work". This suggests that people are aware not only that they have to make a contribution themselves, but also that they can, by offering their participation in the development process, exert pressures on the government to achieve benefits for their communities. Two things follow from this. First of all, the voluntary contributions by people are a great asset to the government, since it can save already scarce financial resources.[24] Secondly, however, the fact that people are aware that they, by offering their voluntary contribution to the development of the society, can affect government responsiveness, is likely to lead to an increase in number of inputs. The burden of demands on the system is, therefore, not necessarily lightened.

It is worth noting that the inclination to mention "voluntary work" is highest in the most distant parishes, Kiruruma and Kabagunda. Here the VDC is meeting less frequently and its role is limited. It seems, therefore, as if input demands in these types of parishes are channeled less through the VDCs than in eastern Buhaya, where these committees tend to be well organized. Even though formal government institutions do not function so well in the distant parts of Buhaya, people are aware of means to influence the course of events.

Voting behavior in the 1965 election

The rest of this chapter will be devoted to an analysis of the voting behavior of the Bahaya in the 1965 general election. As we are interested in the relation between centre and periphery of the Tanzanian political system, our focus will be primarily on how the voters viewed the election process and what it symbolized to them. It means treating the election as an event in the life of the individual citizen and the life of the political system rather than paying attention to "who won and why?" Among other things, we are interested to know whether the general election tended to change political behavior, and, if so, in what way. We have already found, for instance, that participation in political discussion is correlated to level of education. Does this also hold true at election time? Do educated people discuss politics more often? Do they go to the polls in larger proportions than uneducated people?

[24] See p. 50, footnote 63.

The 1965 election in Tanzania was unique in the sense that it was the first serious attempt in any African state to allow for competition within a one-party system. The national leadership of TANU did not make the nominations; these were made at the local level by representatives of the party branches. TANU was more supervising than controling and steering the election.

Among the nominees, those two who had received the highest number of votes at the district conference, which was the selective body, were accepted as official candidates. In only a few cases did the National Executive Committee of TANU, which formally made the final decision, alter the order of preference accepted by the district conference.[25] Each candidate had, for the purpose of identification, to associate himself with a symbol, the "hoe" or the "house". These were used in all constituencies and allocated by the NEC. The symbols are mentioned here, since they came to play a significant part in the election, at least in Buhaya.

70 % of all respondents in our election survey[26] claimed that they went to the polls. This corresponds well to the average in the four Haya constituencies, where roughly two thirds of the registered population used their right to cast a vote. The registered persons were estimated to be approximately two thirds of the total adult population. In Buhaya, age and income did not distinguish voters from non-voters, but education did. On the other hand, attendance at campaign meeting was less a determining variable, as is shown in the following table.

Table 53. Proportion of voters in the 1965 election; by education and attendance at campaign meeting. Absolute number in brackets.

	Education			Attendance at meeting	
	none (143)	some (119)	much (66)	yes (112)	no (165)
voted in the election	51	74	83	71	68,5

That educated people are more likely to vote than non-educated people has been established in electoral surveys in a number of countries[27] and it is found also here, in this relatively isolated part of Tanzania.

Those who failed to vote did so primarily for personal reasons, not because they found technical procedures complicated or politics non-attractive and unimportant. For instance, among the old people physical handicaps were given as reason for non-voting, in the lower age categories "being

25 In 16 out of 208 cases; Cliffe (ed), *op.cit.*, p. 33.
26 *Ibid.*, p. 275.
27 Cf., p. 221, footnote 7.

away from home" was mentioned most frequently. Thus our data suggests that it is personal reasons rather than barriers to suffrage or political alienation which account for non-voting.

The voting pattern in Buhaya differs somewhat from that found in the rural areas of Arusha District in northern Tanzania. There uneducated people turned out in slightly higher proportions than those who had some schooling. Thus, demographic variables do not seem to be powerful predictors of electoral behavior in the rural areas of Tanzania.[28]

The 1965 election was a national event and it helped linking the ordinary member of the Tanzanian political system to the political life of the nation. As such the election did not only help the individual voter feeling a sense of political competence, but it was also bound to affect the legitimacy of the present regime. If a large sector of the population were to feel that the election was rigged, the legitimacy of the regime would decline. Therefore, it was important to the electoral administrators to uphold the rules and regulations and appear impartial to the electorate. As far as our survey data indicates, people by and large felt that the administrators did so. Only 12 % of all *voters* expressed the opinion that the election was not fair. The majority of these people were concentrated to one parish, where dissatisfaction with the presiding officer at one polling station was felt among a certain group of people.

The relative absence of discontent and cynicism with the election is particularly important, as the villagers to a large extent consider voting the most important technique of influencing the government.[29] It is their tool to influence the course of events and it is likely to be of considerable importance to the political system that this first general election in the history of independent. Tanzania was not primarily associated with negative and cynical impressions.

We have noted earlier[30] that quite a large percentage of the respondents attended the campaign meetings which were held in 1965. Our survey data underlines the importance that the villagers are inclined to assign to the election.

Somewhat contradictory is, however, the fact that less than a quarter of the respondents in Buhaya (23 %) report that they have been involved in discussions about the election in the campaign period. This figure is much lower than that registered for political discussions when there is no election (cf., Table 47). Very unexpectedly, those most prepared to discuss the elections were the uneducated people and those who had not attended campaign meetings.

[28] For a more detailed account, see Cliffe (ed), *op.cit.*, p. 275.
[29] See p. 221, Table 46. The same pattern was found in other parts of Tanzania. See Cliffe (ed), *op.cit.*, p. 275 ff.
[30] See p. 219, Table 44.

Table 54. Proportion of respondents discussing the election in the campaign period; by education and attendance at campaign meeting. Absolute number in brackets.

(in %)	Education			Attendance at meeting	
	none (143)	some (119)	much (66)	yes (112)	no (165)
discussed the elections	32	19	14	17	28

These figures suggest several things. We have evidence that most information which was transmitted to the individual respondents about the election came from friends and other family members (57 %). 18 % got this information from campaign meetings, 17 % from radio and newspapers and 8 % from TANU (VDC) leaders. A large amount of information therefore was transmitted from one individual to another in the days before the election. Several people may not have conceived of this information transfer as a "discussion", and that is a possible reason why so few claim that they were involved in "discussions" about the elections. There is an additional aspect of this. Local interviews indicated that in some parts of Buhaya, people disliked to disclose how they should vote. They preferred to be left to make up their minds without "interference" by another person. Showing little interest in political discussion during the actual campaign was therefore not an expression of discontent, not even of indifference. The persons had a latent interest in the election, but did not, for certain reasons, which may be connected with the local culture or the fact that they had already made up their mind and did not want to be "disturbed", express their preferences.

What the figures in Table 54 indicate is the defiance of a conclusion, which has often been drawn in Western countries,[31] that persons who lack education and sophistication about politics exclude political stimuli. In fact, our evidence suggests that the more highly educated people at the time of election were those who excluded the political stimuli.

This rather unusual situation may well have its explanation in the part played by the symbols in the election.[32] With only one party and no real ideological issues at stake the symbols were conceived by several people as the principal alternatives in the election. Such was the case particularly in

[31] Cf., e.g. Almond and Verba, op.cit., pp. 56—57, and 110—13, Lipset, "Political . . .", op.cit., pp. 183—229, and P. F. Lazarsfeld, B. R. Berelson and H. Gaudet, The People's Choice, (New York 1944).

[32] For a detailed account of the part played by symbols in the election, see, G. Hyden, "The Role of Symbols in the Tanzania Election 1965", Mawazo, (Vol I, No 1, 1967), pp. 41—47.

those areas where the candidates were not well-known to the people. As will be shown below, the fact that many voters based their choice on the symbol—as many as 36,5 % of all respondents (54 % of all voters) report they voted for a candidate because of his symbol—does not imply that they did so purely out of affection for one or the other of the two symbols.

There is evidence to suggest that the symbols became major issues in the informal discussions that took place in the rural areas of Buhaya. At any rate our data shows that those who were most often involved in political discussions in the campaign period were those voting by symbols only— respondents who specifically claimed that they voted for a candidate because of his symbol.

Table 55. Electors voting by symbol only, shown as percentages of how often they discussed the election, and when they made up their mind how to vote. Absolute number in brackets.

	Discussed the election:				Made up their mind:			
	every day	once/ twice a week	less than once a week	never	election day	a week before	more than week before	when names were first announced
	(16)	(20)	(63)	(176)	(25)	(39)	(55)	(84)
voted on symbol only	72	72	49	33	44	50	40	31

The figures also reveal that those who voted for a candidate because of his symbol were less inclined to make up their mind until only shortly before election day, or in some cases not until that day. This finding is further corroborated by the fact that in Bugombe, where one of the candidates was very well known, because he lived in a nearby parish, people made up their mind much earlier than elsewhere; a much higher percentage there also claimed that they voted because of "previous services" of the candidate.

To many people the symbols helped making the electoral choice intelligible. Political issues became largely interpreted in the light of the associations that each individual had with the symbol. In Bukoba District, for instance, people favored the "hoe" candidate, the reason being that people by and large believed that this person would be most prepared to help them get more food. At this time there were complaints in the villages that there was not enough of food. In Karagwe, however, and particularly in Kiruruma, which is situated on the edge of real "bush" country, the main concern was with better shelter. In Bukoba most people have "decent" houses, while in many parts of Karagwe, including the Kiruruma area, standard of housing is unsatisfactory.[33]

The final comment to be made is that even people in the villages are quite aware of the importance of voting as a means to influence the course of events. They feel subjectively competent at least to the extent that they believe that their leaders are in power at the discretion of the voters. The 1965 election probably reinforced this belief, as the result was that a large number of prominent politicians were defeated. People do not vote, however, according to whether the candidate reflects the ideology or policy alternative that they themselves support, but rather according to whom can best represent their interest in the National Assembly. The MP is a delegate, and as such he is primarily obliged to fulfill the desires of the members of his constituency. One possible consequence of this style of representation is that the MP becomes an "errand boy". The electors begin raising their demands on the system for certain goods and services. This tendency is particularly likely to appear in an area with a "subject" political culture like Buhaya, where people view the political system primarily as something from which benefits and rewards are to be drawn. The emphasis on the "delegate" role of the MP therefore both increases the burden on the system and limits the freedom of action of the individual MP.[34]

Conclusions

A number of observations about voting behavior made in Western countries have been confirmed by the survey data from Buhaya. For instance, education stimulates participation in both political and non-political activities; educated individuals are more likely to engage in political discussions than other groups, and so forth. We also found, however, that this observation did not hold true at election time. Those most often engaged in political discussion in the campaign period were people with no education. This finding defies the observation made elsewhere that uneducated people shut out political stimuli.

The special situation that we find in Buhaya is likely to be the result of a political education, that almost everyone has gone through in recent years due to the presence of TANU. Villagers are, by and large, aware of

[33] A Haya observer, Bishop J. Kibira confirms this observation. In another context he writes "... people near the Lake (Victoria) with better homes were not concerned much about the 'house', but instead the 'hoe'; whereas far west (Karagwe) where they had done a lot of farming but had poor homes, people chose the 'house' candidate, thinking of he was going to help them get better homes".

[34] Cf., Cliffe (ed), op.cit., pp. 295—97.

the importance of voting, and they have a subjective competence; they believe that they can influence government and the course of political events. The main problem for the political system may grow out of the cultural belief that the political representative of the people is primarily chosen to get his constituents as many services and benefits as possible. To this extent the villagers are still primarily political spectators, although at least in some areas of Buhaya they realize that their own contribution is necessary if the government is to provide e.g., a new school or a better road.

Conclusions, summary and appendices.

Chapter 13.   Conclusions

One important conclusion is that survey research, a method which has successfully been employed for the study of political culture in America and Europe, can be used profitably in a rural African context. It has been possible to confirm, or disprove empirical generalizations established in other parts of the world. For instance, it has been shown that the opinions about economic development of the rural inhabitants are similar to those of peasants in other parts of the world. A second generalization confirmed was that the more highly educated members of society tend to go to the polls in greater numbers than the less educated and illiterate members. The material refutes, however, that the least sophisticated individuals necessarily reject political stimuli. The use of familiar symbols in the 1965 election served indeed as stimuli also for those who did not know the candidates and their records.

Another important finding is that the differences in attitudes and opinions between young and old people are much smaller than expected in a rural area like Buhaya. Other social scientists have supposed this difference to be a typical feature for Africa. The situation in Buhaya may be due to the relatively long educational tradition, the considerable degree of geographical mobility and the presence of a well-organized political party. The situation may well be different where these conditions do not exist. In Buhaya, however, parents are not likely to prepare their children merely for participation in the local communities. The burden of modernizing attitudes and beliefs does not only lie on the educational institutions, as is sometimes assumed.

There is no evidence supporting Lerner's thesis that mass media is principally responsible for the creation of new expectations. People with low and high degree of media exposure do not differ significantly as to their level of satisfaction with certain basic material conditions and their hopes for the future. This, which is supported by findings made in a similar survey in Uganda 1966, can be explained by the fact that media exposure and urbanization affect the process of modernization in a different fashion in East Africa than they have done in the Middle East. Only a small percentage of the total population in Tanzania live in urban areas. There has not yet been in Tanzania, like in several other countries, for instance, in the Middle East, a mass exodus of dissatisfied rural dwellers from the countryside to the towns, where the impact of mass media is likely to be much stronger.

Before proceeding with the conclusions a few remarks are needed. The conclusions in this book are primarily based on the answers of the individual rural inhabitants themselves. Their answers, however, do not tell us whether they would behave in accordance with the way they have indicated orally. Attempts have been made to overcome this shortcoming by relating attitudes and opinions to the type of problems brought before the Village Development Committees. As has been indicated at some places in the text, there does exist a certain correlation. The questions on which the respondents express concern or dissatisfaction, are by and large, also those which are most frequently dealt with by the VDCs.

Secondly it should be emphasized again that Buhaya is not necessarily typical of Tanzania. It has been selected because it is particularly relevant for the study of how the system is trying to overcome developmental problems in the periphery of the society.[1] Despite the limitations of the material in the study, however, it can be used for making certain general statements about the system capabilities in Tanzania.

At the same time, however, it must be noted that the rural environment form only one "constituency", in which the system has to perform. There are other constituencies, domestic and international, which may well be more important for the survival of the system. What has been said, therefore, about the consequences of system performance for the individual members in Buhaya should not be taken as an indication that the same consequences have been achieved among other groups of people in the country. For instance, we do not know how civil servants, urban workers or army officers view the system. The rural population nevertheless has been selected for special attention because it constitutes a vast majority of the total population, because rural problems have been given priority by the government authorities, and because the opinions of rural dwellers have not yet been systematically integrated in studies of this type.

It is now time to draw the conclusions from our closer examination of the centre-periphery relationship. There is enough evidence to show that the new structures established around independence in the local communities of Buhaya are still viable, and that people have reacted favorably to several important changes in the political culture. The political leaders have, to a considerable extent, managed to evoke the support of the rural inhabitants for the goals set by the system.

This finding comes out particularly in the examination of the Haya responses to the problems of identity and legitimacy. The prevalence of a strong identity with the nation and a high degree of loyalty to the regime is likely to serve as an important mechanism for social and political control. People, by and large, have accepted a common set of norms guiding them in their

[1] Cf., pp. 31—32.

relations to other people as well as to the political authorities. This suggests that the system capabilities with regard to the problems of identity and legitimacy have reached a relatively high level. The system has shown itself capable of manipulating various pressures relating to these two types of problems. Innovations and institutionalizations of response patterns to solve problems of identity and legitimacy may have been facilitated by the fact that a certain degree of cultural secularization and structural differentiation had taken place already before independence. The traditional systems in Buhaya had declined in the course of colonial rule, and people had moved into new social and political roles as a result of the spread, among other things, of commercial and educational activities. A new stratification system, primarily based on ownership of economic resources and on educational attainment had around independence largely replaced the traditional one. Certain groups were strong enough to oppose the aims of the new leadership in the country, but the fact that the political organization of TANU grew strong before this new stratification system had become too firmly rooted in Buhaya, helps explain why so little opposition to the regime is recorded in our survey. The presence of TANU values and structures have contributed to the subordination of local interests in Buhaya, which could have become detrimental to the maintenance of various system capabilities.

This does not mean, however, that there exists no distinct local subculture in Buhaya. Values are to a large extent authoritatively allocated by local structures, which, even if they are branches of centrally controlled institutions, perform to some extent within the framework of local cultural values. The fact that this type of values persist has probably contributed to the relatively high degree of assimilation of the Bahaya into the national community. It has been argued that a certain degree of cultural fragmentation will facilitate national assimilation in a country in which the expansion from local to national politics has occurred only recently.[2]

The prevalence of local values is recorded in various contexts. The Bahaya have always been used to a very high degree of regulation of social behavior. It is not surprising, therefore, that a large percentage of the population express concern with the lack of *emilembe*—harmony or peace. The present system, in their mind, is not regulative enough.

Many opinions relating to the problems of penetration and allocation are conditioned by economic factors, such as the small size of the landholdings, lack of cash money, both for agricultural investment and for personal consumption. Several respondents find it hard to accept new methods of cultivation. The Haya coffee farmers grew accustomed to a relatively good cash income during the coffee boom in the 1950s. They have maintained to a

[2] Cf., p. 154.

large extent the expectations and aspirations which were generated in those years, but they lack, today, the financial resources which made the building of better houses, and the buying of new consumption goods, in particular, clothes, possible at that time. This local condition is one explanation why there is a comparatively widespread discontent with certain basic material aspects of life. It is interesting that the distribution of discontent is as prevalent among local political leaders as it is among ordinary members and non-members. One reason for this is that all types of people are recruited to positions of local leadership. Poor and illiterate people are found in positions of local leadership together with rich and educated persons. Once the former reach these positions, however, the social pressures on them to set a good example for the rest of the community, increase. Such persons often perceive their poorly constructed house and lack of education with shame. This, therefore, explains why the discontent is also so prevalent among local leaders who are closely identified with the regime.

On the whole, satisfactory maintenance of the extractive and distributive capabilities are very difficult to achieve in a poor country like Tanzania. Material resources are limited, and its is a difficult task to bring about cultural innovations, which will create a motivational change in the minds of rural inhabitants. This study of Buhaya has illustrated that point. The task of the government to persuade them to become modern coffee farmers is very hard, considering particularly that the economic incentives for growing coffee are less attractive today than they were ten years ago.

In such a situation it is not surprising if the government is blamed for the unsatisfactory material conditions of the people. For instance, the rural inhabitants in Buhaya believe that more money is spent on the MPs than on actual development projects. This belief has also been nurtured by the fact that the political leaders after independence by many have been perceived as a separate group detached from the realities of rural life. Some leaders have become associated with a rather ostentatious way of life, a fact that has not contributed to an increase in their popularity. There is, however, an additional reason for the prevalence of this belief. In the first years of independence the rural dwellers in Buhaya have not seen any spectacular proofs of government investment in development projects. For the building of schools, health dispensaries, and roads, the government has, in fact, relied on voluntary participation by the local population.

The efforts to maximize participation in local self-help projects—*kujitolea*—have, from the government point-of-view, been an educative process, as the idea of collective work has no tradition in Buhaya. People must be educated from their traditional belief that the political system, or the government, exists only to render them rewards. They must be taught that the system also has expectations of its members. This is likely to be almost a precondition for the development of a political system, which has to rely on very scarce material resources.

It is interesting to note, however, that the local population, particularly in the two most distant parishes, view voluntary contributions to development projects as a means to obtain things needed in their communities. The local Bahaya have a certain degree of political confidence, much of which was gained already before independence due to extensive political activities in the area. They prefer, however, to remain political spectators. Their political involvement is rather episodic. It reaches a high point only at times of election. This is a result of their own view of how to affect the course of political events. A large majority believes that the best means by which to exert pressure on the government is through voting rather than by contacting the MP or working through associational interest groups. This is likely to make the individual feel that he has some control over his environment. On the other hand, it may tend to increase his expectations of the system. He may contribute to the politicization of an increased amount of environmental pressures. Our summary of matters brought before the VDCs suggests, however, that the majority of pressures which are politicized through these local institutions are taken care of at that level. They are not transmitted into central government institutions where the load is heaviest. The central government agencies are often unable to bring about a solution to the problems at the local level because of the lack of resources.

One might summarize by saying that the political culture in the rural environment of Tanzania, as it is reflected in our survey in the five Haya parishes, primarily resembles a *subject* culture.[3] It has, however, certain remnants of parochialism and some features of a more participant culture. The members are growing increasingly aware of the input side of the system, and there are tendencies to abandon their strong orientation towards the output side of the system.

The relatively high degree of success in institutionalizing new cultural values in the rural communities is to a large extent due to major structural innovations in recent years, the most important being the organization of TANU. It has become the most valuable instrument in bringing about changes which are necessary to make the political culture more amenable to the demands of a modern political system. The high degree of confidence in the party is a prominent feature of the rural Bahaya. TANU is trusted as the single legitimate authority. When, for instance, it comes to the dissemination of information about agricultural improvement, most of what the farmers learn is obtained from representatives of the party. The agricultural extension service and the cooperative societies are not as prominent in transmitting information relevant for local development. Our material, therefore,

[3] Cf., pp. 165 and 200.

indicates that TANU really functions as a communication media between the centre and the periphery. If TANU, as Bienen concludes[4], is unable to promote economic development in the rural areas, the primary reason is not lack of confidence in the organization. It is rather, as he suggests, the low level of economic development, lack of skilled personnel and so forth, that make the full employment of the TANU organization in the process of economic development impossible.

TANU's contribution to the achievement of social and political change is indicated by the fact that, in terms of prevailing attitudes among the people, no significant differences exist between the five parishes, despite their different social and economic features. People in distant Kiruruma display attitudes similar to those of the people in "sub-urban" Kitendagulo. Differences, therefore, in geographical location, in means of communication, in educational opportunities, and in commercial activities, that could be expected to affect the belief system of the people, are largely neutralized by the presence of a strong political organization. Our survey suggests that several structural and behavioral hindrances to modernization and development have been overcome due to the mobilizational capacity of TANU.

Political mobilization in a rural area, like that of Buhaya in Tanzania, is facilitated by the fact that the number of other social institutions competing for the loyalty of the people is limited. Certainly very few others are involved in major structural and cultural change. People in the rural areas of Buhaya are by and large uncommitted and more readily available for involvement in a political organization.[5] The introduction in these relatively isolated rural communities of a modern political organization, directed to a large extent from a national centre, becomes an even more important factor in the development process as the ability of the inhabitants of these communities to construct and sustain voluntary associations is weak. Modernization and development, therefore, must be achieved mainly through political mobilization, because other institutions are more traditionally-oriented, and the communities are unable, on their own, to achieve major changes. It is true, that Buhaya in this respect is not a typical case, as the traditional orientation of the inhabitants is not prominent. The problem exists also there, but it is likely to be even larger in other areas, where modernization and development has not proceeded so far. This is one reason why government policies in the less developed countries are most often the result of withinputs;[6] of demands by the political elite itself. Inputs from the society are not likely to be conducive to development unless it is mo-

---

[4] Bienen, *op.cit.*, pp. 406—16.

[5] This is the argument of a writer like William Kornhauser. See his, *The Politics of Mass Society*, (New York 1959).

[6] Cf., p. 19.

dern. Allowing for an extensive flow of inputs from traditionally-oriented rural areas would render development more difficult.

In the case of Tanzania, people in the rural areas probably enjoy more opportunities to forward their demands into the system than people in similar positions in most other African countries. This drive to increase the responsiveness of the system to local demands has gained inspiration from the philosophy of President Nyerere himself. It is true that several people, even the majority, do not take advantage of these opportunities. The reason is that they do not know how to go about it; they lack civic competence.[7] In order to reduce the detrimental effects on the development of the system by an extensive flow of local, often parochial, demands, the government has attempted to use the local TANU structures, notably the VDCs, for the institutionalization of new, more modern values. The government has also decentralized the decision-making process, so that the local authorities, the district councils, take care of most local demands. The central authorities only supervise and coordinate. In this way the central authorities are relieved from dealing with a large amount of local demands; there is yet, however, a certain degree of responsiveness from the system.

A current feature of Tanzanian politics, particularly prominent since early 1967, has been the special attention of the government authorities to rural development problems. They have tried to make the goals of the system congruent with the needs of the majority of the people in the country. Some of the government strategies and methods which were used in the first years of independence to bring about improvement in the villages have not been very successful; the best example is the failure of the village settlement schemes. As the material from Buhaya indicates, the villagers have not always viewed the government strategies as beneficial to themselves, as these have often implied increased short-term sacrifices on part of the local population. The high rate of system innovation has occasionally created strains in the society and the process of institutionalization of various response patterns has, therefore, become more complicated. The political leaders of Tanzania have hardly chosen an easy road for themselves. The fact that the system capabilities have been primarily directed towards the achievement of satisfying needs felt among the poor masses of the rural areas, has called for a stronger control and integration of the flow of inputs and outputs. As a result of this, the more privileged groups in the society, including political and other leaders and even the urban workers, have been forced to make great sacrifices. These sacrifices, however, seem necessary, if the more privileged sectors of the population are going to live up to the expectations by the common man in the rural areas.

[7] This concept is used by Almond and Verba in their book, *op.cit.*, p. 136 ff; see also p. 217.

The Arusha Declaration states clearly that the duty of the political leaders is to identify primarily with the needs of the peasants and the workers. It is too early to say whether the system will succeed in this effort. It will depend on whether the system can improve its capabilities; whether it can institutionalize beliefs, like that of self-sacrifice, and structures, thereby guiding human behavior in the direction in which the new values point. This has become particularly pertinent after the Arusha Declaration. The innovations in the society have been both more frequent and more farreaching after February 1967 when the Declaration was approved.

This document was passed after this investigation in Buhaya was completed. It still has a special relevance for this study, because the prescriptions for improvement that are presented there, do point at exactly those weaknesses in the system capabilities that are recorded in our survey. It emphasizes that the rural inhabitants in the first years of independence have suffered from a relative economic stagnation. It records the unfavorable implications of a growing difference between the richer and the poorer sectors of the population. It was on these points that the villagers expressed particular concern and discontent. This study, therefore, confirms the relevance of the recommendations offered in the Arusha Declaration.

The final comment is that, as viewed from the rural environment, the political system in Tanzania shows definite signs of development in recent years. The maintenance of the assimilative, regulative and responsive capabilities have helped the rural population to adapt to the modernization process. The consequence of the emphasis on these capabilities is, by and large, favorable. The individual members in the rural communities feel committed to various components of the system. The maintenance of the extractive and distributive capabilities has been more difficult due to the scarce resources of the country, falling prices on raw material, and so forth. It is very difficult to institutionalize response patterns which can take care of the problems of the local population, relating to improvement of their own economic situation. As is demonstrated in the Arusha Declaration, however, the leaders are aware of this shortcoming of the system. One may conclude, therefore, that the title of the official party song—and of this book—*TANU Yajenga Nchi,* is not just an empty slogan. We have seen in this study that TANU has already to some extent successfully built the new nation and there are plenty of indications that it is still vigorously involved in that process.

System typologies

The last consideration in this book will be whether this investigation can give rise to a redefinition of existing classificatory schemes of political systems, in particular with reference to Africa. It is obvious that the basis for generalizations is limited. All the same, the data presented here indicates some new criteria on which the classification of political systems can be made, the primary reason being that the centre-periphery relationship in an African system not yet been subject of any systematic investigation based on survey data. The centre-periphery relationship is a new dimension with regard to the study of African political system.

The current typologies, to which reference has been made at a number of places, are primarily based on such factors as type of ideology, degree of ideological preoccupation, degree of political mobilization and type of intra-party relationships.[8] This study has focused on an important aspect of the political culture—to what extent there exists some congruence between values professed by the political leaders on the one hand, and their followers, on the other, in one of the new nations in Africa. Buhaya has its own, distinct sub-cultural features; yet the rural population in Buhaya reveal, at the same time, a strong commitment to the system. That this commitment is so strong among the rural inhabitants may be due to special efforts by the political leaders to identify, to a large extent, the system goals with the interest of the masses. Such a commitment does not, however, necessarily exist in a country, even if the leaders are aspiring to achieve this quality of the system. Escalation from a conservative to a more radical ideology, often called "ideological modernization", is important. Nonetheless, more is needed to establish a more viable political system.

Much of the success of the system in solving the developmental problems will depend on the behavior of the political leaders. They must be able to recognize that there are great dangers to the political system, because their societies are not yet fully integrated. Sub-cultural cleavages can very easily create disturbances in the political system. Besides having the capacity, and willingness, to reserve distintegrative tendencies, the political leaders must be able to transcend sub-cultural differences at the centre of the political system. Unless there exists a mutual understanding and willingness to cooperate at the elite level between members of various tribes, religious groups, social classes, and so forth, social and political antagonisms in society are likely to be intensified. Ghana and Nigeria are two cases in point. Political dislocations in those countries are largely due to inability on part of the leaders to cooperate and establish effective means of communications across various types of cleavages. Finally, leaders must also have the ability to find solutions to problems, which attract members of all sub-cultures. This problem is particularly difficult in those countries where there exists a great diversity in developmental levels between various parts of the country. It is

[8] Cf. Coleman and Rosberg, *op.cit.,* Apter, "The Political Kingdom . . .", *op.cit.,* and Rudebeck, *op.cit.*

an allocational problem, which can produce rifts not only between the political leaders, but also between members of the different sub-cultures.

Political elite behavior in Tanzania resembles very much that which is likely to be necessary for overcoming the many complications resulting from the sudden expansion of traditional, local politics to modern, national politics. The political leaders do recognize that a certain type of behavior is necessary in order to bridge the differences, which they have inherited from the colonial period. These countries, in which the leaders do this, have a *consociational* type of political system. The concept was originally used by David Apter[9] to describe political systems in Africa willing to accomodate a variety of groups of divergent ideas in order to achieve a goal of unity. It has later been used to classify those democratic systems, primarily in Western Europe, which have a fragmented political culture, but where cultural differences are bridged by the creation of government by a grand coalition; this involves the institutionalization of a response pattern similar to that of a one-party system.[10] The essential characteristic of the consociational system is, however, not the institutional arrangement, but the type of relation that exists between members of the political elite, and the degree of evocation that can be achieved from the political centre among the population at large.

A political elite behavior of the kind referred to above is a prerequisite for the establishment of a consociational type of political system in a culturally fragmented society. A number of conditions which favor the consociational type should now be examined.

It has been shown in this study how the political leaders in Tanzania have been able to carry the rural population along the path of development. To evoke the support and commitment of the masses is as important for the functioning of a consociational type of political system as is a close cooperation between the leaders. In order to facilitate the evocation of the masses, conflicts at the local level must be kept at a minimum. Attention must be paid to the horizontal relations between groups in society; to the maintenance of the assimilative capability (cf., Figure 13). If the degree of mobilization of people is too rapid, that is, if people are moving into new social and political roles without having developed common means of communication, the efforts by the leaders to carry the masses along may be retarded.

It is often easier to uphold a balance between political sub-cultures if they are numerous, and as in the case of Tanzania all are in minority. It has been shown that Tanzania differs in this respect from its neighboring count-

[9] Apter, "The Political Kingdom . . .", *op.cit.*

[10] See Arendt Lijphart, "Typologies of Democratic Systems", paper presented to the 7th World Congress of IPSA in Brussels, September 18—23, 1967.

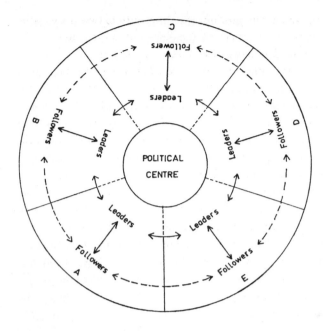

POLITICAL PERIPHERY

Figure 13. Portrait of a consociational political system.

ries Kenya and Uganda. The fear of being dominated has been much stronger in the latter two countries, where the balance of power has tended to be dual; in Kenya between the Kikuyu and the Luo tribes; in Uganda between "Bantu" and "Nilotic" tribes, or between Baganda and non-Ganda peoples. The fear of being dominated has there complicated inter-elite cooperation.

People must favor a one-party system, or government by grand coalition in the case of multi-party systems, if a consociational system is to be successful. In many African countries the one-party system has, a few years after independence, lost its legitimacy. Some of its critics have called it "inefficient"; others have labeled it "undemocratic"[11] We have seen in the investigation of political attitudes in rural Tanzania that people by and large favor the one-party system, and there have in that country been fewer signs of discontent with the experience of a one-party system than in most other African states with a similar party arrangement.

The consociational type of political system is primarily a response to divisions in the domestic environment; in the society in which the political system is a part. It is a response to a national emergency situation. At some occasions, however, external threats have contributed to a reinforcement

[11] These are the points which, for instance, the militaries have used to justify their intervention in politics in a number of African countries recently.

of the consociational pattern. Changes in the international environment which may be detrimental to the goals of the system are often used to re-create the need for a close cooperation at the national elite level.

Finally, it is obvious that a political system with a fragmented culture, cannot carry too heavy a load of demands without threats to its future development. If the consociational pattern is established an improvement in the capabilities of the system is likely to occur. This depends, however, partly on whether local structures can be created, which are able to carry some of the load of the system; to solve some of the problems that enter the system. In Tanzania, such a situation exists to a large extent. Both VDCs and district councils are involved in the process of problem-solving. Partly because of this, the management of sub-cultural cleavages do not require much of the energies and skills of the political leaders at the centre.

Tanzania fits quite well the consociational pattern. The political leaders have accomodated, and to a large extent, have overcome disagreements between various sub-cultures. It is probably true to say that the environmental conditions in Tanzania are better than in most other African countries, since the political sub-cultures have never been openly hostile to each other, and the balance between them is multiple rather than dual. Not many political systems in Africa are likely to have achieved such a high degree of cooperation and tolerance at the elite level and such a high degree of evocation among the masses as has the Tanzanian system. These two qualities are necessary for counteracting disintegrative tendencies in a system with a basically fragmented political culture, and the fact that the Tanzanian system has achieved them is likely to explain the relative success in the first years of independence.

The opposite to the consociational type of system in Africa is the *centrifugal* one.[12] Like the consociational pattern it has a fragmented political culture, but instead of accomodating differing sub-cultures, there is a tendency among members of the political elite to pull in different directions. Hence open political conflicts are not unusual. Cleavages may be based on different ideological outlooks or on different ethnic or tribal origins, and so forth. Regardless of the institutional patterns in these countries, whether they are one-party states or not, a typical feature of post-independence politics has been one of relative decay. The political system has not been able to respond to the many environmental pressures. There has been a crisis in the centre-periphery relationship, in the intra-elite cooperation, or in both. The trend, therefore, has been contrary to that of the consociational systems. Various components of the system have begun to fall apart, the government authorities, the regime, and in the worst cases, the community itself. The latter has been the case in Nigeria.

[12] Lijphart, *op.cit.,* p. 40.

The attempt here to classify the political systems in post-independence Africa is, of course, tentative. It is based on a limited amount of data. It has been included in this study mainly because classification based on these criteria may suggest some new and further steps of research. We need more depth in our studies of African political systems. It is necessary to present more material on the political culture particularly at the mass level. Classification according to type of ideology prevailing in the system, its organizational patterns, and so forth is, no doubt, important, but it hardly tells us anything how political systems *really* differ in terms of to what extent they are able to satisfy the needs of the majority of the population and to what extent they are able to solve developmental problems emerging in the environment of the system. The typological distinction between consociational and centrifugal political systems is based on other differentiating factors. It may, therefore, indicate a new avenue towards a fuller understanding of the functioning of political systems in Africa.

Muhtasari

Kitabu hiki ni juu ya mabadiliko yaliyotokea vijijini katika wilaya za Bukoba na Karagwe (Buhaya—Tanzania) tangu kabla ya utawala wa kikoloni mpaka hivi sasa.

Hasa kinahusika na madaraka ya TANU katika bidii zake za karibuni za kuendeleza maendeleo. Habari zilizoandikwa katika kitabu hiki zilikusanywa kati ya Novemba 1964 na Novemba 1966. Naishukuru sana serikali ya Tanzania iliyonisaidia katika kuufanya uchunguzi huu uwezekane; na pia kwa kila mmoja katika wilaya za Bukoba na Karagwe walioshiriki katika uchunguzi huu.

Sehemu ya kwanza ya kitabu hiki ni ya utangulizi. Hapo naeleza mambo yaliyotumika katika uchunguzi huu. Naeleza maana ya maendeleo ya siasa, kuwa ni kuongezeka kwa uwezo wa serikali katika kuondoa matatizo nchini —yakiwa ya uchumi au ya siasa. Matatizo haya ambayo ni ya lazima kuondolewa yanaweza kujumlishwa kwenye aina kubwa tano:

1) Yale yahusikanayo na maendeleo ya umoja wa taifa;
2) Yale yahusikanayo na namna ya kuifanya serikali ipate imani ya wananchi;
3) Yale yahusikanayo na uongezekaji wa mali ya serikali ya kutumika kwa maendeleo, kwa mfano wa kodi au bidii zaidi za kazi za kujitolea;
4) Yale yahusuyo ugawanyaji wa mali ya serikali; kama ikitumiwa kwenye viwanda au kilimo,—kwa watu wachache tu au kwa kila mtu;
5) Yale yahusuyo namna ya kuifanya serikali ijibu mahitaji ya watu; kuna nafasi gani kwa watu kushiriki katika mambo ya siasa.

Swala la jinsi gani haya matatizo matano ya maendeleo yanavyodhuru watu linazungumzwa katika sehemu kubwa ya kitabu hiki. Katika sura ya pili, ninaeleza jinsi serikali ya Tanzania ilivyojaribu kuondoa matatizo haya. Ni hatua gani zilizochukuliwa na serikali ili kuyashinda?

Kitabu kinaeleza pia jinsi serikali ya Tanzania ilivyojaribu kushinda ukabila; na sehemu muhimu ambayo lugha ya Kiswahili imefanywa kutumika katika juhudi hizi. Inatiwa mkazo jinsi ilivyo muhima ya kwamba lugha hii ya taifa (Kiswahili) ni lugha itumiwayo na karibu kila mwananchi; wala si kusema inatumiwa na watu wachache tu walioelimika, kama ilivyo kwenye hizo nchi ambako Kiingereza au Kifaransa kimefanywa kuwa ndiyo lugha ya serikali.

Kilicho muhimu pia ni kwamba, kwa kusudi la ushirikiano wa taifa zima, TANU ilikwishapata nafasi kubwa isiyoshindika mapema hata kabla ya uhuru. Baada ya mwaka wa 1961, serikali ilichukua hatua ya kama kuwahamisha watumishi wa serikali na wanasiasa kutoka mkoa hadi mkoa; na hii ililleta kuweko na mchanganyiko mkubwa kati watu wa makabila tofauti. TANU, vilevile, ilifanya bidii kubwa ya kuzuia ubaguzi wa dini uliokuwepo nchini kabla ya uhuru. Umuhimu wa uhusiano mwema kati ya viongozi na watu ulitiwa mkazo hasa katika azimio la Arusha. Hatua nyingine ilikuwa kuyafanya mashirika mbali ya taifa, kama NUTA na mashule, kutumikia matakwa ya taifa au watu kwa ujumla, na siyo kundi fulani la watu wachache.

Jambo kuu katika azimio la Arusha ni kubadili mkazo uliokuwepo wa kutegemea fedha, na badala yake, kutegemea bidii za watu. Inaonyeshwa hapa jinsi azimio la Arusha linavyokuwa ni jitihada ya kuufanya uchumi wa nchi upatane na makusudi ya viongozi wa siasa. Utoaji wa zaidi wa wananchi katika maendeleo ya nchi ni lazima kulipwa na kuinuka kwa hali ya maisha ya watu wa vijijini. Watu hawa wanahitaji kutiwa moyo; na azimio la Arusha pia linatia mkazo katika jambo hili. Uchukuaji wa madaraka ya mabanki ya kigeni na serikali ni njia mojawapo serikali imechukua ili kujaribu kuendeleza maendeleo kwa usawa zaidi. Kwa kuziendeleza fedha kutoka mijini kwenda sehemu za vijijini, serikali inaweza kufaulu kupunguza tofauti iliyopo kati ya sehemu zilizoendelea na zisizoendelea sana.

Tatizo katika serikali nyingi ni kulinganisha matakwa ya watu au vikundi mbali mbali, na yale yanayopendekezwa na viongozi. Katika nchi nyingi serikali imelazimika kupunguza kukubali matakwa yote yanayopendekezwa na watu wake. Katika nchi ambamo kila mtu hupewa haki ya kupiga kura kabla uchumi timamu haujaendelezwa nchini, serikali inaweza kujiona kuzidiwa na mzigo wa matakwa ya raia wake. Serikali haina nguvu ya kuweza kutosheleza matakwa yote. Tanzania hasa ina mpango mzuri, kwani ijapokuwa nchi bado ni maskini, imeruhusu ushirika kwa wote katika siasa. Hii imewezekana kwa sababu ya kiasi kikubwa sana cha bidii iliyowekwa na watu pamoja na viongozi wao katika kutimiza kusudi lililo moja la taifa zima, — jambo lililoelezwa mara nyingi baada tu ya uhuru.

Sehemu ya pili ya uchunguzi huu inaeleza juu ya historia ya Bukoba na Karagwe kabla ya kufika kwa watawala wa kwanza wa kikoloni, na wakati wa utawala wao. Yanayoelezwa pia ni tabia ya kizamani ya kifalme katika Buhaya. Pia desturi ya Kihaya ya kuwa na mashamba ijulikanayo kama *nyarubanja,* iliyoondilewa na serikali mwaka wa 1965. Desturi hii ilisababusha kuwepo na upungufu wa ardhi pamoja na uongezeko wa thamani ya kuwa na ardhi. Wafalme (Bakama), badala ya kutoa mifugo kwa waliowapenda kwa kufuata mila na desturi ya kiasili, walianza mashamba. Uhusiano kati ya upungufu wa ardhi katika wilaya ya Bukoba na kuwepo kwa nyarubanja, inaonyesha wazi ni kwa nini mtindo huu haukutokea katika wilaya ya Karagwe kulikuwa bado kuna ardhi kubwa na wafalme waliendelea kutoa mifugo kwa waliowapenda ikiwa ndiyo mali ya thamani kuliko zote.

Jambo jingine linalofaa kukumbukwa kuhusu mazoea ya Wahaya ni kwamba watu wa huko hawajapata kutamaliwa chini ya ufalme mmoja kama ilivyokuwa kwa majirani wao wa Buganda. Watawala walikuwa wanageuza mipaka mara nyingi na ugomvi kati ya jamaa wa ukoo wa watawala ulikuwa wa kawaida. Mamlaka ya siasa katika utawala wa kizamani ulitolewa kwa aina mbili za watu: Wana wa wafalme (balangira)— wote wakiwa ni wa ukoo wa kifalme; na wafuasi wa wafalme (batekwa) ambao hawakuwa wa ukoo wa kifalme. Balangira walifanywa kuwa na mamlaka katika kundi la vijiji (bakungu). Wafuasi wa wafalme, mara nyingine, walipewa mamlaka kwenye tawala ndogo (gombolola).

Tofauti ya mali kati ya balangira na watu wa kawaida (bairu), ulifikiriwa kuwa ni hali isiyowezekana kubadilishwa katika Buhaya inayofuata desturi za zamani. Mpango huu wa nyarubanja uliwafanya watu wengine wategemee huruma za hawa wafuasi wachache wa wafalme. Kushiriki kwa watu wa kawaida katika mambo ya utawala kulikuwa hakuruhusiwi; na upendano wa kipekee na wafalme au mmoja wa jamii yake ilikuwa mara nyingi ndiyo njia tu kwa mtu wa kawaida (mwiru) kupata ulinzi wa maisha au mali yake. Watu hawakuwa na njia ye yote ya kuonyesha ya kuwa hawakuridhika na utawala wa wafalme.

Kuanzishwa kwa utawala wa kikoloni kulibadili kidogo tabia nyingine za kizamani katika Buhaya. Walakini, ni lazima ikumbukwe ya kwamba utawala wa kizamani wa Buhaya haukubadilishwa sana na utawala mpya wa Kijerumani kama ilivyokuwa katika sehemu nyingine za Tanganyika, kwa sababu hawa watawala wapya hawakuyavunja mamlaka mengi ya watawala wa kizamani wa Buhaya. Hawa watawala wa mbeleni waliachwa kutawala kama ilivyokuwa mbeleni, pakiwepo na tofauti ya kwamba sasa walikuwa chini ya askari mkuu wa Kijerumani aliyekuwa anakaa kwenye boma lililokuwepo mjini Bukoba. Wajerumani walitaka utii kutoka kwa wenyeji, na pia watu hawakutakiwa kupinga au kulaumu wafalme wao.

Mojawapo ya mambo yaliyofuata miliki ya Wajerumani ilikuwa kuanzishwa kwa misheni katika Buhaya. Wamisheni wa Roman Katoliki walikuwa wa kwanza, na kituo chao cha kwanza kilijengwa mwaka wa 1892. Kwa muda mrefu Waprotestanti walizuiwa na Wajerumani kuanzisha kazi yao katika Buhaya, sababu ikiwa kwamba walifikiriwa kushirikishwa na shughuli za Waingereza waliokuwa wakitawala upande mwingine wa mpaka wao—yaani Uganda. Hata hivyo, mwaka wa 1910, chama cha Waprotestanti wa Kijerumani kilifungua kituo chao Bukoba; hasa kwa kufuata maombi ya wenyeji kadhaa waliogeuzwa kuwa Waprotestanti walipokuwa matembezini katika Buganda. Kuenea kwa dini ya Kiislamu kulitokea wakati mmoja na dini ya Kikatoliki; nayo ilienezwa na wafanyibiashara wa kwanza Waarabu waliokuja kuishi katika sehemu hiyo.

Elimu ya kisasa katika sehemu hiyo ilianzishwa kwa mara ya kwanza na vyama vya wamisheni. Utawala wa Kijerumani ulitia mkazo katika kilimo cha kahawa kwa kusudi la kuuza. Pamoja na kahawa iliyokuwepo ya aina ya "Robusta" (Kihaya), Wajerumani walileta kahawa nyingine ya aina ya "Arabica" (Kizungu).

Waingereza walichukua madaraka ya utawala kutoka kwa Wajerumani mwaka wa 1916. Waingereza, kama Wajerumani, walitegemea sana wafalme wa Buhaya kwa kuweza kuitawala sehemu hiyo. Tatizo kubwa lilikuwa kwamba wafalme wengi walikuwa hawana elimu ya kutosha ya kuweza kuchukua madaraka ya utawala waliyopewa na Waingereza.

Wakati wa utawala wa Waingereza, uongozi kati ya Wahaya ulianza kuhamishwa kutoka kwa viongozi wa asili. Baadhi ya watu wengine wa kisasa walioelimishwa walijiunga wenyewe katika chama kimoja cha siasa mwaka wa 1924. Chama chao kilichojulikana kama *Bahaya Union* na baadaye kikaitwa *African Association,* kilikuwa ndilo onyesho la kwanza nchini Tanganyika la jinsi wananchi wasivyoridhika na utawala uliokuwepo, kwa sababu Waingereza hawa kuonyesha kuwa na nia ya kusikiliza mahitaji ya watu. Kusudi la chama hiki halikuwa kudai uhuru, bali viongozi wa hiki chama walikuwa wanahusika na kuendeleza mbele hali za kuishi kwa watu.

Siasa katika Buhaya ilibadilika kati ya mwaka wa 1935 na wa 1940, wakati watu walipoanza kupinga wenyewe mipango mipya ya maendeleo ya kilimo ambayo Waingereza walitaka kuianzisha. Mwaka wa 1937, ghasia zilitokea katika sehemu mbali mbali za Buhaya. Kupinga huku kwa huu mpango mpya wa Waingereza wa kilimo kuliendelea mpaka baada ya mwaka wa 1940. Huku kutoridhika pamoja na kuenea kwa chuki kati ya watu, kulifanya tawi la Bukoba la *Tanganyika African Association* (TAA) kuwa na nguvu sana. Chama hiki kilichofuata Bahaya Union, kilikuwa siyo chama cha kisiasa peke yake. Katika ufalme wa Kianja, wata kadhaa ambao hawakuridhika na utawala wa Waingereza pamoja na wa wafalme, walianzisha chama kilichoitwa *Kianja Labour Association.* Chama hiki hakikusudia kubadili utawala kabisa, lakini kilisaidia kuunda ufahamu mpya wa siasa kati ya watu.

Kwenye mwaka wa 1950, Buhaya ilikuwa sehemu ya kwanza katika Tanganyika kujulikana katika shughuli za siasa, na katika muda huo Waingereza walianza kubadili tawala za mitaa ili kuwafanya watu washiriki zaidi katika mambo ya siasa. Hatua hizi zilichukuliwa kwa sababu ya uzito wa maombi ya wenyeji. Badiliko la kwanza lilikuwa ni kuanzishwa kwa Baraza la Wilaya (District Council) kuwa ni badala ya Baraza la wafalme (Council of Chiefs).

Kuenea kwa shughuli za kisiasa katika Buhaya mwanzoni mwa mwaka wa 1950, kuliandalia njia ya TANU. Tawi la Bukoba ambalo baadaye liliitwa "West Lake Branch" liliandikishwa serikalini mwaka wa 1956, baada ya Waingereza kujaribu kuzuia muda wa kuandikishwa kwake. Baadhi ya viongozi wa kwanza wa TANU katika Buhaya, wamekuwamo waliokuwa wakijishughulisha na shughuli za chama cha TAA. Mwanzoni kulikuwepo na mabishano kidogo juu ya uongozi wa chama hiki mtaani kati ya kizazi cha vijana na cha wazee, lakini mpaka mwaka wa 1958 huku kuhitilafiana kulikuwa kumerekebishwa; walioshindwa walikuwa ni wa kizazi cha wazee.

Wale waliolazimishwa kuacha kamati ya TANU ya jimbo, wamekuwa viongozi wa chama kipya cha upinzani, — yaani *Tanganyika African National Congress* (TANC), kilichoanzishwa mwaka wa 1958. Uongozi wa taifa wa chama hiki ulitaka kugeuza mambo mengi ya serikali kwa nguvu na upesi zaidi kuliko viongozi wa TANU walivyotaka. Baadhi ya viongozi wa chama hiki cha TANC katika Buhaya walitaka desturi za kizamani za wafalme zirudishwe. TANC na chama kingine kilichoundwa nchini Tanganyika kabla ya uhuru — *United Tanganyika Party* (UTP), havikufanikiwa katika Buhaya ingawa UTP ilipata msaada kutoka kwa utawala wa Waingereza. Vyama hivi viwili vilishindwa kabisa katika Buhaya kama vilivyoshindwa pia katika sehemu nyingine za Tanganyika.

Wakati wa kupata uhuru, TANU ilikuwa imekwishapata hali ya juu zaidi ambayo haikuwezwa kupingwa, — ingawaje miongoni mwa baadhi ya wanachama wengine walikuwa bado wanapigania kuwa na ushawishi. Kundi lililojulikana ni la walimu waliodharau viongozi wa vijijini ambao waliwafikiria kutokuwa na elimu ya kutosha. Kundi hili lilipingana na viongozi wa TANU kwenye uchaguzi wa "Buhaya District Council" katika mwaka wa 1963. Wachache wao walifanikiwa. Matokeo haya yaliongeza wasiwasi na ugomvi kati ya vikundi mbali mbali vilivyokuwa vikipingana katika Buhaya na hatimaye serikali kuu ikaamua kulivunja Baraza hili jipya lililochaguliwa. Walimu waliambiwa washikilie kazi yao na wasishiriki katika mambo ya siasa. Watu waliopendelea desturi za wafalme wa kizamani, na wafuazi waliobakia wa TANC waliendelea na upinzani wao kwa muda mfupi baada ya uhuru. Walakini katika mwaka wa 1964, upinzani karibu wote ulikuwa umetoweka.

Sehemu ya tatu ya kitabu hiki ni juu ya uchunguzi uliofanywa wa mawazo ya watu kuhusu mabadiliko mbali uliofanywa mingoni mwa kikundi kilichochaguliwa katika mitaa mitano ya Buhaya:— Bugombe, Kitendagulo, Bwatangabo, Kabagunda na Kiruruma. Watu 328 waliulizwa maswali yahusikanayo na matatizo matano ya maendeleo yaliyotajwa mwanzoni mwa muhtasari huu.

Watu wakaao vijijini katika sehemu hii ya Tanzania wana fikara gani juu ya hali ya maisha yao, serikali, na mabadiliko yaliyotokea karibuni? Jambo moja ni wazi na labda si la kushangaza: Watu wa vijijini wana upendo mkubwa sana kwa taifa jipya la Tanzania. Wengi wanafikiri kuwa ni jambo la maana kuwafunza watoto wao kujitolea kujenga taifa. Karibu nusu ya watu walioulizwa maswali walisema ya kuwa sifa ya kwanza ya Tanzania ni uhuru, kwa sababu ulipatwa kwa amani na tena tangu baada ya kupata uhuru mwaka wa 1961 hali ya nchi imekuwa tulivu na ya amani. Mapigano yaliyotokea katika nchi za jirani ya Tanzania: Uganda, Rwanda na Kongo, labda yaliwafanya watu waliamini sana taifa la Tanzania, — na TANU vivyo hivyo. Majibu yanaonyesha wazi kwamba TANU kwa halisi ni chama cha watu wote. Katika Buhaya yapata watu 67 kwa kila mia ni wanachama wa chama hiki. Hii inaonyesha nguvu TANU inayopata kutoka kwa watu wa vijijini. Zaidi ya hayo, karibu watu wote waishio Buhaya ni wa kabila moja—la kihaya. Wageni waliotoka sehemu nyingine za Tanzania au nchi nyingine hawakuamia kabisa Buhayani; bali walifanya kazi tu na kurudi makwao. Kwa sababu hiyo mashindano ya ukabila hayakutokea.

Ni jambo la maana kwa serikali kujaribu kuendeleza maarifa ya ushirikiano wa makabila mbali mbali, kwa sababu kama watu hawakushirikiana maendeleo yatakuwa magumu. Nchini Tanzania serikali ilikwishatambua umuhimu wa jambo hilo.

Jambo jingine linaloelezwa katika kitabu hiki ni makubaliano ya watu wengi na madhumuni makuu ya serikali: (1) usawa wa watu wote; (2) maendeleo ya haraka; na (3) kufanya kazi chini ya chama kimoja cha siasa.

Ingawa tofauti kati ya watu ilikuwa desturi maalum Buhayani mpaka karibu na mwisho wa mwaka wa 1950; watu siku hizi wanakubaliana na siasa ya usawa kati ya watu. Wengi walioulizwa maswali walifikiri kuwa uhuru ni jambo muhimu lililoleta kubadilisha kwa tabia za watu.

Sehemu kubwa ya watu inaunga mkono mpango wa kuwa na chama kimoja cha siasa, na wanapenda chama kimoja tu kichukue mamlaka yote. Hii inakuwa ni kwa sababu watu hawakuzoea kuamini kuwa utawala unaweza kuendeshwa na zaidi ya chama kimoja. Zaidi ya nusu ya watu walioulizwa maswali walisema kuwa watu wanaopinga siasa ya TANU au viongozi wake wangalitiwa vizuizini. Kati ya hao wasiokubaliana na maoni haya, wengi ni wenye elimu ya "Secondary School".

Zaidi ya watu themanini kwa mia walioulizwa maswali wanapenda serikali ifanye maendeleo kwa upesi, lakini wengine wengi wanafikiri kuwa serikali inazidi kutazamia vitu vingi mno kutoka kwa wananchi, — kama vile kodi na kufanya zaidi kazi za kujitolea. Kati ya watu wanaofikiri hivyo, wengi ni wenye elimu ndogo na mashamba madogo madogo.

Watu wa vijijini wengi wanafikiri serikali haina nguvu ya kutosha: kwa mfano serikali haichukui hatua ya kutosha katika kupunguza matendo ya wahalifu nchini, — hasa wizi ambao umekuwa mzigo mkubwa kwa watu wa vijijini na mijini. Kwa sababu ya hali hii watu wengine wanasema kwamba wanakosa nguvu kama za utawala wa zamani wa wafalme.

Wakaaji wa vijijini waliulizwa maswali mengine kuhusu maendeleo ya kilimo. Katika sehemu ya mashariki ya Buhaya watu wengine hawaupendi mpango wa kung'oa mibuni ya zamani na kupanda mipya. Ni jambo la maana kuona kuwa kati ya watu wanaopinga mpango huu wengine wana bidii ya kuendeleza mashamba yao, lakini wanakosa fedha. Njia moja ya kuwasaidia watu hawa ingalikuwa serikali iwakopeshe fedha kusudi waweze kuendeleza mashamba yao. Miongoni mwa wale wanaopinga ung'oaji wa kahawa ya zamani ni watu waishio vijijini wasiokuwa na njia nyingine ya kupata fedha, ila wanategemea mashamba yao tu.

Kwa kawaida wakulima karibu wote wa Buhaya wanataka kutumia fedha kwa maendeleo ya kilimo. Hili lilijibiwa katika swali wakulima waliloulizwa kuhusu jinsi gani wangalitumia nyongeza ya fedha zao. Wengi sana walijibu kwamba kilimo cha ndizi ni cha maana zaidi kuliko kilimo cha mibuni. Walikaza kilimo cha vyakula zaidi kuliko kilimo kingine chochote.

Wakulima walisema kuwa wanategemea sana viongozi wa VDC (Village Development Committee) na "Village Executive Officer", siyo kwa ajili ya siasa peke yake, bali pia kwa ajili ya maendeleo ya kilimo. Wanafikiri kuwa wanapata habari chache kutoka kwa wahalmashauri wa chama cha ushirika na Mabwana Shamba (Agricultural Extension Officers).

Kwa kawaida watu wengi vijijini hupata habari kutoka kwa watu wengine ambao hupata habari za nchi kwa njia ya redio au magazeti. Majibu ya watu yanaeleza kwamba watu wasiosikiliza redio au wasiosoma magazeti wanajiona kuwa na mategemeo makubwa ya maisha ya baadaye kama wale wanaosikiliza redio na kusoma magazeti.

Watu walipoulizwa ni tofauti gani iliyo ya maana kati ya watu vijijini; nusu ya walioulizwa walisema ya kuwa tofauti kubwa ni ya uchumi. Kuna wengine waliosema kuwa tofauti kubwa ni kati ya watu wa amani na wanaogombana hovyo. Walipoulizwa maswali juu ya fedha ya nchi wengi walisema serikali haijatumia fedha nyingi ya kutosha kwa manufaa ya maendeleo vijijini. Walisema fedha nyingi inatumiwa kwenye viwanda na maendeleo ya mijini.

Jambo la kushangaza ni kwamba wakati watu walipoulizwa haya maswali mwaka wa 1965 — kabla ya uchaguzi wa wajumbe wa Bunge — zaidi ya nusu ya watu walifikiri kuwa serikali ilikuwa inatumia fedha nyingi mno kwa kulipa mishahara ya Wabunge kuliko kwenye shughuli za maendeleo. Pia walifikiri ya kwamba elimu na bidii ya kazi ni vitu muhimu sana ili kuweza kufanikiwa kwenye siasa kuliko ushirikiano wa kirafiki na viongozi, au kutoka kwenye ukoo bora.

Watu wengine walisema ni mara chache wanahudhuria mikutano ya siasa vijijini. Mazungumzo ya siasa mara nyingi yalizungumziwa katika vilabu vya pombe; na watu 75 kwa mia walisema ya kuwa wamekwishawahi kushiriki katika mazungumzo ya namna hiyo. Watu waliowahi kwenda shule walishiriki zaidi katika mazungumzo ya siasa kuliko wale ambao hawakuenda shule. Kwa upande mwingine kwenye uchaguzi wa mwaka wa 1965, watu wasiokuwa na elimu walijishughulisha sana na mazungumzo ya siasa kuliko wale wengine. Waliopiga kura kwa sababu ya alama ya mchaguliwa ni wale walioongea zaidi juu ya uchaguzi wenyewe. Wahaya wanaamini kwamba kupiga kura ni jambo la maana sana katika kushawishi mwenendo wa matukio ya siasa. Wengine wanafikiri pia ya kuwa kupiga kura ni bora kuliko kuandika barua kwa Wabunge au kuonana na kuzungumza nao, au kufanya kazi kwenye mashirika ya taifa kama vile NUTA au vyama vya ushirika. Mbunge anaonekana kuwa kama kiongozi wa watu aliyechaguliwa ili kuwawakilisha serikalini na kusaidia kuwapa wapiga kura vitu vinavyowapa faida za mwili. Watu wa vijijini zaidi ni wachanga katika kushiriki katika mambo ya siasa. Mara nyingi hupenda kuona watu wengine wanashiriki kwenye siasa kwa miaba yao. Hata hivyo, wanatambua ya kuwa ili kuweza kupata msaada wa serikali ni lazima watoe mchango wao wenyewe, kwa mfano, kwa njia ya kufanya kazi za kujitolea.

Kwa kumaliza, majibu tuliyoyapata yanaonyesha kwamba TANU inafanya kazi muhimu katika kuendeleza maendeleo ya wakaaji wa vijijini. Watu hufikiria chama kuwa ni chenye utawala wa haki, na huwaendea viongozi wao wawasaidie katika matatizo yao. Shida kubwa ambayo TANU imepata ni katika maendeleo ya kilimo na katika kugawanya faida ya nchi kwa kufuatana na matumaini ya wananchi. Lakini hii shida ya pili ni tatizo linalokabili kila serikali, hasa katika nchi iliyo maskini.

Appendix 1.   How the data was gathered

Data for this study was gathered between November 1964 and November 1966, most of it in the course of 1965. Events in Tanzania during 1967 have been considered as far as they are of relevance for this investigation. I arrived in Tanzania on the 29th of October 1964, and left for Bukoba three weeks later after clearance had been arranged with the Tanzanian government and the Head of the Department of Political Science at the University College, Dar es Salaam, Professor David Kimble. I stayed permanently in Bukoba for twelve months before moving to Kampala, Uganda, as a Visiting Lecturer in the Department of Political Science. This assignment was terminated in December 1966.

Immediately upon my arrival at Bukoba I sought a research assistant, who could also serve as an interpreter, as my knowledge of Kiswahili at that time was limited, and I did not know the vernacular at all. My choice fell upon Mr Dominic Joseph Rutabingwa, a former secondary school student, who during 1964 was working half-time as instructor in adult education courses in Bukoba. Mr Rutabingwa was my permanent companion until I left Buhaya. While I was in Kampala, he was gathering material on his own.

Our first objective was to obtain some background material by talking to various people in the regional and district administration, in TANU, and in voluntary agencies, like the Protestant and Catholic churches. Later we began to look for parishes which would be representative for various parts of Buhaya, and used as primary units in the planned survey. The selection was made after a number of trips to various divisional and sub-divisional headquarters, where the local statistics were most easily available.

Five parishes were selected, each in different divisions or chiefdoms. They were chosen as representative of various parts of Buhaya on the basis of the following criteria: distance from Bukoba township, number of regular bus connections with Bukoba, number of schools, age of these schools, and degree and type of commercial activities. Educational and commercial activities pursued in adjacent parishes were also considered, as it is common that people go to a neighboring market or send their children to school in a nearby parish.

The local statistics contain information about the number of people living in the parishes, number of cattle, and number of coffee trees. These census figures are, however, not very reliable, since they are collected by untrained local Village Executive Officers. The total population of one parish was listed as being at the end of 1962: 2135; at the end of 1963: 1789; and, at the end of 1964: 2246. The only reliable list was that of the taxpayers, mainly because it was identical to the list of the households. Every household pays local poll-tax, and each such unit is registered in the name of its head.

Our strategy was to visit one parish at a time. We spent approximately seven-eight weeks in each place. The first to be visited was Bugombe. We came there the first time in early January 1965. We followed the same working schedule everywhere. We started by contacting the Village Executive Officer or the chairman of the Village Development Committee. They called a public meeting at which we were given opportunity to present our project and the reasons why we were there. The parish leaders also helped us in our efforts to legitimize the project.

After that we arranged interviews with all members of the VDC and the VEO himself; we read through the minutes of the VDC and interviewed selected village elders, who were likely to tell us something about the history of the parish area. At all these occasions I put the questions myself and Mr. Rutabingwa interpreted. We found that because we had our credentials from the office of the President people had no fears to be interviewed. This also meant, however, that some people regarded us as government officials. We did everything to eliminate this misconception. Information about our research was spread to neighboring parishes. In a few cases we were called upon by the leaders in these parishes to do research there too. The reason for this "competition" was in most cases pride; they believed that their parish was as good as that one we had selected. They could not understand the reasons for our selection. In some cases we came across the belief that our research was going to give the parishes in which we worked immediate material benefits. We also found a few individuals who were interviewed in our survey holding the same notion. It was, however, discouraged.

We were, to a large extent, participant observers in the local communities. We usually stayed there the whole day. In the more distant parishes we slept over-night in the parish or its immediate neighborhood. We used to drink with the local people, privately or in the public bars, in order to get as deep an impression as possible of life in these rural communities.

The survey research that we conducted in the parishes towards the end of our stay was consequently well prepared. Accordingly, we encountered little difficulty in winning the confidence of the people. The problem rather lay in the technical task of drawing the sample, writing the questions and getting the interview assistants well-trained.

There existed, at the time of this research, neither in the parishes, nor elsewhere in the country, any complete list of all members of each household. As mentioned earlier, the local government statistics register each household in the name of only one person, and there is no reference to how many people live with that person. The local religious institutions keep a more detailed track of the composition of the households, but only of those which are affiliated with the respective churches.

The sample, therefore, had to be drawn from the list of the taxpayers. It means that, since the list contains mainly male persons, the sample is biased in that direction. A number of women on the list have also been included in the sample. There is no indication that it exists any significant difference between the male and the female sector of the population in terms of the attitudes and opinions under investigation. By and large, a household in Buhaya consists of two adults and a varying number of children under 18—20 years of age. We came across some families who were living with their old parents, as well as some households which only consisted of a woman and her children.

The sample size was decided to be 15 % of all households in order to achieve a high degree of precision. The sample was drawn in each parish in the presence of the Village Executive Officer; every seventh name from his list was selected for interviewing. In the five parishes the following total number of interviewees was obtained:

Bugombe 58

Kitendagulo 56

Bwatangabo 98

Kabagunda 72

Kiruruma 44

Total 328

Every thirtieth name was selected as a "reserve". In the five parishes, of those only five had to be used, one in Bugombe, two in Kitendagulo, and two in Bwatangabo. In all, therefore, 333 persons were approached. Among those five who could not be reached, one had recently died, two were away working elsewhere, and two refused, supposedly because they feared to be interviewed.

The second problem was that of writing questions which would make sense to the interviewees. Here we were caught between the desire to apply as much as possible questions of a general character, which have been used elsewhere, and the desire to make the questions as understandable to the local people; to include local events, institutions, and so forth. A preliminary questionnaire worked out by members of the Cross-National Project in Social and Political Change, led by Gabriel Almond and Sidney Verba, was helpful in the initial preparatory efforts. All questions were originally written in English, and later translated into Luhaya by Mr Rutabingwa.

The translation was also cross-checked by Miss Else Orstadius, a Swedish missionary, who at this time was involved in a new translation of the English Bible into Luhaya. The vernacular was chosen as it was assumed a number of people would not know Kiswahili. This way we could also avoid troubles in the course of the actual interviews.

Some pre-testing of the questions was done with selected individuals in Bugombe and Kitendagulo; all together 29 persons were approached. The testing of our instrument revealed that certain questions were written in such a way that they were too difficult to the interviewees. In some cases it was the original wording of the question which was too complicated, in others it was difficult to find the correct translation so that the meaning of the question was not altered. Some open-ended questions had to become closed-choice questions. When structuring these questions, however, we only used those alternatives, which had been offered to us in the course of the pre-testing, in order to avoid the creation of alternatives, which did not exist in the minds of the interviewees. We wanted, for instance, to know which institutions in society that the adults considered most important; for which they wanted to teach their children to work. The answers which came out in the course of the pre-testing indicated "the nation", "the family", "the village" and "the church". No mentioning was made of "the tribe" or "the chiefdom". When, therefore, we constructed the question, we used the first four alternatives.

In order to make some questions less embarassing to the respondents, they were read as statements, and we asked subsequently whether they agreed or disagreed with the statement. On the whole we were very careful not to use questions, which could be regarded as sensitive. Nevertheless, we were able to ask questions on a great variety of matters.

The fact that we could get people to answer our questions satisfactorily was much due to the availability of local, and good interview assistants. Besides Mr Rutabingwa I had for interview purposes temporarily employed five other persons. Like Mr Rutabingwa they had completed Upper Primary School, and continued studying after that, without, however, reaching a full secondary school certificate. They were all from the rural areas and were familiar with the language and culture of the villagers. It took some time before we got hold of these people, and we had to turn away a few persons, who were too young or who lacked the qualifications we considered necessary. Of the five assistants we selected, three worked with us all the time, while one had to retire early since he was moving out of Buhaya. He was then replaced by another person, our fifth assistant. Before we went out in the field we had briefing sessions with the assistants in order to make them familiar with interviewing techniques. They were told about the difficulties they should anticipate. They were asked to behave impartially, casually, and friendly. The questions should be put in a conversational manner. They were instructed to record comments and remarks as they were given; stress was laid upon the fact that it was the first meaningful reaction that should be recorded, not changes in the original answer.

For some of the assistants it was difficult to follow these instructions in every detail. For instance, I was often told that they found it difficult to press for an answer if the respondents said "don't know". They might have been able to obtain a meaningful answer, but sometimes they felt that they lacked the authority to ask an old man for his opinion, if he had already indicated he did not know or he did not want to answer the question. This was one of the handicaps using young interviewers in these communities, where people of age are so highly respected.

It should be added that the interview assistants were asked to write the answers to open-ended questions in English, but if they did not know exactly the English words, they should use Kiswahili. An average interview lasted for about an hour, and every assistant could accomplish four or five interviews a day.

The survey research was completed in the five parishes by October 1965. In Kiruruma, however, it coincided with a post-electoral survey, organized by the Political Science Research Programme at Makerere University College, Kampala, Uganda, to find out people's opinion about the 1965 general election. The same persons, who had been selected in our survey was also included in the post-electoral survey. In the other four parishes we returned to interview the respondents again as part of that survey. In Bwatangabo and Kitendagulo, in particular, it was difficult to find people again, not because they refused to answer our questions, but because they were, for a variety of other reasons, not available. All together 285 out of the 328 respondents in our original sample were interviewed in the post-electoral survey. Some of the results from that survey have been recorded in Chapter 12 of this book.

Thirty-six people were later, in the beginning of 1966, approached for answers supplementary to those of the original questionnaire. These persons were selected to represent certain categories of respondents in each parish, small, middle-size and large farmers, educated and illiterate peoples, and so forth. The objective of these supplementary interviews was to probe a bit further into the minds of the people on certain important matters. We encountered no difficulty in approaching these people again.

Finally, it should be mentioned that the answers were coded, and the data organized on punch-cards in the East African Institute of Social Research in Kampala. The basic analysis of the material was also made there, using the machine available. A final analysis was made in Lund during 1967.

Appendix II. Description of the five parishes and their populations

Bugombe, Kitendagulo, Bwatangabo, Kabagunda and Kiruruma, each constitutes a parish, in Luhaya *nkungu*. They have their own local government officer, the Village Executive Officer, or *mukungu* in the vernacular. Each parish also has its own Village Development Committee, the lowest political authority in the Tanzanian political system. Kitendagulo differs slightly from the other four units, because its VEO has since 1963 responsibility for an administrative area which is larger than that included in this study. This difference, however, does not affect the comparability of the five parishes.

Here follows a description of the characteristics of the parishes and their population, first the data available in the parishes, and secondly the data generated by this study itself.

A. The five parishes:

1. Distance in miles from Bukoba township by nearest road:

	Distance:
Bugombe	23
Kitendagulo	2
Bwatangabo	37
Kabagunda	60
Kiruruma	103

2. Number of villages (*byalo*) in each parish:

Bugombe	4
Kitendagulo	4
Bwatangabo	6
Kabagunda	5
Kiruruma	4

3. Regular bus connections with Bukoba:

Bugombe	twice a day in both directions
Kitendagulo	buses are passing in both directions at least twenty times a day
Bwatangabo	six-seven times a day in both directions
Kabagunda	one in each direction
Kiruruma	no direct bus connection with Bukoba. People have to walk six miles to catch the bus which runs in both directions twice a week between Nyabuyonza and Bugene, the main trading centre in Karagwe District; see, map, p. 64.

4. Number of schools in the parish or in its immediate neighborhood:

Type:	Lower Primary School (St I—IV)					Extended and Upper Primary School (St V—VIII)					
Agency:	Govt	Cath	Prot	TA-PA*	Musl	Govt	Cath	Prot	TA-PA*	Musl.	Total
Bugombe	—	1	—	—	1	—	—	—	1	—	3
neighboring	—	2	2	—	—	—	—	2	—	—	6
Kitendagulo	—	—	—	—	—	—	—	—	—	—	—
neighboring	—	2	1	—	1	1	2	1	—	1	9
Bwatangabo	—	2	—	—	—	—	2	—	—	—	4
neighboring	—	3	1	—	1	—	1	1	—	1	8
Kabagunda	—	—	1	—	—	—	—	—	—	—	1
neighboring	—	3	2	—	—	—	1	—	—	—	6
Kiruruma	—	1	—	—	—	—	—	—	—	—	1
neighboring	—	1	—	—	—	—	—	1	—	—	2
Total	—	15	7	—	3	1	6	5	1	2	40

* = Tanganyika African Parents Association

As "neighboring" schools have been considered only those schools which are within "walking distance" for school children; that is, in this area, around 7 miles at the most. It should be pointed out that this table does not cover all educational activities in the parishes. In Kabagunda, for instance, there is a "bush school", an unregistered primary school in which children are taught reading, writing and counting. In each parish there is also adult education.

There are five secondary schools in the two districts, all located in Bukoba or its immediate vicinity.

5. Age of educational institutions:

	oldest LPS years	oldest UPS years
Bugombe	38	5
neighboring	29	35
Kitendagulo	—	—
neighboring	60	30
Bwatangabo	19	10
neighboring	17	26
Kabagunda	19	—
neighboring	30	8
Kiruruma	2	—
neighboring	12	12

6. Types of commercial activities:

	public market	shops		bars		tailors
		big	small	local beer	ordinary beer	
Bugombe	no	3	6	1	1	7
Kitendagulo	no	—	8	6	1	14
Bwatangabo	no	3	6	5	2	10
Kabagunda	yes	—	7	5	1	5
Kiruruma	no	—	1	1	—	0

People living in Kitendagulo can of course much easier than inhabitants of the other four parishes derive advantage from the big public market in Bukoba, which is open every day. In Bugombe and Bwatangabo most of the commercial activities are concentrated to one "village street". In Kabagunda commercial buildings are clustered at the lakeshore and there most trade of fish and other goods takes place, except twice a week, when a public market is held in another part of the parish. People in Kiruruma have access to a public market, which is held eight miles away, once a week.

7. Average land unit per farmer in acres:

	acre
Bugombe	2
Kitendagulo	2
Bwatangabo	3,5
Kabagunda	3,5
Kiruruma	4

8. Number of clans per parish:

	clans
Bugombe	19
Kitendagulo	31
Bwatangabo	42
Kabagunda	46
Kiruruma	22

In the old times each village (*kyalo*) used to be inhabited exclusively by one clan. Due to migrations, however, this pattern began to change already at an early period. Today one finds representatives of each clan in almost any part of Buhaya. In the five parishes studied here the original village clans were still among the biggest, but a large number of other clans are also found.

B. *Basic characteristics of the respondents in this survey:*

1. Age: (approximate)

(in %)	Bugombe	Kitendagulo	Bwatangabo	Kabagunda	Kiruruma
18—30	5 (3)	26 (15)	15 (15)	32 (24)	27 (12)
31—40	10 (6)	16 (9)	24 (23)	20 (14)	25 (11)
41—50	28 (16)	16 (9)	19,5 (19)	22 (15)	21 (9)
51—60	28 (16)	26 (15)	17,5 (17)	11 (8)	17 (7)
61—70	18 (10)	7 (4)	14 (14)	6 (4)	4 (2)
over 71	11 (7)	7 (4)	9 (9)	8 (6)	4 (2)
no infor	— —	2 (1)	1 (1)	1 (1)	2 (1)
	100 (58)	100 (56)	100 (98)	100 (72)	100 (44)

In the text, all people under 40 are considered as "young", those between 41 and 60 as "middle-aged" and those above 60 as "old".

2. Housing situation:

87 % of the villagers in Bwatangabo live in a rectangular mud-house, *ibanda* with a corrugated iron roof; also in the other four parishes this type of house is predominant. The stone-house, *ibale*, is most common in Kitendagulo (18 %) and the traditional conical hut, *mushonge*, is most frequent in Bugombe (28 %).

Three quarters of the respondents in each village own only one house. In average, six to seven people live in each house.

3. Occupation:

(in %)	Bugombe		Kiten-dagulo		Bwatan-gabo		Kaba-gunda		Kiru-ruma	
farmer	91	(53)	60	(34)	98	(96)	65	(47)	91	(40)
skilled worker	—	—	12	(7)	—	—	—	—	4	(2)
fisherman	—	—	2	(1)	—	—	25	(16)	2,5	(1)
white-collar	—	—	9	(5)	1	(1)	—	—	—	—
house-wife	—	—	4	(2)	—	—	1	(1)	—	—
teacher, rel.occ.	2	(1)	5,5	(3)	—	—	—	—	—	—
trader, shop-keeper	7	(4)	5,5	(3)	—	—	9	(6)	—	—
other	—	—	2	(1)	—	—	—	—	2,5	(1)
no infor	—	—	—	—	1	(1)	—	—	—	—
	100	(58)	100	(56)	100	(98)	100	(72)	100	(44)

Except for some respondents in Kitendagulo and Kabagunda, where non-farmers are most frequent, all respondents are self-employed. In Kitendagulo and Kabagunda one third of the sample claim that they work regularly with others. Most of the respondents who employ others are found in Kitendagulo and Bwatangabo. In the latter, quite many have others employed to assist in the coffee pruning.

The equipment used by the farmers in their daily work is typical of peasant farming: the hoe, the knife (*panga*), billhook, and axe.

5. How the farm has been acquired:

The farm, or the land plot, is the most valuable asset of all respondents. The majority have only one farm, but in Bugombe as many as one quarter of the sample own more than one. The following table illustrates the way the respondents have originally acquired their land:

(in %)	Bugombe		Kiten-dagulo		Bwatan-gabo		Kaba-gunda		Kiru-ruma	
Inheritance	72	(42)	52	(29)	63	(62)	63	(45)	25	(11)
Purchase	14	(8)	20	(11)	25	(24)	22	(17)	63	(29)
No infor	14	(8)	28	(16)	12	(12)	15	(10)	12	(4)
	100	(58)	100	(56)	100	(98)	100	(72)	100	(44)

6. Size of coffee farm:

Almost all farmers have only one source of cash income, the coffee farm. The number of trees that a person has, therefore, determines to a large extent his financial situation. Those who have only a few trees, by and large, have old trees, which are very unproductive. Those who have very many trees, have uprooted the old ones and planted new, more productive trees. The following table shows the distribution of trees by respondent:

(in %)	Bugombe		Kiten-dagulo		Bwatan-gabo		Kaba-gunda		Kiru-ruma	
less than 10	12	(7)	7	(4)	2	(2)	33	(24)	9	(4)
10—20	12	(7)	28,5	(16)	10	(10)	30,5	(22)	31,5	(14)
21—50	29,5	(17)	25,5	(14)	12	(12)	16,5	(12)	18,5	(8)
51—100	26	(15)	12,5	(7)	29	(28)	7	(5)	18,5	(8)
more than 101	20,5	(12)	7	(4)	40	(39)	7	(5)	9	(4)
no trees	—	(0)	7	(4)	—	(0)	—	(0)	—	(0)
no information	—	(0)	12,5	(7)	7	(7)	6	(4)	13,5	(6)
total:	100	(58)	100	(56)	100	(98)	100	(72)	100	(44)

In the text, respondents with less than 20 trees are considered as having "small" farms, people with 21—100 trees as having "middle-size" farms, and those with more than 100 trees as having "large" farms.

7. Tax-paying:

In Bwatangabo, Kabagunda and Kiruruma more than 90 % pay the lowest poll-tax rate—1965, 45 shs. This means that their annual cash income is not supposed to exceed 1000 shs. In Bugombe the equivalent figure is 80 %, in Kitendagulo 71 %. Only people with large coffee farms and those who are licensed to conduct commercial activities are compelled to pay higher rates.

8. Language:

(in %)	Bugombe	Kiten-dagulo	Bwatan-gabo	Kaba-gunda	Kiru-ruma
Luhaya only	31 (18)	29 (16)	36 (35)	45 (32)	61 (27)
Luhaya+ Kiswahili	50 (29)	43 (24)	49 (48)	42 (30)	9 (4)
also third language	19 (11)	28 (16)	13 (13)	12 (9)	28 (12)
no infor	— —	— —	2 (2)	1 (1)	2 (1)
total:	100 (58)	100 (56)	100 (98)	100 (72)	100 (44)

The reason why so many respondents in Kiruruma claim they know a third language is that quite number are originally from Rwanda.

9. Educational attainment:

(in %)	Bugombe		Kiten-dagulo		Bwatan-gabo		Kaba-gunda		Kiru-ruma	
Highest level of education:										
St I—II	12	(7)	11	(6)	9	(9)	12	(9)	4	(2)
III—IV	20	(13)	17	(10)	38	(37)	31	(22)	10	(4)
V—VI	23	(14)	16	(9)	11	(11)	4,5	(3)	7	(3)
VII—VIII	5	(3)	9	(5)	3	(3)	6,5	(4)	7	(3)
secondary s.	—	—	11	(6)	—	—	—	—	—	—
teacher train.	—	—	4	(2)	—	—	—	—	—	—
no education	40	(23)	32	(18)	39	(38)	46	(33)	72	(32)
total:	100	(58)	100	(56)	100	(98)	100	(72)	100	(44)

Those with only lower primary schooling are in the text referred to as having "some" education, those with upper primary or more as having "much" education. This should, of course, be viewed in relation to the spread of education in the area.

10. Religious affiliation:

(in %)	Bugombe		Kiten-dagulo		Bwatan-gabo		Kaba-gunda		Kiru-ruma	
Roman Cath.	56	(32)	62	(35)	80	(78)	39	(28)	52	(23)
Protestant	13	(8)	16	(9)	2	(2)	30	(22)	22	(9)
Muslim	12	(7)	12	(7)	11	(11)	17	(14)	—	—
Animist	19	(11)	10	(5)	6	(6)	14	(10)	26	(12)
no information	—	—	—	—	1	(1)	—	—	—	—
total:	100	(58)	100	(56)	100	(98)	100	(72)	100	(44)

11. Media exposure:

a) Radio:

(in %)	Bugombe		Kiten-dagulo		Bwatan-gabo		Kaba-gunda		Kiru-ruma	
Listens:										
every day	16	(9)	19	(11)	9	(9)	6,5	(5)	—	(0)
once or twice a week	22,5	(13)	37	(21)	16	(16)	18	(13)	9,5	(4)
less than once a week	22,5	(13)	30	(17)	41	(40)	15,5	(11)	31,5	(14)
never	39	(23)	14	(8)	32	(31)	50	(36)	43	(19)
no infor	—	(0)	—	(0)	2	(2)	10	(7)	16	(7)
total:	100	(58)	100	(56)	100	(98)	100	(72)	100	(44)

b) Newspaper:

(in %)	Bugombe		Kiten-dagulo		Bwatan-gabo		Kaba-gunda		Kiru-ruma	
Reads:										
every day	12	(7)	10,5	(6)	2	(2)	1,5	(1)	—	(0)
once or twice a week	27,5	(16)	30	(17)	13	(13)	26,5	(19)	4,5	(2)
less than once a week	12	(7)	5,5	(3)	29	(28)	3	(2)	4,5	(2)
never	46,5	(27)	54	(30)	55	(54)	63,5	(46)	75	(33)
no information	2	(1)	—	(0)	1	(1)	5,5	(4)	16	(7)
total:	100	(58)	100	(56)	100	(98)	100	(72)	100	(44)

Table a) and b) have been brought together in the text, and respondents divided into four categories: Those who listen or read every day are considered to be exposed "very often", those who listen once or twice a week "often", those who read or listen less than once a week "not so often", and those who never read or listen as "never" exposed.

12. Geographical mobility:

(in %)	Bugombe		Kiten-dagulo		Bwatan-gabo		Kaba-gunda		Kiru-ruma	
Has travelled outside:										
village	19	(11)	21,5	(12)	32	(31)	22	(16)	31,5	(14)
district	29,5	(17)	28	(16)	22	(22)	50	(36)	21	(9)
nation	51,5	(30)	46,5	(26)	46	(45)	14	(10)	45,5	(20)
no information	—	(0)	4	(2)	—	(0)	12,5	(9)	2	(1)
total:	100	(58)	100	(56)	100	(98)	100	(72)	100	(44)

13. Membership in TANU:

(in %)	Bugombe		Kiten-dagulo		Bwatan-gabo		Kaba-gunda		Kiru-ruma	
member	76	(44)	54	(30)	73	(71)	65	(47)	75	(33)
not member	13,5	(8)	10,5	(6)	5	(5)	32	(23)	23	(10)
has no card but believe in TANU	2	(1)	4	(2)	—	(0)	—	(0)	—	(0)
no information	8,5	(5)	31,5	(18)	22	(22)	3	(2)	2	(1)
total:	100	(58)	100	(56)	100	(98)	100	(72)	100	(44)

This information was obtained in the special electoral survey. Thereby the high percentage of "no information" in Kitendagulo and Bwatangabo can be explained. In the text people who claim they believe in TANU have been put together with the non-members into one category.

List of figures

1. Geographical map of Tanzania.
2. Summary of the analytical scheme used in this study.
3. Selected major tribes on mainland Tanzania.
4. Geographical map of Bukoba and Karagwe Districts, Buhaya.
5. Rainfall and hydrography of Buhaya.
6. African population of Buhaya, 1957.
7. Percentage composition of population by tribe in selected Lake districts.
8. Interlacustrine tribes of East Africa.
9. The traditional political organization in Buhaya.
10. Coffee production in Buhaya 1905—60.
11. The organization of the centre-periphery relationship in the traditional political systems of Buhaya, in the colonial system and in the present Tanzanian political system.
12. Total number of respondents preferring to grow coffee rather than bananas, divided into major categories.
13. Portrait of a consociational political system.

List of tables

23. Proportion of young and old small farmers with no formal education of the total number of respondents answering that the government expects too much of the people; by parish.
24. Opinions about personal qualities for which the respondents want to be admired; by parish.
25. Matters brought up before the Village Development Committees between March 1963 and March 1965.
26. Opinions about whether the abolition of chiefly power has left a vacuum in society; by parish.
27. Attitudes towards various aspects of agricultural improvement; by parish.
28. Differences in attitudes towards agricultural production; by age, education, size of farm and media exposure.
29. Attitudes of certain categories of respondents towards coffee rejuvenation and farm cultivation.
30. Answers from where the respondents get their information about politics; by parish.
31. Distribution of answers how the respondents obtain additional information about politics; by parish.
32. Answers from whom the farmers get agricultural information; by parish.
33. Opinions about which type of leaders has the greatest impact on the local population; by parish.
34. Degree of satisfaction felt among the respondents with regard to their income, housing situation, job and education; by parish.
35. Proportion of respondents who express some degree of dissatisfaction with education, income and job; by age, education, size of farm and occupation.
36. Proportion of some selected categories of farmers reporting dissatisfaction with income.
37. Proportion of respondents who express some degree of dissatisfaction with education, income and job; by media exposure, geographical mobility and party membership.
38. Distribution of opinion about their income, housing situation, job and education among local political leaders, members of TANU, and non-members.
39. Beliefs about government allocation of money; by parish.
40. Beliefs about how government allocates its resources; by age education and party membership.
41. Preferences about how government should allocate its resources; by parish.
42. Opinions about what is most important in order to succeed in life; by parish.
43. Proportion of those who believe "good personal contacts", "good family background" and "intelligence" determine success in life; by age and education.
44. Attendance at campaign meetings in the 1965 general election; by parish.
45. Attendance at other meetings than those organized by the VDC; average for all five parishes.
46. Opinions about the most effective technique to influence government; by parish.
47. Frequency with which respondents discuss political matters; by parish.
48. Proportion of respondents who discuss politics at least once a week; by education, media exposure and political involvement.

49. Knowledge of the name of certain key political leaders and dates of selected national events; by parish.
50. Proportion of those who can name at least three key political leaders and two national events; by education, frequency of political discussion and media exposure.
51. Beliefs about whether people can do anything or not to make government provide a service for their home area; by parish.
52. What "competent" villagers report that they would do to make the government provide a service to their community; by parish.
53. Proportion of voters in the 1965 election; by education and attendance at campaign meetings.
54. Proportion of respondents discussing the election in the campaign period; by education and attendance at campaign meeting.
55. Electors voting by symbol only, shown as percentages of how often they discussed the election, and when they made up their mind how to vote.

Bibliography

Books

Afrifa, A. A., *The Ghana Coup: 24th February, 1966*, New York 1966.
Allardt, E. and Littunen, Y., *Cleavages, Ideologies, and Party Systems*, Helsinki 1964.
Almond, G. A. and Coleman, J. S., *The Politics of the Developing Areas*, Princeton 1960.
Almond, G. A. and Powell, B. Jr., *Comparative Politics: A Developmental Approach*, New York 1966.
Almond, G. A. and Verba, S., *The Civic Culture*, Princeton 1963.
Apter, D., *The Gold Coast in Transition*, Princeton 1955.
Apter, D., *The Political Kingdom in Uganda*, Princeton 1961.
Apter, D., *The Politics of Modernization*, Chicago 1965.
Banfield, E. C., *The Moral Basis of a Backward Society*, (Second Edition), New York 1967.
Barongo, E. B. M., *Hotuba ya Bwana Mheshimiwa Nyerere*, Bukoba 1958.
Benettsson, H., *Östafrikansk verklighetsuppfattning och människosyn*, Uppsala 1966.
Berelson, B. R., Lazarsfeld, P. F. and McPhee, W. N., *Voting*, Chicago 1954.
Bienen, H., *Tanzania: Party Transformation and Economic Development*, Princeton 1967.
Binder, L., *Iran—Political Development in a Changing Society*, Los Angeles 1964.
Bretton, H. L., *The Rise and Fall of Kwame Nkrumah—A Study of Personal Rule in Africa*, New York 1966.
Brokensha, D. (ed.), *Ecology and Economic Development in Tropical Africa*, Berkeley 1965.
Chidzero, B., *Tanganyika and International Trusteeship*, London 1961.
Cliffe, L. (ed.), *One Party Democracy—The 1965 Tanzania General Elections*, Nairobi 1967.
Coleman, J. S. (ed.), *Education and Political Development*, Princeton 1965.
Coleman, J. S. and Rosberg, C., *Political Parties and National Integration in Tropical Africa*, Los Angeles 1965.
Cory, H., *The History of Bukoba District*, Mwanza 1957.
Cory, H. and Hartnoll, M. M., *The Customary Law of the Haya Tribe, Tanganyika Territory*, London 1945.
Deutsch, K. W., *Nationalism and Social Communication* (2nd Edition), New York 1966.
Dumont, R., *L'Afrique noire est mal partie*, Paris 1962.
Easton, D., *A Framework for Political Analysis*, New York 1965.
Easton, D., *A Systems Analysis of Political Life*, Chigago 1965.

Fallers, L. A. (ed.), *The King's Men,* New York 1964.

Fitch, B. and Oppenheimer, M., *Ghana: End of Illusion,* New York 1966.

Forde, D., *African Worlds,* London 1954.

Fortes, M. and Evans-Pritchard, E. E. (eds.), *African Political Systems,* New York 1940.

Geertz, C. (ed.), *Old Societies and New States,* New York 1963.

Hance, W. A., *The Geography of Modern Africa,* New York 1964.

Hellberg, C. J., *Missions on a Colonial Frontier West of Lake Victoria,* Lund 1965.

Herskovits, M. J., *The Human Factor in Changing Africa,* London 1962.

Herskovits, M. J. and Harwitz, M. (eds.), *Economic Transition in Africa,* New York 1964.

Hirschman, A., *Journeys Towards Progress,* New York 1965.

Ingham, K., *A History of East Africa,* London 1965.

Kibira, J., *Aus einer afrikanischen Kirche,* Bielefeld 1960.

Kornhauser, W., *The Politics of Mass Society,* New York 1959.

Lane, R. E., *Political Life: Why People Get Involved in Politics,* New York 1959.

LaPalombara, J. (ed.), *Bureaucracy and Political Development,* Princeton 1963.

LaPalombara, J. and Weiner M. (eds.), *Political Parties and Political Development,* Princeton 1966.

Lazarsfeld, P. F., Berelson, B. and Gaudet, H., *The People's Choice,* New York 1948.

Lerner, D. and Schramm, W. (eds.), *Communication and Change in the Developing Countries,* Honolulu 1967.

Lerner, D., *The Passing of Traditional Society,* New York 1958.

Lipset, S. M., *America—The First New Nation,* New York 1963.

Lipset, S. M., *Political Man,* New York 1960.

Listowel, J., *The Making of Tanganyika,* London 1965.

Lwamgira, F. X., *Amakuru ga Kiziba n'Abakama Bamu,* Bukoba 1949.

MacDonald, A., *Tanzania—Young Nation in Hurry,* New York 1966.

Meister, A., *L'Afrique peut-elle partir?,* Paris 1966.

Milbraith, L. W., *Political Participation,* Chicago 1965.

Millikan, M. F., and Backmer, D. L. M., *Emerging Nations,* Boston 1961.

Montgomery, J. D. and Siffin, W. J. (eds.), *Approaches to Development: Politics, Administration and Change,* New York 1966.

Murdock, G. P., *Africa: Its Peoples and Their Culture History,* New York 1959.

Nyerere, J. K., *Democracy and the Party System,* Dar es Salaam 1962.

Nyerere, J. K., *Tanzania skall byggas med hängivelse,* (Tanzania itajengwa na wenye moyo), Uppsala 1967.

Oliver, R. and Mathew, G. (eds.), *History of East Africa,* New York 1963.

Organski, A. F. K., *Stages of Political Growth,* New York 1965.

Parsons, T., *The Social System,* London 1952.

Post, K. W. J., *The Nigerian Federal Election of 1959,* London 1963.

Pye, L. W., *Aspects of Political Development,* New York 1966.

Pye, L. W. (ed.), *Communications and Political Development,* Princeton 1963.

Pye, L. W. and Verba, S. (eds.), *Political Culture and Political Development,* Princeton 1965.

Redfield, R., *Peasant Society and Culture,* Chicago 1956.

Rehse, H., *Kiziba—Land und Leute,* Stuttgart 1910.

Richards, A. I., *East African Chiefs,* London 1960.

Rudebeck, L., *Party and People—A Study of Political Change in Tunisia,* Uppsala 1967.

Shils, E., *Political Development of the New States,* The Hague 1962.

Smith, M. G., *Government in Zazzau,* London 1960.

Southall, A. W. (ed.), *Social Change in Modern Africa,* Chicago 1961.

Southall, A. W. and Gutkind, P. C., *Townsmen in the Making,* Kampala 1957.

Spiro, H. J., *Africa: The Primacy of Politics,* New York 1966.

Stanley, H. M., *In Darkest Africa,* London 1890.

Stuhlmann, F., *Mit Emin Pasha ins Herz von Afrika,* Berlin 1894.

Sundkler, B. G. M., *Bantu Prophets in South Africa,* London 1948.

Taylor, B. K., *The Western Lacustrine Bantu,* London 1962.

Taylor, J. C., *The Political Development of Tanganyika,* Los Angeles 1963.

Thomas, W. I. and Znaniecki, F., *The Polish Peasant,* New York 1958.

Trimingham, J. S., *Islam in East Africa,* London 1962.

UNESCO, *Social Change and Economic Development,* Leiden 1963.

Ward, R. and Rustow, D. (eds.), *Political Modernization in Japan and Turkey,* Princeton 1964.

Weber, M., *The Theory of Social and Economic Organization,* (edited by Talcott Parsons), New York 1964.

Welbourn, F. B., *East African Rebels,* London 1961.

Welbourn, F. B., *Religion and Politics in Uganda 1955—62,* Nairobi 1965.

White Fathers' Mission, *Edini Omuli Buhaya,* Bukoba 1941.

Wilson, G. and M., *The Analysis of Social Change,* New York 1945.

Young, C., *Politics in the Congo: Decolonization and Independence,* Princeton 1965.

Zolberg, A., *Creating Political Order: The Party-States of West Africa,* New York 1966.

Articles

Almond G. A., "A Developmental Approach to Political System", *World Politics,* (Vol XVII, January 1965).

Austen, R., "Notes on the Pre-History of TANU", *Makerere Journal,* (No 9, March 1964).

Balandier, G., "Messianisme et Nationalisme en Africa Noire", *Cahiers Internationaux de Sociologie,* (Vol XIV).

Befu, H., "The Political Relation of the Village to the State", *World Politics,* (Vol. XIX, July 1967).

Bennett, G., "An Outline History of TANU", *Makerere Journal,* (No 7, July 1963).

Blair, T., "Social Structure and Information Exposure in Rural Brazil", *Rural Sociology,* (Vol XXV, March 1960).

Copeland Reining, P., "Haya Land Tenure: Landholding and Tenancy", *Anthropological Quarterly,* (Vol 35, April 1962).

"Extracts from Mengo Notes", *Uganda Journal,* (Vol 11, September 1947).

Fernandez, J. W., "African Religious Movements", *Journal of Modern African Studies,* (Vol 2, No 4).

Glickman, H., "Dialogues on the Theory of African Political Development", *Africa Report,* (Vol XII, May 1967).

Gray, J. M., "Ahmed bin Ibrahim—the first Arab to reach Buganda", *Uganda Journal,* (Vol 11, September 1947).

Gulliver, P., "Incentives in Labour Migration", *Human Organization,* (Vol 19, No 3, 1960).

Gusfield, J., "Tradition and Modernity: Misplaced Polarities in the Study of Social Change", *American Journal of Sociology,* (Vol 72, January 1967).

Harris, B., "The Tanzanian Election", *Mbioni,* (Vol II, No 5).

Huntington, S. P., "Political Development and Political Decay", *World Politics,* (Vol XVII, April 1965).

Hyden, G., "The Role of Symbols in the Tanzania Election 1965", *Mawazo,* (Vol I, No 1, 1967).

Jervis, T. S., "A History of Robusta Coffee in Bukoba", *Tanganyika Notes and Records,* (No 8, December 1939).

Junod, V., "Community Development and National Planning: The Tanganyika Case", *International Review of Community Development,* (Rome 1966).

Karlsson, G., "Voting Participation among Male Swedish Youth", *Acta Sociologica,* (Vol III, fasc. 2—3).

Lasswell, H., "The Policy Sciences of Development", *World Politics,* (Vol XVII, January 1965).

LeMarchand, R., "Village-by-Village Nation-Building in Tanzania", *Africa Report,* (Vol X, February 1965).

Liebenow, G. J., "Responses to Planned Change in a Tanganyika Tribal Group", *American Political Science Review,* (Vol L, No 2, 1956).

Mayer, Ph., "Migrancy and the Study of Africans in Towns", *The American Anthropologist,* (Vol 64, 1962).

Mazrui, A. A., "Nkrumah—The Leninist Czar", *Transition,* (No 27, 1966).

Mc Auslan, J. O. W. and Ghai Y., "Innovation and Stability in Tanzania", *Journal of Modern African Studies,* (Vol 4, No 4).

McMaster, D. N., "Change of Regional Balance in Bukoba District of Tanganyika", *Tanganyika Notes and Records,* (No 56, March 1961).

Milne, G., "Essays in Applied Pedology, III: Bukoba: High and Low Fertility on a Laterised Soil", *East African Agricultural Journal,* (Vol IV, 1938).

Mitchell, J. C., "Africans in Industrial Towns in Northern Rhodesia", *Report of the Duke of Edinburgh's Study Conference,* (Vol II, Oxford 1957).

Montague, F. A., "Some Difficulties in the Democratization of Native Authorities in Tanganyika", *Journal of African Administration,* (Vol III, January 1951).

Nyerere, J. K., "Education and Self-Reliance", *Africa Report,* (Vol. XII, June 1967).

Rokkan, S., and Campbell, A., "Norway and the United States of America", *International Social Science Journal,* (Vol XII, No 1).

Pennock, J. R., "Political Development, Political Systems, and Political Goods", *World Politics,* (Vol XVIII, April 1966).

Rogers, E. M., "Mass Media Exposure and Modernization among Colombian Peasants", *Public Opinion Quarterly*, (Vol 29, No 4).

Shepperson, G., "The Politics of African Church Separatist Movements In British Central Africa", *Africa*, (Vol XXIV, No 3).

Wallerstein, I., "Ethnicity and National Integration in West Africa", *Cahier d'Etudes Africaines*, (No 3, 1960).

Ward, R. E., "Introduction to Village Government in Eastern and Southern Asia: A Symposium", *Far Eastern Quarterly*, (Vol XV, February 1956).

Wright, Q., "The Nature of Conflict", *Western Political Quarterly*, (Vol IV, June 1951).

Government and TANU publications

Baines, D. L., "The Anglo-German War", *Bukoba District Book*, Bukoba 1919.

Hall, R. de Z., "The Social Organisation in Karagwe", *Bukoba District Book*, Bukoba 1928.

"The Primitive Native Education System 'Muteko'", *Bukoba District Book*, Bukoba 1928.

The Bukoba Native Cooperative Union Ltd, *Annual Reports for the Union's years 1959/60 and 1960/61*, Bukoba.

Colonial Office, *Report 1958*, London 1959.

Constitution of the African Association, Bukoba 1932.

East African Statistical Department, *Tanganyika Population Census 1957*, Nairobi 1958.

Malcolm, D. W., "Sukumaland—An African People and Their Country", *Mwanza District Book*, Mwanza 1938.

Nyerere, J. K., *After the Arusha Declaration*, Dar es Salaam 1967.

Nyerere, J. K., *Principles and Development*, Dar es Salaam 1966.

Nyerere, J. K., *Socialism and Rural Development*, Dar es Salaam 1967.

Tanganyika African National Union, *Sheria na Madhumuni ya Chama*, Dar es Salaam.

The Republic of Tanganyika, *African Census Report 1957*, Dar es Salaam 1963.

The Republic of Tanganyika, *The Tanganyika Five-Year Plan for Economic and Social Development*, Dar es Salaam 1964.

The Republic of Tanganyika, *Tanganyika Gazette*, Dar es Salaam.

The Republic of Tanganyika, *Tanganyika Local Government Ordinance*, Dar es Salaam.

The United Republic of Tanzania, *First Year Progress Report on the Implementation of the Five-Year Development plan (Public Sector) 1st July, 1964 to 30th June, 1965*, Dar es Salaam 1966.

The United Republic of Tanzania, *Our Economy 1965—67*, Dar es Salaam 1966.

The United Republic of Tanzania, *Report on Rules for the Nomination Process and Conduct of Election Campaigns for the National Assembly*, Dar es Salaam 1965.

The United Republic of Tanzania, *The Report of the Presidential Special Committee of Inquiry into the Cooperative Movement*, Dar es Salaam 1966.

Unpublished papers

East African Institute of Social Research and University of East Africa Social Science Conference Papers and other documents

Austen, R., "Political Generations in Bukoba 1890—1939", (June 1963).

Austen, R., "The Study of Indirect Rule in a Tanganyika Province", (December 1963).

Cliffe, L., "Nationalism and the Reaction to Agricultural Improvement in Tanganyika during the Colonial Period", (December 1964).

Copeland Reining, P., "Village Organization in Buhaya", (June 1952).

Harris, C. C., "Development of Local Councils and Re-organization of Local Government, Bukoba District", (June 1952).

Koff, B. and Von der Muhll, G., "Political Socialization in Kenya and Tanzania —A Comparative Analysis", (December 1966).

Low, D. A., "Religion and Society in Buganda 1875—1900", (Studies Material, 1956).

Miller, N., "Village Leadership in Tanzania", (December 1964).

Morrison, B., "Educating Citizens for Tanzania", (December 1966).

Ranger, T. O., "Connections between 'Primary Resistance' Movements and Modern Mass Nationalism in East and Central Africa", (December 1966).

Tanner, R. E. S., "Conflict within Small European Communities in Tanganyika", (July 1962).

Tordoff, W., "Regional Administration in Tanganyika", (December 1964).

Others

Copeland Reining, P., "Progress Report on Research among the Haya", paper presented to a conference arranged by "Centre de Recherches Scientifiques du Ruanda-Urundi de l'Institut pour la Recherche Scientifique en Afrique Centrale", Astrida 1952.

Hyden, G., "Attitudes among School Children and Adults in a Rural Area in Tanzania", The Political Science Research Programme, Makerere University College, Kampala 1966.

Hyden, G., "Problems of Village Administration in Tanzania", The Political Science Research Programme, Makerere University College 1966.

Kaombwe, A. E., "The Buhaya District Council—Historical Background", Bukoba 1965.

Kibira, J., "A Study of Christianity among the Haya Tribe; West Lake Region, Tanganyika", M. A. Thesis, Boston University School of Theology 1963.

Klingelhofer, E. L., "Studies of Tanzanian Students", University College, Dar es Salaam, 1967.

Lijphart, A., "Typologies of Democratic Systems", paper read at the 7th World Congress of the International Political Science Association in Brussels, September 18—23, 1967.

Luykx, N., "The Role of Rural Development in Agriculture in Thailand" Comparative Administration Group: Occasional Papers, Bloomington 1964.

Mazrui, A. A., "Political Superannuation and the Trans-class Man", paper read at the 7th World Congress of the International Political Science Association in Brussels, September 18—23, 1967.

Moris, J., "Education and Training of the Farmer", paper read at the Conference on Education, Employment and Rural Development at Kericho, Kenya, September 25—October 1, 1966.

Obershall, A., "Media Exposure, Information Level and Aspirations in Rural Uganda", Department of Sociology, Yale University, August 1967.

Pye, L. W., "Typologies and Political Development", paper read at the 7th World Congress of the International Political Science Association in Brussels, September 18—23, 1967.

Von der Muhll, G., "Education, Citizenship, and Social Revolution in Tanzania", paper prepared for 10th Annual Meeting of the African Studies Association in New York, November 1—4, 1967.

Wamala, M., "The Cooperative Movement in Tanganyika", Bukoba, undated.

White Fathers' Mission, "Enquete sur les moeurs et coutumes indigenes", Kashozi, Bukoba, undated.

Wipper, A., "Penetration", paper prepared for the Political Science Research Programme, Makerere University College, 1965.

Zolberg, A., "The Structure of Political Conflict in the New States of Tropical Africa", paper read at the 7th World Congress of the International Political Science Association in Brussels, September 18—23, 1967.

Newspapers and Periodicals

Bukoba Cooperative News, (Bukoba).

Bukya na Gandi, (Bukoba).

Rumuli, (Bukoba).

Ija Webonere, (Bukoba).

Kiongozi, (Tabora).

Tanzania News Bulletin, (Stockholm).

The Nationalist, (Dar es Salaam).

The Standard, (Dar es Salaam).

Uganda Argus, (Kampala).

Index